D1559517

DARKEST CHRISTMAS

DARKEST CHRISTMAS

December 1942 and a World at War

PETER HARMSEN

CASEMATE

Philadelphia & Oxford

Published in the United States of America and Great Britain in 2022 by
CASEMATE PUBLISHERS
1950 Lawrence Road, Havertown, PA 19083, USA
and
The Old Music Hall, 106–108 Cowley Road, Oxford OX4 1JE, UK

Hardback Edition: ISBN 978-1-63624-189-0
Digital Edition: ISBN 978-1-63624-190-6

A CIP record for this book is available from the British Library

Printed and bound in the United Kingdom by TJ Books

Typeset in India by Lapiz Digital Services, Chennai.

For a complete list of Casemate titles, please contact:

CASEMATE PUBLISHERS (US)
Telephone (610) 853-9131
Fax (610) 853-9146
Email: casemate@casematepublishers.com
www.casematepublishers.com

CASEMATE PUBLISHERS (UK)
Telephone (01865) 241249
Email: casemate-uk@casematepublishers.co.uk
www.casematepublishers.co.uk

Cover illustration by Declan Ingram.

Contents

Preface

The idea behind this book is a simple one. It is to "follow the sun" as it appears around the globe on a single day in the history of the planet, taking as the starting point the dateline in the mid-Pacific and moving from time zone to time zone until, at the end of the book, the account has come full circle. In principle, any day could be described in this way. Especially as we get closer to our own time, and the available sources become more abundant, it would be possible to find enough information to write such a book without being repetitive or having to skip certain parts of the globe. However, the one day that will be the subject of this book is Christmas Day 1942.

One may ask: why? Why Christmas? The answer is that Christmas is a time of heightened emotion. Christmas at a time of war is all the more so since young men and women pass the holiday torn from their loved ones, in a situation where they cannot know if they are even to survive until the next Christmas. And why 1942? Because it was a unique time. Much remained undecided that fateful December. Modern historians may argue that the Allies had effectively already won the war at this stage, but this was far from obvious for the actors standing in the middle of the maelstrom of history. The big German defeats at Stalingrad and Kursk lay in the future. Japan still ruled much of the Pacific. Even many Americans, safe behind the two oceans, might ask themselves if this was their last Christmas spent in freedom. To us, the thought might seem absurd. To them it was not.

There is another, more practical reason for picking Christmas as the subject for a book about "one day in World War II." For soldiers at the front and their relatives at home, most days during the war resembled any other and were frankly unremarkable, filled with the mostly dreary routine of life in wartime. However, Christmas stood out and imprinted itself in the memory of most. Even decades later, they were able to recall where they were and what they did during Christmas 1942. This has resulted in a large mass of source material that the historian can pick from.

Still, it is my objective with this book not merely to provide a listing of events around the world that happened to take place within the same short span of time on a single day in late December 1942. I aim to reach a deeper level of understanding of what Christmas meant to people, and what it did to them. What was the significance to them of being at war, of killing and facing the risk of being killed oneself, while commemorating the biblical annunciation to the shepherds of "on earth peace, good will toward men"? The answers to these questions may lay the groundwork for a cultural and spiritual history of World War II, seen through the lens of Christmas. It may seem a narrow lens, but in fact it is not, as ultimately it encompasses the entire human experience of being at war.

* * *

All history is written from a vantage point. This is also true for this book. Europe was at war again for the first time in decades when I was putting the finishing touches to these chapters. While Russian bombs were exploding over Kiev and Kharkov, or Kyiv and Kharkiv as the cities are now known, I was writing about events that took place 80 years ago not far away from where the present battles were raging. It is a reminder that even though historical conflicts can be experienced at a safe distance, peace is not guaranteed, and that, sadly, more often than not we fail in our effort to study history in order not to repeat past tragedies.

The book was also written at a time when a particular era in the history of mankind might be coming to a close. The age of globalization could be approaching an end, or at the very least globalization as we know it may be about to be transformed into something else. A devastating pandemic halted the trend of ever-increasing international travel that had been taking place in an uninterrupted fashion since 1945 and for a moment brought civilian air traffic back to a level where it had not been for eight decades. At the same time, theorists of international relations described a future world which might to a greater extent be divided into separate political, cultural and economic blocs.

If this is indeed the case, this book is fittingly about the beginning of that period in history. Globalization can be traced back for centuries, but a world in which any inhabited place was within reach of any other inhabited place within usually no more than 24 hours, and in which the same cultural habits seemed to be predominant at least in the capitals and big cities—that world is very much the product of conditions created by World War II. I have written this book without making any value judgments about the merits and otherwise of globalization, and merely describing a fact of life that has set the general tone for the modern world over the past three or four generations.

* * *

Given the subject at hand, it is inevitable that religion plays a prominent part in the following chapters. Most of the nations at war were cultures built on the Christian faith. To be sure, it was a secular age in a variety of ways, and science-based rationality was taking hold in many of the societies, while Germany was moving towards a new, strange kind of faith, seeking to gradually replace inherited liturgy with "Germanic" rituals. However, a basic set of Christian traditions lived on everywhere—fueled by the religious revival which many belligerent nations experienced—and Christmas was the most important of these.

Many soldiers and sailors who took part in the war were intensely religious, or they became that way. As American military chaplain William Thomas Cummings reportedly said during the desperate battle for the Philippine peninsula of Bataan in 1942, "there are no atheists in the fox holes."[1] In our more cynical and secular age, it is easy to shrug off such religious feelings. However, that also entails the historian's cardinal sin of failing to approach the past on its own terms. My attitude has been not to explicitly assume any position on the religious beliefs that emerge from the sources but to describe them as faithfully and precisely as possible.

More generally, I have decided to let the sources speak for themselves to the greatest extent possible. This means that even when the sources express views and opinions that will strike most readers as callous, unreasonable or hypocritical, I have refrained from adding my personal comment, for example when citing sources using derogatory terms typical of the age such as "Jap." Personally, as a reader I prefer not to be told what to think, and I trust that many others feel the same way. An example of what this entails are the excerpts of German Propaganda Minister Joseph Goebbels' diary, which express great regret at his inability to spend more time with his five daughters and one son, entirely disregarding the many Jewish parents who could not see their children because they were dead. I believe that the readers are able to reach their own conclusions about Goebbels' inherently insensitive nature.

It is in the nature of the subject, aiming to provide an account of the world and what took place in it within the span of 24 eventful hours, that the full story of the persons who appear on the broad global canvas cannot be told.

They quickly emerge from the massive, anonymous flow of history, move briefly into sight, and then disappear again. This may leave some readers wanting to know more about what happened afterwards to the individuals who appear in this book. Therefore, I have added a list at the end of the book briefly outlining their fates after Christmas 1942 to the extent that these are known. Such a list can easily become unwieldy and drown in biographical detail, and therefore I have limited myself to only the most basic information. In many cases, I have merely stated that a person "survived the war."

A few remarks on the rendering of foreign names, inevitable in a book spanning the entire globe: German names are given in the original spelling, e.g. the Nazi party newspaper is *Völkischer Beobachter* rather than *Voelkischer Beobachter*. Likewise, the Norwegian surname Næss is rendered in its original spelling, not Naess. The same for the Czech surname Vašek instead of Vasek. Chinese names, always a source of some confusion, are transliterated using the modern pinyin system, which is now almost universally accepted. The only exception is cases where earlier transliteration practices have stuck. Therefore, China's leader at the time is spelled Chiang Kai-shek, not, as pinyin would have it, Jiang Jieshi. For both Chinese and Japanese individuals, the East Asian practice is adopted in that surnames come before given names. All spellings of place names are used as they would have been spelt at the time and may not reflect their current or modern spelling.

* * *

No book is entirely a one-man enterprise, and every author of a non-fiction title will necessarily be indebted to others who helped make the work come to fruition. I would like to direct thanks to the following individuals, all specialist in their fields: Christopher Bell, Dalhousie University; Marcus Faulkner, King's College London; David Kohnen, Naval War College; Joe Perry, Georgia State University; and Marks-Hirschfeld Museum of Medical History, Faculty of Medicine, University of Queensland. Also special thanks to Robert Schott and his father, World War II veteran Joe Schott. This is my sixth book for Casemate, and once again I must credit the professional and friendly support I have received from the earliest drafts to the final publication. In particular, I wish to thank Ruth Sheppard, Felicity Goldsack, Alison Griffiths and Declan Ingram. Needless to say, any errors and misinterpretations are my responsibility alone. Finally, as always thanks to my wife Lin Hui-tsung and our two daughters Eva and Lisa for their patience.

"White Christmas"

Globalization by other means

In December 1942, it was a "White Christmas" for millions. No one could be in doubt after listening to the season's number one hit rendered in Bing Crosby's unique low baritone, switching effortlessly in and out of bass. Humming along, his fans knew it was a Christmas of glistening treetops and sleighbells in the snow. The tender tune of "White Christmas," a celebration of the holiday as it ought to be in times of peace, accompanied a generation of young Americans as they headed out to war in places where there was no snow, but blistering sand, frothy sea and steamy jungle. It was the right song for the time, sad and wistful but also strangely comforting with its unspoken promise of one day being able to return to the life that had been left behind.

Joseph Schott was a 19-year-old sailor on board the troop transport SS *Westernland*, about to depart Hoboken, New Jersey, for the British Isles, when he heard the song the first time that December. "I was ordered to be on deck patrol duty, so I did not get to try my hammock until late that night. At around midnight, I was out on deck as the ship eased its way away from the dock. Down on the dock, there was a little wooden shack for a civilian watchman. He had his radio on, and the beautiful and popular song, 'White Christmas,' was playing with Bing Crosby singing. It was probably the perfect music for me to hear during those first few minutes of what was to become a sixteen-day voyage across the Atlantic Ocean. A little later, as we got under way, I could just about make out that we were passing the Statue of Liberty."[1]

"White Christmas" struck a chord at a point in history when the United States was beginning to shoulder the actual burden of global war. It had been made to face the challenge of confronting tyranny in its various guises after the Japanese attack on Pearl Harbor the previous year, but it could not become a full-fledged belligerent overnight. Its overseas commitments had been built up in the course of 1942, and now, by the end of the year, they were complete.

American forces were fighting in North Africa, on islands in Oceania, and in the air over Europe. Almost 380,000 Army and Navy personnel had been sailed across the Atlantic, and another 470,000 had been sent to the Pacific. One year after it had been dragged into the war, the United States was involved on a worldwide scale. In this sense, 1942 was America's first true war Christmas.

Just like America's war participation, "White Christmas" had been underway for about a year. Irving Berlin, a Russian-born Jew who did not celebrate Christmas himself, had composed the song in 1941, while being separated from his wife, who was a Christian. He had delayed its release because he specifically wanted Bing Crosby to sing it and had to wait for the star's schedule to become free.[2] That was his great luck, although it was not immediately obvious. When it came out in May 1942 as part of the soundtrack for the movie *Holiday Inn*, other songs in the film initially fared better. But as Christmas drew nearer, while a significant number of young men and women departed for distant destinations, many more could relate, and it gradually gained appeal. On October 24, it soared to the top of the hitlist for sheet music, replacing Glenn Miller's "Kalamazoo."[3] One week later, it was also the best-selling retail record,[4] and yet two weeks on, it dominated the airwaves, too.[5]

The sensation was immediate and obvious, and good news for Decca, Crosby's record company. "Decca's Bing is getting to be Santa Claus of the music shops," the *Billboard* trade magazine gushed.[6] That was just the beginning. The song was disseminated by Armed Forces Radio Network across the globe, and later it was brought to yet more troops through the medium of the V-disc, or "victory record." At the same time, soldiers around the world found their own ways to listen to the song if official channels were too slow. Men of the 1st Battalion, 11th Marines on Guadalcanal heard the song via their TBX radio transmitter, which was strictly for service use but could be tuned to KWID/KWIX San Francisco and other American short-wave stations when not required for military purposes.[7]

Like Schott, the young sailor, many would later remember with astonishing clarity the first time they heard the song. Geraldine MacAdoo of Wolfe Island, Ontario, was a nurse at a 1,700-bed military hospital in Pretoria, South Africa, where casualties from the desert campaign at the other end of the continent were being treated. It was hard work from dawn till dusk, but there was time for Christmas and a party in the middle of the sunny summer of the southern hemisphere. It was hot enough that the doctors attended in their shorts. One of the nurses brought a recording she had acquired in Detroit. "It was Bing Crosby's 'I'm Dreaming of a White Christmas'," MacAdoo reminisced nearly four decades on.[8]

The original version of the song was set in "Beverly Hills, L.A." where "orange and palm trees sway." It was about a person located in the heat of southern California, wishing to be in a place where snow could add to the Christmas atmosphere. It made it clearer why the song should be about *dreaming* of a white Christmas. Those lyrics were later removed, but even though the internal logic of song suffered, it still made sense to the fans. Its subject was dreaming about a mythical America, not necessarily the America that people actually hailed from. A large number of servicemen were from places where there was no snow, no treetops and certainly no sleighbells, but it was all the same to them. The song expressed longing, which, along with boredom and occasional terror, was perhaps the dominant mental state during the war years.

It was reflected in the popular culture of the age. Dreaming was a central theme in the songs heard in barracks and on board troop transports. Titles that found a ready audience in the early 1940s included "Thanks for the Dream," "I Had the Craziest Dream," "A Soldier Dreams of You Tonight," "I Dream of You," "I'll Buy That Dream," "My Dreams Are Getting Better All the Time," and simply "Dream."[9] Dreaming remained pivotal to "White Christmas" even when GIs substituted their own bawdy poetry for the original lyrics. In North Africa, American soldiers lost in a foreign world that was nothing like home changed the opening words to "I'm dreaming of a white mistress."[10]

Dreaming, however, was not just about the past and what had been lost, but also about what lay ahead and might still be gained. Carl Sandburg, a poet and winner of the Pulitzer Prize, described the meaning of "White Christmas" in an essay published in the *Chicago Times* on the first anniversary of the Pearl Harbor attack. "This latest hit of Irving Berlin catches us where we love peace. The Nazi theory and doctrine that man in his blood is naturally warlike, so much so that he should call war a blessing, we don't like it… The hopes and prayers are that we will see the beginnings of a hundred years of White Christmases—with no blood-spots of needless agony and death on the snow."[11]

The century of peace described by Sandburg was in a distant future, beyond a hundred battles, and until that time, the mood that the song primarily produced was inevitably also sadness. "White Christmas," similar to songs like "I'll be Home for Christmas," was, in the words of one historian, an "anthem for homesickness."[12] Donald Brydon, a young soldier in the Army Air Corps from Maine, was undergoing basic training in Miami Beach, Florida, as the song filled the barracks. "I can remember listenin' to Bing Crosby on the radio singin' 'White Christmas' and being so homesick I could hardly stand it," he said.[13]

It was a universal feeling. Donald G. Speyer, who was training as a radio operator at the Naval Air Station at Alameda, California, reported a raw emotional impact from "White Christmas." "That is the only one thing that makes me want to come home," he wrote in a letter to his parents in Indiana.[14] Carl Bosenberg, an enlisted man in the Coast Guard, heard the song on an island in the Pacific. "That was a real tear jerker out there," he said.[15] Fred Redwine, a welder with a bomb squadron, was in Guadalcanal, suffering from repeated bouts of malaria when he heard the song for the first time. "Talk about making a man homesick," he told a reporter half a century later.[16]

From the Solomon Islands to Tunisia, from Iceland to Australia, the majority of young Americans who were spending Christmas away from home were doing so for the first time, united in their longing to go back stateside expressed so eloquently with Bing Crosby's reassuring, avuncular voice. They were also united in the experience of belonging to a generation born into a time of unusual sacrifice. It was one they shared with their peers from other nations also forced into a conflict which found them in unlikely places, spread to all corners of the world by the winds of international war.

* * *

Indian nationalist leader Subhas Chandra Bose spent Christmas 1942 in Vienna with his Austrian wife Emilie Schenkl. Both of them were focusing their attention on their new-born daughter Anita, and Bose, a conservative man who after five years of marriage still addressed his wife as "Miss Schenkl" in his letters, had somewhat hesitantly reconciled himself with the fact that his first child was not a son. It was an opportunity for quiet family bliss before Bose was to embark on the most hazardous move of his career. He was about to return to Asia in hopes of leading Indians in what he believed would become a Japanese-backed fight for independence from the British Empire.

Within weeks, he would set out in a German U-boat, headed for the Indian Ocean, where he would be transferred to a Japanese submarine. From there, he would move on to territory occupied by the Japanese, recruiting Indian prisoners of war for an army that was to fight on the Japanese side against the old British masters. It was a perilous journey, to be carried out at a time when the Axis powers were being increasingly challenged on the oceans by strong and technologically sophisticated Allied navies. "There is a certain amount of risk undoubtedly in this undertaking, but so is there in every undertaking," he wrote in a letter to German Foreign Minister Joachim von Ribbentrop in December.[17]

To summarize: Bose was an Indian subject of the British Empire, spending Christmas with his Austrian wife in a large city of the Greater German Reich, while planning to go to Asia with the aid of the Japanese. Clearly, his story was peculiar. Still, it highlighted a central aspect of the ongoing conflict, as it uprooted people from their native places and scattered them across the continents to remote lands that they would, in times of peace, never have seen and perhaps not even heard about, bringing them into contact with others in the same situation, often violently. Christmas 1942 saw people and places combined in ways that would have been exceedingly odd in peacetime: Americans in the Solomons, Italians in Russia, Indians in North Africa, Japanese in New Guinea, Poles in Iran, and Chinese in Bengal.

Oklahoma's largest department store John A. Brown made a similar point, probably inadvertently, when on December 25 it ran a full-page ad in *The Daily Oklahoman* in honor of its own employees now in uniform, and of every young member of the community who had left for the war. In most cases, they were young men who might otherwise rarely have crossed the boundary to neighboring Arkansas and might never have left the United States: "On this Christmas Day we propose a toast. To Joe on a submarine off the Alaska coast. To Bill in the tank corps on Africa sands. To Harold flying bombers over faraway lands. To our 36 boys in the air, on land and sea. And to your boys too, wherever they may be."[18]

At the same time in Germany, the Nazi party newspaper *Völkischer Beobachter* also reflected in its pages, in its own sinister way, how the war had scattered an entire generation across the map, as it published death notices for young members of the armed forces who had lost their lives on different battle fronts. Hans Prinz, a 22-year-old non-commissioned officer with an armored regiment, had been killed in North Africa.[19] Hermann Schwee, a 29-year-old field surgeon, had died from his wounds near Smolensk in Russia. On a different section of the vast Eastern Front, Lieutenant Franz Kunz, 26, had been killed south of the city of Rzhev. Gottfried Huber, a 22-year-old sergeant in an armored unit, had died in the Caucasus. Manfred Gesenberg, also just 22 years of age, had lost his life in occupied France.[20]

If war is politics by other means, world war is globalization by other, violent means. In 1942 this was more evident than perhaps at any previous time in the history of human conflict. The world war was commonly seen as having begun in 1939 with Germany's attack on Poland. Some might even say that its actual starting point was 1937 with the Japanese invasion of China. Strictly speaking, however, they were two separate regional conflicts that only became linked up with the US entry into the war in late 1941 and the gradual deployment of American troops overseas in the course of the following 12 months. That made Christmas 1942 the first truly global Christmas of the war.

The notion that this was a global Christmas was not lost on those in the midst of things. Nikolai Belov, a Russian soldier, felt an acute sense of relief when he heard about the Allied invasion of Northwest Africa thousands of miles from where he himself was fighting. "It's a long way, but it seems it's also quite close," he wrote in his diary.[21] There was a quiet awe at the way in which the war had shrunk the world, linking individuals in places previously accessible only to the most adventurous. "You may be serving for the first time in Gibraltar, in Malta, in Cyprus, in the Middle East, in Ceylon, or in India," Britain's King George VI said in his Christmas broadcast, addressing soldiers defending the sprawling empire. "Perhaps you are listening to me from Aden or Syria, or Persia, or Madagascar or the West Indies."[22]

Similarly, in his Christmas message Australian Prime Minister John Curtin made a virtual tour of the world as he listed the places where his compatriots were serving: "Sailors on the seven seas; soldiers in embattled Britain, in the deserts of the Middle East, in steaming, fetid New Guinea and Papua, in the guerrilla lairs of Timor, at battle stations in and around the Commonwealth; airmen in Britain, Canada, the Middle East, India, Rhodesia, Russia, Iceland, Malta, Iraq and Australia's front line; women's auxiliaries everywhere Australians stand to arms—you are our sword and buckler."[23]

The 1930s had been a time when international travel was rarely undertaken, not just because the gathering storms of war made it less safe to venture abroad, but also because technology and infrastructure placed strict limits on where one could go. War changed all that. Ken Marks of the US Army Air Force had been trained as a flight engineer on a B-17 bomber, with one final week of getting used to the specifics of the B-24, and it was on a B-24 that he left Miami on Christmas morning. "We didn't know where we were going," he told an interviewer after the war. "We were supposed to fly a certain course for an hour and then open up our orders. Our orders were to go to the 7th Bomb Group in India. We were all set to go to England."[24] They thought they were traveling to Britain. Instead, they went to India. The world had indeed become smaller.

It was particularly paradoxical for the American public, many of whom had hoped until the previous year to stay aloof in isolationist complacency from the war raging beyond the oceans. Now, the war brought the world closer to their homes than at any earlier time in their history. An editorial writer at the *Cincinnati Enquirer* reminded his readers of this fact, describing how "most of us, on this Christmas Day, will find our merriment restrained; for we shall be thinking of clear-eyed young men in the humid heat of Guadalcanal or the knife-edged winds of Iceland—or on the sleet-swept, turbulent waters of the North Atlantic. On Christmas Day, they will be thinking of us, and we of them."[25]

* * *

Christmas highlighted the connection between battlefront and home front, in the United States and in most other countries where there was a tradition for celebrating it, not least Germany. Through letters and on very rare occasions by radio, soldiers and sailors were able to connect with their loved ones at home and in this way, they were once more reminded what they were fighting for. Still, it was a double-edged sword for military authorities concerned with morale in the rank and file, for at the same time, too much Christmas paved the way for sentimentality and nostalgia taking hold in dangerous ways. It was a balancing act and the result of a development that had lasted for more than a century. As Christmas had become a bigger event in people's lives across the western world, it had also become a more dominant feature in wartime.

John Milton in his ode *On the Morning of Christ's Nativity* written in 1629 famously juxtaposed Christmas and war:

> No war or battle's sound
> Was heard the world around;
> The idle spear and shield were high uphung;
> The hooked chariot stood
> Unstain'd with hostile blood;
> The trumpet spake not to the armed throng;
> And kings sate still with awful eye,
> As if they surely knew their sovran Lord was by.

Every American schoolchild knows that George Washington crossed the Delaware River on Christmas 1776 to lead a surprise attack on Hessian troops in New Jersey. The holiday did play a role in the action, inasmuch as the German soldiers were partly incapacitated by the previous night's revelry, but nevertheless it did not quite have the impact with the American nation as one might expect, looking back at the event with modern eyes. Christmas had simply not become the grand celebration, heavy with emotion and memory, that we know today. That only came in the course of the 19th century.

As the American identity was gradually strengthened during the decades after achieving independence, Christmas emerged as a holiday that could forge the nation together across confessional dividing lines, as the religious element in the celebrations was comparatively modest. Railways and roads contributed to better communication, facilitating the spread of common understandings of how Christmas should be celebrated. Especially in the North, where closely-knit village life gave way to large towns and cities, the need was felt particularly keenly for new traditions that could recreate some of the lost sense of community.[26]

The lawyer Isaac Mickle was astonished by the sight that met him in Philadelphia in December 1842. "I never saw so many people turned out to celebrate Christmas," he wrote in his diary. "The main streets were literally jammed."[27] It added to the popularity of the holiday that immigrant communities could readily fit in, contributing their own traditions brought from the Old World, not least German immigrants, who were arriving in ever greater numbers.[28] The trend was further helped along by popular culture. The author Clement Clarke Moore laid part of the foundation for the modern Santa Claus, describing him in his poem "A Visit from St. Nicholas" as "tubby and plump, a right jolly old elf."[29]

During the Civil War, Christmas was not yet an American public holiday, but nevertheless it was an important event in the lives of a majority of the soldiers and civilians, many of them deeply religious, and it was celebrated in ways recognizable to a 21st-century public. Christmas carols such as "Jingle Bells" and "It Came Upon the Midnight Clear" had been written in the preceding decade and were sung by troops in the field. The German-born artist Thomas Nast included Santa Claus in his patriotic illustrations, showing him handing gifts to Union troops and transforming him definitively into the jovial, barrel-bellied character loved by future generations.[30]

One of Nast's wildly popular illustrations for *Harper's Weekly* highlighted one of the lasting themes of Christmas at war. Created for Christmas 1862, it showed a Union soldier in the field and his wife at home hundreds of miles away, kept apart by physical distance but united in prayer.[31] One year later, Nast drew the same fictional couple, now in each other's arms, as the husband had been allowed home on furlough. The separation from loved ones, which had been a circumstance accompanying war since the beginning of history, was felt particularly keenly during Christmas, which had been emerging in the preceding decades as not just a religious holiday, but also an occasion for getting together with family and giving gifts.

This view of Christmas was still not universally appreciated, and some northerners considered it a betrayal of the holiday's original meaning. Likewise, up the chain of command there was considerable ambivalence regarding the advisability of letting the troops get carried away with the holiday spirit. In some instances, officers even banned any celebration of Christmas among the troops. Others had a deeper understanding of how to keep morale high. President Abraham Lincoln praised Nast as "our best recruiting sergeant,"[32] while General Ulysses S. Grant said he "did as much as any one man to preserve the Union and bring the war to an end."[33]

In Europe, too, Christmas increased in importance, in peace and at war. The Franco-Prussian War saw the German Army camped outside Paris during Christmas 1870. It was the first mythical "War Christmas," even though for the participants there was often nothing glamorous about it. "The French never stopped sending us their holiday greetings, at the usual hour, in the form of bombs and grenades," a Bavarian soldier reminisced later.[34] In the romanticized memory of the war, however, the holiday spent at the gates of the French capital came to be seen as a national event of great importance, uniting home and front. Christmas trees, which had a history dating back to the 16th century, were distributed among military camps and hospitals, and from then on, they were seen as truly and essentially German. "Nowhere else in Christendom is the holiday celebrated with such sincerity and warmth as in the German lands," claimed a patriotic book from the post-war years.[35]

This German view of a patriotic Christmas was maintained for nearly half a century and carried into World War I. The almost mystical link between the army in the field and the people at home was felt even more intensively. "Our thought rushed as if on a golden bridge from here to the homeland, where they were also getting ready for Christmas in church and family," according to one account of a Christmas mass on the western front.[36]

One incident above all others stood out: the Christmas truce of December 1914. As the holiday approached, on certain parts of the Western Front the opposing sides stopped firing at each other, and eventually, after having built up enough mutual confidence, met in no man's land. For the next few hours, they chatted, sang songs, exchanged gifts, and played football. Officers on both sides immediately understood that this type of fraternizing was devastating for morale, and quickly reined it in, never allowing it to be repeated. Still, for those who experienced the remarkable event, it left an indelible mark. "People don't believe it," said Archibald Stanley, a British veteran. "We had this unofficial truce. We met in no man's land on Christmas Day 1914. We shook hands—they were Saxons—and I heard one fellow talking English."[37]

The Christmas truce attained almost mythical status, due to the great attention it attracted in the mass media and popular imagination later. Still, it was atypical. It only happened in a few places in 1914, and for the rest of the war, Christmas was no different from any other time of the year. The German Catholic chaplain Fridolin Mayer, for one, described a dreary Christmas in the freezing mud of the Western Front in 1916. Christmas Day was taken up partly with the burial of a soldier from the engineers who had been killed on Christmas Eve while fetching food. "So, now I've experienced the third Christmas at war," he wrote in his diary on December 28, noting that reports suggested growing belief in imminent peace. "At the front, they are pessimists and consider the possibility of a fourth war Christmas."[38]

* * *

War and Christmas had a long prehistory by the time the world descended into global conflict for a second time within just decades. December 1942 already saw the fourth war Christmas for the European belligerents. For adherents of the Christian faith in China and Japan, who had entered into conflict in the summer of 1937, it was the sixth. The belligerents were confronting each other with greater fury and a more implacable attitude than in perhaps any other modern war, since the national differences that usually animate conflict were exacerbated by ideological and especially racial hatreds. Still, for a few precious hours, they were united, often reluctantly, by a common observance of Christmas.

An elderly British woman spoke for many, on both sides of the conflict, when she wrote in her diary, "A very happy Christmas we had to be sure, and here is to a very happy and perhaps peaceful 1943."[39] That did not happen, and most observers directing a cool, analytical eye at the frontlines by late 1942 would have known that the war could not possibly end that fast. It was fanciful to imagine that Christmas 1942 could have become the last war Christmas.

Still, those who paused, however briefly, in December 1942 to ponder the situation realized they were experiencing a time that would never be entirely erased entirely from memory. The Norwegian architect and resistance fighter Odd Nansen, who was kept by the Germans at their internment camp at Grini near the occupied capital of Oslo, felt it keenly. "While other Christmas Eves," he wrote in his diary, "will be merged increasingly in one continuous image of children and candles round the unifying symbol and center of the Christmas fir, this Christmas Eve will always stand out—let us hope alone—in our memory."[40]

It was a story like no other, and it played out again and again across the globe, even as the titanic struggle for the future of mankind raged on. It is a story that can be told in many different ways—perhaps as many as there were people experiencing it. Our story begins in the Pacific, where one year earlier the Americans had been brutally awakened from their slumber and confronted with the ugly necessity of war. Of all places, it happened in their own version of paradise, the sunny islands of Hawaii.

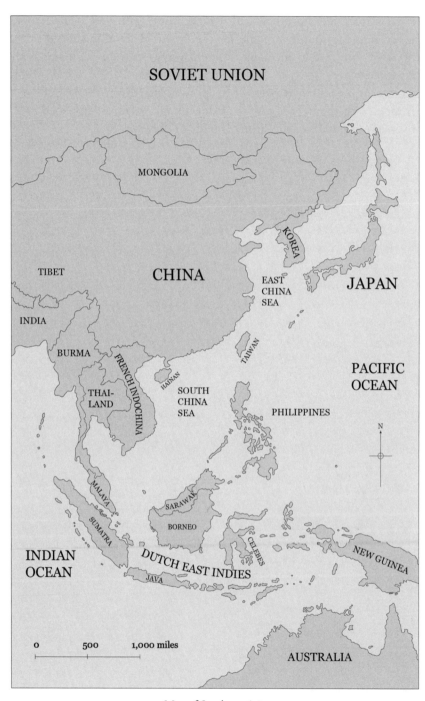

Map of Southeast Asia

CHAPTER I

"Mele Kalikimaka"

The Pacific

Hawaii was where it had all begun little more than a year earlier. On a lazy Sunday morning, Japanese planes had swooped in over the blue waters of Pearl Harbor and brought death and devastation to the US Pacific Fleet. Altogether 2,403 Americans had been killed. Many of the young casualties had spent the final hours of their lives carrying out last-minute Christmas shopping in Honolulu, just in time to have the presents shipped back to family in the continental United States ahead of the holiday. No wonder, then, that in December 1941, the people of Hawaii had lived through a somber Christmas, full of apprehension of what the future might bring. They had still been reeling from the lightning strike and reminded of it by the foul smell of burned and rotting bodies that had continued to hang over the naval base.[1]

Now it was 1942, and once again Christmas was coming around. In the year that had passed Hawaii had seen greater change than any other US territory. It had been transformed into one of the main staging areas for the ambitious drive that American planners were preparing to take back the Pacific. Men and women forced into uniform by the sudden entrance of the United States into the global conflict were in evidence everywhere. The white uniforms of the Navy and the olive hues of the Army and the Marine Corps filled the streets. Almost none of the young soldiers and sailors had been in Hawaii before, and they tried to get used to the tropical temperatures, so different from the cooler weather that most of them knew from home, while also practicing how to wish a "Merry Christmas" in the local language: "*Mele Kalikimaka.*"[2]

The climate made it hard to get in the right mood, and the scarcity of Christmas decorations in the local stores did little to change the atmosphere. Wartime necessity rendered it impossible to ship in Christmas trees from the American northwest, as had usually been done, and local *ersatz* trees had to be found instead. "On Oahu some pines are available, but algarobas and ironwoods also are performing wartime duty as Christmas trees," a correspondent noted.[3] Brightly lit outdoor Christmas trees were banned, even though the blackout that had been imposed in the early tense days after the Japanese assault had been replaced with a "dim-out." It still left Hawaii a sinister place after dark, since the only lights allowed were 25-watt bulbs—often reconverted Christmas tree lights—that had been painted black except for a one-inch circle at the bottom.[4]

It was a time for quiet contemplation for the men in the armed forces, some little more than boys torn away from their loved ones for the first time in their lives. Still, in the overall atmosphere of quiet melancholy, there were also moments of magic where the holiday brought strangers together in unexpected ways. In one of the many tent camps scattered across the Hawaiian Islands, the soldiers were getting ready to sleep on Christmas Eve, trying not to think too much about home, when they heard a strange, slender voice reaching them through the night. They made their way out of the tents, alone and in groups. "There on a mountaintop in Hawaii, in a moment of stillness in a world at war, a woman who had never seen snow sang, 'I'm Dreaming of a White Christmas'," recount two historians of World War II Hawaii. "It was her gift, and she knew it was not enough."[5]

At the same time, in a residential area near Honolulu, Wilfred Jay "Jasper" Holmes, an ex-Navy man and a professor at the University of Hawaii who had been called back to active service working for intelligence, held a Christmas gathering at his home, mostly in order to entertain those among his officers who had come from stateside and were feeling lonesome on this special evening. Among them was Lieutenant Joseph Finnegan, a Japanese language specialist, who almost made the evening too memorable: "When Finnegan stood up and led the language officers in an emotional rendition of 'Kaigun Kōshin Kyoku,' the Japanese Navy song, in Japanese, his Irish tenor must have been heard to the uttermost limits," Holmes wrote in his memoirs. "I thought we might all end up in jail for the night."[6]

That fear was not baseless. A mood of caution and suspicion permeated Honolulu and the rest of Hawaii, as it had ever since the Japanese had struck. Academic staff at the University of Hawaii were investigated after they were overheard singing German Christmas carols. A strict curfew was in force, and military police patrolled the streets looking for violators.[7] Military rule had been imposed immediately after the Japanese attack, resulting in unprecedented powers being handed to government. Citizens down to the age of six had been forced to submit fingerprints, and although the internment of Americans of Japanese descent was not as sweeping here as it had been along the US West Coast, altogether 1,450 who were considered potential security threats had been detained, and in November, 107 of them had been transferred from Hawaii to Jerome Relocation Center in Arkansas.[8]

The anxious mood could not change the fact that on the whole, there was a sense that after a tense 1942 things were finally moving in the right direction for America and its Allies. The immediate fear of a Japanese invasion was gone. Lieutenant General Delos Emmons, commander of the Hawaiian Department and in this capacity ultimately responsible for the islands' garrison, congratulated the men under his command on a year during which much had been accomplished, but at the same time warned that the guards could not be let down. "There must be no relaxation nor any indication of a feeling that the job is completed," he said in his Christmas message. "The military security of these islands must be assured, and it is the primary duty of each one of us to contribute to the utmost of his ability to that assurance."[9]

Despite widespread understanding that the national emergency made extraordinary measures necessary, a growing note of impatience was emerging in the public debate, and dissenting voices appeared in the press, stating with surprising candor that the situation was neither normal, nor desirable and ought to end as soon as possible. An unnamed official with the Interior Department told the United Press news agency in an interview that Joseph B. Poindexter, the eighth governor of the Territory, had interrupted a venerable tradition for civilian rule when declaring martial law in the wake of the Pearl Harbor raid. "The situation became pretty awful," the anonymous official said. "It has been the first military government on American soil."[10]

A return to normalcy was still a long way off in December 1942, and Admiral Chester W. Nimitz, the 57-year-old commander of US forces in the Pacific, could promise little more than blood, sweat and tears. He had arrived in Pearl Harbor to assume the position exactly one year earlier, on Christmas Day 1941,[11] and he could now look back on 12 months during which Japan, seemingly invincible in January, had been forced onto the defensive. There were many feats to be proud of, with the surprise victory at Midway in June as the crowning achievement, but while he used the occasion to thank those who had made it all possible, he reminded them how much was still left to be done. "To all fighting men in the Pacific: On this holiest of days I extend my greetings with admiration of your brave deeds of the past year. The victories you have won, the sacrifices you have made, the ordeals you now endure, are an inspiration to the Christian world," he said, concluding: "As you meet the Jap along this vast battle line from the Aleutians to the Solomons, remember, liberty is in every blow you strike."[12]

* * *

One of the blows described by Nimitz was struck in the early hours of December 24. In the middle of the black Pacific night, a group of 26 bombers, B-24D Liberators, were heading west at an altitude of 10,000 feet. They were from the 307th Bombardment Group, activated earlier in 1942. Their base was Oahu in Hawaii, and their target was Wake Island, an atoll in the Western Pacific which had formerly been under US control but had wound up in Japanese hands after an invasion one year earlier. The aircraft stopped over for refueling on the island of Midway, extending their radius significantly and allowing them to cross a vast expanse of ocean with their heavy load of 135 general-purpose bombs weighing in at 500 pounds each, as well as 21 incendiaries.[13]

This was the first large-scale air raid on Wake since the Japanese occupation. Only scattered American reconnaissance planes had been anywhere near the island in the intervening period, and it was unclear how well-prepared the Japanese defenses were. Time would tell. The B-24Ds crossed the International Date Line before making the final approach towards the target. As the isolated island appeared in front of the heavy planes as a black spot that was rapidly growing larger amid the dark silvery glow of the ocean, the Japanese garrison seemed fast asleep. There were no searchlights, no tracer bullets ripping through the air, no planes being scrambled. The bombers had made the entire journey undetected, and now they were favored by the element of surprise.

War correspondent Olen W. Clements was in the lead plane and reported on the attack in vivid terms: "It's one minute after midnight Christmas Eve day. What a surprise package the Japs are going to get pretty soon now."[14] With just seconds to go, the bombers commenced a dive to 4,000 feet, the altitude where they would release their cargo in a single bomb run. "On and on we plunge," Clements wrote. "The speed is terrific, the wind mad. I'm thinking about friends and relatives and wishing I was a little boy. Then I wouldn't be here." Suddenly the pilot leveled the bomber off. "Wham! Wham! Bombs go off below. The bomber shoots out over the water. My knees almost collapse. It's over, and we are still alive."[15]

The bomber crews were unable to assess the exact damage they had inflicted on the Japanese installations, as the targets were covered in smoke by several fires, but it was clear they had scored a tactical triumph, proving not for the first time that the arrogance of the Japanese could be used against them.[16] The Japanese, unwilling to contemplate the idea that they could be attacked so far away from the nearest American base, only started firing at the planes after the first bombs had already fallen, and then it was too late.

The B-24Ds headed back towards Midway, with only two of the planes having sustained superficial damage. By the time they touched down in Oahu, after one more refueling stop on Midway, they had covered more than 4,300 nautical miles. "This raid and others like it will not alone eject the enemy from Wake," Admiral Nimitz stated after the attack. "Such raids will, however, serve notice on the enemy, as well as give assurance to our own countrymen, that we have the men with the spirit, resolution and skill to handle the tools that are going to drive the Jap back to his own islands."[17]

Vice Admiral Ugaki Matome, chief of staff of Japan's Combined Fleet, was at the receiving end of the American determination to strike back. He was furious as he jotted down the details of the attack in his diary. He described, erroneously, how Wake had been hit by a fleet of B-17 Flying Fortress bombers, and he noted, also in error, that four of the enemy bombers had been shot down, while six others had been hit, before they had turned around. While he referred to the alleged enemy losses with some satisfaction, a sense of anger, even betrayal, seeped through in his diary entry for the day: "Did they carry it out last night hoping to make it a Christmas present for us? Last year we specifically ordered that our submarine on the West Coast of the States withhold bombardment on Christmas Eve. If they're going to treat us in such a way, we'll treat them in the same way."[18]

Amid the fury, however, there was also something akin to reluctant admiration. After a similar daring raid carried out by the US Navy against another Japanese base in the Pacific 10 months earlier, the vice admiral had grudgingly acknowledged the special élan displayed by his American adversaries, stating in his diary that "adventure is one of their characteristics."[19] This was only part of the story. It was not just resourcefulness and boldness that had carried the Americans to where they were now. Technology and the ability to bring huge industrial resources to bear across the vast ocean played an equally important part.

The Christmas attack on Wake showed that the United States military was already establishing the infrastructure that was to assist it in taking back the Pacific from the Japanese. All parts of the vast American military machine were needed in this endeavor, but the US Navy's powerful submarines, which had been in an offensive role since a few hours after Pearl Harbor, were essential. The members of the silent service demonstrated their importance again this Christmas. As the B-24Ds from the 307th Bombardment Group made their way across the dark ocean towards Wake, they were guided by a network of submarines signaling from the surface below.

One of them was the USS *Triton* under the command of Charles C. Kirkpatrick. Once the mission was completed, the sub's crew spotted the mast of the Japanese transport ship *Amakasu Maru* en route to Wake Island. Rather than slipping away in the safe knowledge that he had accomplished his primary mission, Kirkpatrick opted for attack. Closing to a distance of 1,000 yards, the submarine fired two torpedoes, both of which hit, sending the vessel to the bottom of the ocean with the loss of the lives of 12 Japanese crew members.[20]

This was no isolated incident. At the exact same time, but more than 4,000 miles away, the submarine USS *Thresher* was patrolling waters off the city of Soerbaya in the occupied Dutch East Indies when the crew spotted a coastal convoy of freighters, protected by an escort of two destroyers, a number of submarine chasers and two aircraft. Despite the size of the enemy force, the *Thresher*'s commander, Moke Millican, decided to attack, sending five torpedoes in rapid succession against the three leading transports.

Some of the torpedoes missed or malfunctioned, but two explosions ensued, and when the submarine rose to periscope depth, Millican saw one 7,000-ton freighter sinking, and another enveloped in smoke.[21] The escorting vessels immediately went into action and almost got *Thresher*. "They came after us with depth charges," Jacques Abels, a junior officer on board, told a reporter many years later. "It was really scary. The water was only 150 feet deep. We had to do evasive action to get away from the destroyers."[22]

The American submarine crews were facing nerve-wracking risks on their missions, but they knew they were backed by a logistical apparatus with immense resources at its disposal. The American submarine force was roaming almost at will and had done so since the earliest days of the war, making even the Japanese home islands a warzone. Most Japanese did not realize this, and probably they would not have believed it if they had been told, but just days after Pearl Harbor, they were being watched by enemy vessels lurking in the waters only miles off their coastline.

Thus, on Christmas Eve 1942, the submarine USS *Trigger* was in a position off Tokyo Bay, looking for prey among the vessels sailing in and out of the enemy's capital city. One of the enlisted men suggested hooking the record player to the PA system, allowing the entire crew to listen to Christmas carols. A member of the crew, Edward Beach, had a lump in his throat "the size of a watermelon." He later recalled the special feeling as the music, amplified by two speakers on the deck, drifted away into the ominous dark: "For the few minutes that those magic, so-well-remembered strains filled the air we were transported away from the battle, and the danger, and the lurking terror."[23]

* * *

By Christmas 1942, the Americans were already making large parts of the Pacific their ocean, from the warm waters near the Equator to the frozen expanses in the far north. Chief Commissary Steward Worth Smith arrived in Alaska on board a US Navy vessel just before Christmas, braving a 60-mile gale. The men had not been near a radio ever since they had left the contiguous United States, and only now did they find out how popular "White Christmas" had become. They had difficulty sympathizing with Bing Crosby's wish for a snow-covered holiday, since they themselves had to toil all their waking hours to scrape ice off of guns and every piece of exposed equipment. "It took us every minute of Christmas Day to get rid of our 'White Christmas', and we were ready to make a Jap out of the guy who wrote the song," Smith told a reporter a few months later.[24]

Further west, in the wind-swept Aleutians, American forces were preparing to roll back the Japanese advance in this part of the Pacific. Here, in June, Japanese troops had occupied the two islands of Attu and Kiska, becoming the only Axis forces to take possession of American soil. US forces were now getting ready for the counterattack, and it was as part of this effort that Lieutenant Commander Joseph C. Bronson, the commander of the United States Naval Construction Battalion 4, arrived on the island of Adak, 250 miles from the nearest Japanese forces, shortly before Christmas Eve. The American ground forces slated to hit the Japanese needed ports and warehouses to stay supplied, and Bronson was there to build them.[25]

However, immediately after setting foot on Alaskan soil, he went down with the flu and was unable to attend a Christmas party on the base. Gifts sent from the Navy Wives Club in Seattle were handed out at the gathering, and J. R. Ritter, an officer on the base, brought some to the incapacitated lieutenant commander. "Joe was just like a little kid getting toys for Christmas," Ritter wrote in his memoirs.[26] It was all testimony to the main factor that made America an awe-inspiring opponent in the war. Bronson and Ritter were posted in one of the most inhospitable and thinly populated places in the world, and yet the means were available to arrange a Christmas party and distribute presents sent from afar.

It was part of a larger story about who was going to win the war and why. The conflict that was shaping up in the almost impossibly huge Pacific, covering roughly one third of surface of the Earth, was primarily one of logistics, and the United States, as the predominant industrial power, second to none in the mass utilization of state-of-the-art technology, was superbly equipped to fight that kind of war. Japan had bitten off more than it could chew at Pearl Harbor, and by December 1942, the almost absurd mismatch in the capabilities of the two sides was already becoming apparent.

That Christmas, at the other end of the Pacific, the US Navy was showing off its might in the form of its aircraft carriers, ready to beat the Japanese at their own game. Off the French territory of New Caledonia, east of Australia, James E. Wilson, a Marine, remembered the wonder he felt at seeing the enormous hull of aircraft carrier USS *Enterprise* and the comforting feeling of knowing that this man-made giant was on his side. "The people on the *Enterprise* shared their Christmas dinner with us," he said.[27]

To be sure, supplies were not inexhaustible, even for the United States, but it was important to at least give the impression that they were. The fact that each submarine was carrying turkey on board to be served for the crews during Christmas suggested a level of material plenty their opponents could only dream of, even if it was not entirely real and there was an element of make-believe.[28] George C. Marshall, the US Army chief of staff, encouraged efforts to go to great lengths in order to spoil the troops, especially during Christmas and other holidays. "Many of our people forget the importance of little things to morale," he said. "The men think if there is candy up forward, things can't be so bad."[29]

It was a reflection of this very philosophy that officers at the US Navy's Advance Base 1 at Noumea, capital of New Caledonia, tried to create a Christmas atmosphere, even though it was hard in a part of the southern hemisphere where summer was at its most verdant, with bougainvillea and poinsettia in full bloom. Undeterred, Navy engineers erected a large Christmas tree, shipped in from colder climes, and crushed shiny white coral, spreading it on the ground in a radius of 25–30 feet to make it look like newly fallen snow.

Among the spectators was Dick Wood, a young sailor who had only weeks earlier survived the sinking of the destroyer USS *Meredith*. On Christmas Eve he chanced upon a high-school friend, who was now serving on board the battleship USS *North Carolina*. "Homesick? Terribly!" he reminisced many years later. "Two 19-year-old boys sitting here on Christmas Eve, 10,000 miles from homes and families on a hot tropical island, looking down upon a scene that reminded us so much of Christmastime at home."[30]

Still, the real business of the Navy was fighting, and Admiral Bill Halsey, its commander of the South Pacific Area with headquarters in Noumea, did not forget that. In the morning of December 24, he carried out an air attack on Munda, a Japanese stronghold on the island of New Georgia in the Solomons to the north. Nine Douglas SBD Dauntless dive bombers under fighter escort dropped their load on a nearly complete Japanese air strip, as well as on landing barges anchored nearby. "It is reported that the landing strip is considerably damaged," an after-action assessment stated.[31]

Halsey, who was already a household name at home and had made it to the front page of *Time* magazine the month before, knew it was just a temporary triumph, and the air strip would indeed be operational again within a week, but it was a small step on the long way to Tokyo. "Having hung up a record that day, we hung up our stockings that night with extra cheeriness. My staff procured some small, imitation Christmas trees, and our Filipino mess attendants festooned them with 'flowers' carved from radishes and carrots," he wrote in his memoirs.[32]

The American presence inevitably left a large and not always welcome imprint on New Caledonia, previously a sleepy colonial backwater. Paul F. Wachholz, a junior officer in the US Army stationed in New Caledonia, was reminded of this fact when he received an invitation from a French resident by the name of Emile Roland to join him for Christmas dinner at his home. Wachholz knew the place well. When he had first arrived, he had set up his unit of 50 men and four water-cooled, tripod-mounted .50 caliber machine guns in Roland's tropical garden, ruining his carefully nurtured papaya and mango trees. Using the Christmas party to apologize, he was surprised to see the Frenchman shrug his shoulders. Remembering the Americans who had come to the rescue of France during the previous war, he considered it a small price to pay. "*C'est la guerre*," he said. "That's war."[33]

* * *

There was something downright uncanny about Christmas in the tropics, combat correspondent Mack Morriss thought. Most important and inescapable of all, there was the temperature. The heat was the first thing he noticed after he touched down on the island of Guadalcanal on board a B-17 aircraft on December 24. The moment the propellers of the bomber stopped turning, beads of sweat started rolling down his face. "This is the hottest Christmas Eve I've ever spent," he wrote in his diary.[34] Attempts to instill the Christmas spirit in this unlikeliest of places disintegrated into absurd theater. The Christmas balls and the red and green rope decorating the mess shacks looked dramatically out of place against the dark green jungle. Listening to Army bands playing

"Joy to the world" while sinking into the mud created by a sudden violent shower sent shivers down his spine.[35]

Morriss had traveled to Guadalcanal expecting to witness the fighting that had been going on since the summer, but he initially saw few signs that he was in a combat zone. On Christmas Day, 24 hours after arriving on "the Canal," he still had not seen or heard much of the war, except the faint rumble of distant artillery, which might just as well have been thunder to the untrained ear. "Nobody seemed to have an idea that the Japs were anywhere within a thousand miles—they're about four," he wrote in his diary.[36] Bomb craters and palm trees mangled by shrapnel showed that it had not always been this peaceful. "War has been here," Morriss wrote. "That it is still here, I have to find out."[37]

In fact, by Christmas, the nearly five-month-long battle for Guadalcanal was approaching an end. From the US point of view, the campaign had initially been aimed at protecting the vital sea lane between the American West Coast and Australia with the secondary purpose of laying the groundwork for the long-term endeavor of pushing back the Japanese forces in the South Pacific. During a fall season marked by grueling combat, much of it hand-to-hand and all of it brutal, it had gradually become less defensive in nature and had transformed into America's first offensive.

In the waning days of 1942, the Japanese forces on the island, reduced by disease, injury and hunger to just 12,000 men fit for fight, had been pushed into a narrowing perimeter, and they were now centering their efforts on keeping a toehold on Guadalcanal around a series of hills in the northwestern part of the island. Morriss, eager to see action, arrived at the hills, known as Mount Austen to the Americans, a few days after Christmas. He reached positions held by the 132nd Regiment, which had landed on Guadalcanal in early December and had been deployed directly in the frontline, just as news about an ill-fated patrol was filtering in. "They were serious and, I think, mad," he wrote in his diary.[38]

The patrol, consisting of 18 soldiers led by 2nd Lieutenant Albert D. Swacina, had set out on Christmas Eve and made its way through 1,000 yards of dense jungle to reconnoiter the Japanese positions and gauge enemy strength. The first half of the patrol went well, but its members committed the cardinal error of making their way back along the same route that they had used on the way out. The Japanese, knowing that their enemy was still green and inexperienced, had expected them to make exactly that mistake and had set up an ambush. In a hail of gunfire, several members of the patrol were killed or injured.

Swacina received a bullet to his neck and died within minutes. Without a leader, panic erupted among the soldiers, many still new to combat. "The sergeant ran off hollering, just about losing his mind," Private Anthony Martinez, who had his baptism of fire, told a reporter after the war. "We went after him and brought him back."[39] Most of the patrol managed to scramble to the safety of the American lines, but one injured soldier who had been hit by shrapnel was left behind. In the morning, as he heard Japanese voices through the thicket, he started crawling back and eventually reached US-held positions.[40]

The Christmas patrol at Mount Austen was not the only time that the untried soldiers of the 132nd Regiment showed themselves inferior to the battle-hardened Japanese, and morale was at rock bottom for many of the newly arrived Americans. This gave Christmas particular significance. It could be a time when the mood deteriorated even further, or it could be an opportunity to give the soldiers and Marines on Guadalcanal a morale boost which would pay off in terms of their future performance on the battlefield, as General Marshall had advised. The officers on Guadalcanal did their utmost to make sure it was the latter.

Marine Roy H. Elrod, who spent Christmas on the banks of the Matanikau River near Mount Austen, was one of the beneficiaries and was served his first real meal since he had landed in early November. It was turkey with all the trimmings. "They brought it up in heated and insulated containers and they just dipped it out into our mess gear," he wrote later. "It was a little bit on the cool side, but we would've eaten it raw."[41] The 1st Battalion, 11th Marine Regiment, also received a special treat on Christmas Day. They, too, got turkey, and Christmas packages and mail from home were sent in by plane. A tropical plant with a good enough resemblance to a pine was decorated with cotton balls and colored paper strips to serve as a Christmas tree.[42]

Some Americans were so close to the sharp end that their Christmas provisions could not be brought to them by conventional means. This was true for Battery H, 3rd Battalion, 10th Marines, which had an eventful Christmas Eve. The Japanese had located the battery's position on a ridge and fired mortar round after mortar round at the artillerymen. The Marines fired back every few minutes, calling it "a Christmas present for Tojo's soldiers," referring to Japanese Prime Minister Tojo Hideki, whose round glasses and thin moustache had made him one of the most widely known Axis leaders in the American public. In the middle of the life-and-death duel, a column of local bearers known as the "Cannibal Battalion" arrived along a winding hill trail with a special Christmas treat for the men—sandwiches and a can of cranberry sauce for each Marine.[43]

The efforts of the officers to lift morale during Christmas were not universally successful. Johnny Coldiron, an infantryman, was too preoccupied with the business of survival to think about Christmas. "We didn't know when Christmas came that year," he said after the war. "We knew it was December but we didn't have too much time to think too much."[44] For some, Christmas even turned into a time of heightened frustration. Marine Robert Leckie's unit had received Christmas packages, mostly food, a few days early. They were about to ship out of Guadalcanal, and there were limits to what ordinary Marines could bring onboard. Leckie and his comrades devoured what they could and tossed out the rest. Only officers were allowed to carry seabags, even though they had actually been issued to enlisted men. "The officers would satisfy their covetousness by forbidding us things rightfully ours, and then take them up themselves, much as politicians use the courts to gain their ends," Leckie wrote with lingering bitterness in his memoirs.[45]

Even if they tried, the officers could only do so much to lift the mood of their men. Word from home mattered far more, and the lucky ones who received mail for Christmas were reminded what they were fighting for. One of them was James V. Edmundson, the commander of the 431st Bombardment Squadron, which flew B-17s out of Henderson Airfield on Guadalcanal. Being somewhat used to the military, his young wife probably understood better than most what life in the field entailed, and she sent him a parcel which arrived shortly before Christmas, full of items that he needed: socks, razor blades, soap, shaving cream, toothbrushes and Air Mail stamps.[46] Edmundson was delighted but did nothing to conceal how much he regretted the separation. "Christmas has always been such a big day for me that I hate to let one go by," he wrote back in a letter. "But at that, we are both alive and can look forward to being together again in six months or so. At least it's a better prospect than we had last Christmas."[47]

It was a desperate hope, and Edmundson may have known that he was unlikely to be reunited with his wife so soon. Even so, hope was important, whether it was hope of seeing loved ones again, or the kind of hope provided by religion. Frederic Gehring, a Navy chaplain, performed Christmas services for those on Guadalcanal who wanted to attend, and he was busy. His tent had been destroyed by Japanese shells, and the entire ceremony took place with the sounds of the continuing war as a constant, unsettling backdrop. "In the darkness we could hear the crackle of gunfire as the Japanese tried to infiltrate the Marine perimeter," Gehring said after the war.[48]

A pump organ had been transported from the nearby island of Tulagi, and the only man available to play it was a former professional boxer by the name of Barney Ross. Having grown up in a Jewish family, Ross did not know "Silent Night," but after fellow soldiers hummed it to him, he familiarized himself with the tune well enough to assist in the service. Ross knew that the Marines, soldiers and sailors on Guadalcanal were like himself, mostly just big boys who missed their mothers, and when he was done with the Christmas carols, he addressed the crowd of worshippers.

He touched on a subject that united them all, across religious dividing lines. "I've been thinking about my mother, too," he said, "and I've got a favorite song I'd like to play and sing in her honor."[49] He then proceeded to perform "My Yiddshe Momme." Few understood the Yiddish lyrics, but the song nevertheless struck a chord, Ross told an interviewer after the war: "There was a Jewish kid playing an organ and singing in Yiddish about his mama and a Catholic priest standing next to him with a violin trying to help it sound nice, and all around there were guys who came from every religion and some of them didn't even have one, but they were all crying and thinking about the same thing."[50]

At the same time, roughly 100 miles away, Marine 1st Lieutenant Emmett N. Carter was experiencing an even stranger encounter across a seemingly unbridgeable cultural chasm. Since mid-November, he had been in command of a small group of men on a lonely vigil on Rennell Island south of Guadalcanal. Their job was to observe Japanese movements in waters near the island and report back. The island was already inhabited by Polynesians, and before Carter and his men had been deployed, they had received a chilling warning that it was not known if the inhabitants were "friendly or cannibalistic."

The indigenous people, settled near Lake Tengano on the island, turned out to be sufficiently amicable to abstain from eating the new arrivals, and curious enough about the outside world to want to talk. In fact, missionaries from the Church of England had garnered a following there in the pre-war years, and Christmas provided common ground and an occasion to get together for the young Western soldiers and the locals, distant relatives on a planet divided by war. "I was invited to give the Christmas story to the entire Lake [Tengano] population on December 25," Carter wrote after the war. "It was questionable whether they received very much from my story."[51]

CHAPTER 2

Austerity Christmas

New Zealand, Australia and New Guinea

Gisborne, a town in northeastern New Zealand nested amid verdant pastures, was near the spot where British explorer Captain James Cook first set foot in October 1769. A little more than 173 years later, this community of roughly 15,000 inhabitants received new visitors. Fifty-two American Marines arrived on a special train and spent their Christmas with families in the area.[1] Most of them were patients from Silverstream Hospital near the New Zealand capital of Wellington, where they were being treated for malaria or injuries sustained in South Pacific battles.[2] Gisborne had never seen such an influx of Americans before. "This occasion will be remembered by our children and our children's children," Mayor N. H. Bull said.[3]

The Americans, still reeling from their hellish experiences fighting the Japanese, were spoiled by the locals. "It was […] summertime there, and it was right on the beach and all we had to do was roll out of the house and go for a swim," said Norman T. Hatch, a Marine combat photographer. "Everybody had a grand time. Beer was flowing like mad, and there were great, big parties on the beach."[4] The day before they departed, the Americans played baseball against a team of Gisborne residents, in front of a large crowd. "The local opposition were mainly cricketers, who took to the new game with such zest they were able to defeat the Americans by 10 runs to eight, the fielding of the local cricketers being a factor in their success," the *Gisborne Herald* reported with hardly suppressed pride.[5]

By Christmas 1942, New Zealand had been at war for nearly 40 months, having declared war on Germany on September 3, 1939, the same day as Britain, and subsequently it had sent its young citizens to fight Germany and Italy in remote battlefields with names that had once sounded exotic but had long since acquired a familiar ring: Maleme, Galatas, Tobruk. It had been a somber period, but the previous Christmas had been a particularly bleak one. Back then in late 1941, the island nation had been in shock from the rapid Japanese advance across the Pacific, which had suddenly brought the war much closer.

New Zealand was now "within the theater of war," as Prime Minister Peter Fraser had said in a Christmas message to his British counterpart Winston Churchill. "Days of difficulty and disappointment may lie ahead of us all," he had predicted ominously.[6] Now, a year on, there was light at the end of the tunnel. In his 1942 Christmas message to New Zealand troops fighting in the Middle East, Fraser promised a peace "which will bring you home and restore to you and us the right to live our own lives unmolested here in our own land."[7]

The optimism expressed by the premier was also palpable among the public at large. The *New Zealand Herald* noted a clear improvement in the mood from a year earlier. "There has been a buoyant Christmas spirit abroad during the past few days," it said in an editorial. "The contrast with last Christmas has been marked. The war position, particularly as it might have affected New Zealand, was serious last year. America had just been attacked and her weight had not yet been visibly exerted. Today the change in the war situation, generally, has had a stimulating effect upon the people. The spirit of confidence buttressing the will to victory is expressed in the buoyancy of the crowd."[8]

The triumphs that New Zealand's own forces were reporting back from the Middle East were a clear morale booster, but it was undeniably very far away, and the significance to the nation's own defense was not entirely clear. More important in terms of creating an immediate sense of security was the arrival of the Americans. At any one time for two years beginning in June 1942, there were between 15,000 and 45,000 American soldiers and sailors in New Zealand,[9] and during the entire period a total of 100,000 passed through on their way to Pacific battlefields or on their return journey away from them.[10] It was both a blessing and a curse.

It was not easy to miss the foreign presence in the cities and towns of New Zealand, with the different uniforms, strange accents and endearingly simple-minded questions about local customs. Their big, well-groomed smiles, testimony to an American obsession with teeth, were also noticed.[11] Still, many New Zealanders had a hard time understanding the roundabout logic of sending their own soldiers to fight European foes, with the consequence that troops had to be sent in from America to counter the more immediate Japanese threat. "Why are you sending New Zealand boys away and bringing Americans here?" an angry and bewildered citizen asked Defense Minister Frederick Jones in a meeting with voters in Christchurch.[12]

As an example of the problems it could entail, the Marine Raider battalion, which had been through fierce fights on Guadalcanal, spent Christmas 1942 in Wellington. For the men, it was the first real vacation since they had enlisted, and simple, half-forgotten pleasures like eating ice cream while strolling through city parks were suddenly possible. "Ate dinner off of a table, saw movies, went to dances and had a rip-roaring time," Corporal Lee Minier wrote in a letter home.[13]

For soldiers who had been in combat for an extended period of time and now returned to civilized life, often broken in body and soul, not all pleasures were equally innocent. Rear Admiral Kelly Turner, who ferried the Raiders to New Zealand aboard his flagship, the USS *McCawley*, had guessed as much. "When I remember what grand fighters all of you are, I also realize that I will have to stand responsible for all your misdeeds and explain them to my boss," he wrote in an apprehensive message before unloading the troops onto New Zealand soil. "I hope all of you have a grand time—but please remember to maintain the grand name you have established." Turner could not have done much more, and it did not help. One of the first days on land saw an epic street fight between the Raiders and New Zealand troops, later named the "Battle of Wellington."[14]

There were other fights like this, universally ignored by the local newspapers keen to maintain a flawless image of a fraternal cross-Pacific alliance, and often they were over sex. New Zealanders described the Americans dismissively as "bedroom commandos" who took advantage of lonely women whose husbands or boyfriends were away fighting.[15] Still, it did not stop romantic liaisons, and a total of 15,000 New Zealand women ended up marrying their American boyfriends and emigrating to the United States. Besides, the well-paid visitors helped the local economy as part of the courting routines. "Thanks to American servicemen, florists found this Christmas one of the best they had experienced," a journalist remarked in December 1942. "Indeed, with the limited range of flowers available at the moment and rather short supplies of those, some shops were unable to satisfy customers as the day wore on."[16]

The American interactions with the New Zealand population were complex and never unambiguous. This applied for all age groups, including the children, who loved the glamorous new visitors with an intensity bordering on hero worship, and who saw their affection richly rewarded: "One time they put on a Christmas party for all the kids in the neighborhood," a New Zealander recalled. "They got their names and their ages. There was a present for every child and a ride in the jeep too. There were games and paper hats and a real feast afterwards."[17]

Still, the American encounter even with young New Zealanders was also mixed, and an element of mendacity crept in. Teenagers and children down to the age of six quickly learned that there was good money to be made shining shoes for the Americans, and soon they started crowding around places known to be popular with GIs. "The entrance to a club was so congested with shoe-shiners that only one person could pass through at a time," a newspaper reported from Wellington. "To intercept even this small passing traffic a boy planted himself right in the gang way." This could not go on. Shortly before Christmas, the Wellington City Council decided to put an end to the chaotic practice, ordering that shoe-shiners keep off public streets.[18]

* * *

Like New Zealand, Australia had been changed in profound ways by the Americans. The Japanese entry into the war one year earlier had suddenly made the global conflict move closer to the Australians, but it had also entailed US participation on the Allied side, and with it, a guarantee that the Rising Sun flag would never be hoisted over Canberra's Government Building. Prime Minister John Curtin made that a point in his Christmas message to the troops. "Australians approach this Christmas period, after three years of war, without knowing the horrors of physical contact with war," he said. "To you, our fighting men, and to the forces of the United States, holding the approaches to Australia in the South-west Pacific, we owe a debt of gratitude we feel incapable ever of discharging."[19]

The prime minister was not entirely correct in his assertion that Australia had evaded direct attack. Parts of the nation had actually been bombed during 1942. Japanese planes operating off both aircraft carriers and land bases had raided the northern port city of Darwin several times, and there had been hundreds of casualties. Midget submarines had even slipped into Sydney Harbor. On the other hand, it was true that the Japanese military never had any concrete and detailed plans to invade Australia. Still, that was unknown at the time, and hard to imagine when looking at a map and realizing that the Japanese were entrenched in an arc around the northern shores of Australia from the East Indies over New Guinea to the Solomons.

It was, therefore, welcome news to see Americans arrive in huge numbers in the course of 1942. The influx was hard to miss. Reporting from Melbourne at the end of the year, *The Age* noted that much larger crowds than usual thronged the churches to take part in the special Christmas services. "Everywhere men and women in uniform formed a big proportion of the congregations, but this year these uniformed men and women were not only Australian," the newspaper's journalist remarked. "On this fourth war-time Christmas members of the fighting forces of other nations shared in Melbourne's observance of the festival."[20]

It was good to have representatives of the new powerful ally around, but it was also strange for both parties. It was odd to the Americans to find themselves in a country where Christmas was celebrated in mid-summer. It was an equally mystifying encounter to the Australians.[21] The change brought by the Americans was in evidence everywhere, and smaller communities sometimes were transformed beyond recognition and even beyond recovery. The town of Ballarat was typical. "We turned from a little conservative country town into this surging rage of men," one resident said. "Everybody came out to welcome them. You know, we looked at all these men as though they'd come from outer space."[22]

In Australia, too, the presence of the Americans led to a series of romantic liaisons, some ending in marriage. Similar to New Zealand, it triggered considerable anger, since the Yanks took the place of local men fighting in distant battlefields. A young woman offered a rationale for breaking up with her boyfriend, who had been taken prisoner by the Japanese in the early months of the war and was now languishing in a camp somewhere: "It's very hard at 22 to wait for someone when you don't know if they're going to be alive or dead or what's going to happen."[23]

Wartime brought a new moral codex, and in the opinion of some, declining standards. Crime was also on the rise, even though the contemporary press tried to avoid the topic at times. During Christmas 1942, Sydney police raided gambling dens in the Surry Hills district, arresting 94 people. Several of them were Chinese, who according to a local magazine "after witnessing the horrors of bombings in New Guinea and Darwin, have turned from hard-working and thrifty people into avaricious gambling fiends."[24]

The overall drabness of life in wartime may have attracted some to crime. It was a Christmas marked by scarcity. The government called for an "Austerity Christmas," and in a bid to forestall excessive consumption during the holiday, the authorities introduced a ban on Christmas advertisements. Minister of War Organization J. J. Dedman published the decision in November, meeting with criticism and derision. The magazine *Truth* derided him as "a modern Scrooge," and the department store Anthony Hordens, in a move that bordered on civil disobedience, sought to evade the ban by referring to Santa Claus as "an old friend," while his sleigh was described as "a fairy coach."[25]

More was at stake than just semantics. The limitations on private spending were real enough. Interstate trains were reduced to 10 percent of their peacetime normal during Christmas 1942, meaning that half a million people were squeezed into the 31 departures that did go ahead.[26] In Melbourne, ice makers and vendors were ordered to leave storage space for butter and other food items deemed essential. This passed the buck down to households, who were facing the problem of milk and other foodstuffs spoiling over Christmas, during some of the hottest weeks of the year.[27] Meanwhile, the press carried advice about how to prepare Christmas treats with the ingredients available. The *Australian Women's Weekly* published a recipe for "Christmas fruit mince pie" consisting mainly of apple and orange, while a range of other ingredients, from apricots to raisins and rum, were left out.[28]

Everyone in Australia knew someone who was serving in the armed forces, and despite the scarcity at home, there was a keen willingness to send the best the country could afford to the men in uniform. The Australian Comfort Fund, established during the previous world war, became operational again, collecting and packaging hampers for the country's soldiers and sailors. The hampers contained "Christmas cake and pudding, fruit and cream in tins, and sweets, chewing gum, tobacco, cigarette papers, razor blades, boot polish, tooth paste, and brush and shaving soap," according to a contemporary newspaper article.[29]

The *Sydney Morning Herald* reported how the Royal Australian Air Force was using every available non-operational aircraft "to play Santa Claus," covering thousands of miles picking up and distributing Christmas parcels and mail. The paper described an ingenious method to get mail to and from soldiers in the Australian Outback who could not otherwise be reached: "Special Christmas packages, extra rations, and beer have been dropped by parachutes, or in special containers, to soldiers at lonely outposts in this area where planes cannot land. Soldiers at these posts who have letters and parcels to be sent to their families, place them in bags which are suspended between two long poles. Pilots swoop down and pick up the bags by means of hooks attached to the bodies of the planes."[30] The Outback was a lonely place. Still, it could be worse, the soldiers knew. They could be in much more terrifying places. They could be in New Guinea.

* * *

The damp, green jungles of New Guinea seemed as far away from Christmas as one could possibly get in December 1942. "Whoever," quipped war correspondent Murlin Spencer, "heard of a Christmas where the temperature was 100 degrees and it was a question whether you'd live until night?"[31] In the months that had gone before, the Japanese had been pushed back across the mountainous, forest-covered island, and now they were fighting a desperate battle against the pursuing Americans and Australians in an attempt to keep a toehold rather than be forced into the sea whence they had come less than a year earlier. The Japanese defenders had built fortifications around the towns of Buna, Sanananda and Gona, determined to hold on to their thin slices of jungle at any cost, including their own lives.

Even in the absence of a ruthless and tough enemy, New Guinea would have been an intensely uncomfortable experience for the advancing soldiers, possessing some of the most inhospitable environments on the planet. It would take five or six hours to walk a single mile, as the soldiers often had to edge along cliff walls and grasp for vines to move on.[32] "Our strength is about gone," Sergeant Paul R. Lutjens of the 126th Infantry, 32nd Infantry Division, wrote in his diary. "Most of us have dysentery. Boys are falling out and dropping back with fever. Continual downpour of rain. It's hard to cook our rice and tea. Bully beef makes us sick. We seem to climb straight up for hours, then down again. God, will it never end?"[33]

General George Kenney, the commander of air forces in the area, recorded the poor state of the 32nd Division, formed from National Guard units recruited in Michigan and Wisconsin. "The troops were green and the officers were not controlling them," he wrote in his post-war memoirs. "They threw away their steel helmets and then wouldn't go forward because they didn't have them. They were scared to death of snipers and were beginning to imagine that every coconut tree was full of them."[34] It was the first American division to be deployed overseas in its entirety, and some of its units buckled under the raw realities of combat. Soldiers were seen "crying and begging to go to the rear." Some were hugging the ground so tightly that, according to the testimony of one who was there, "you couldn't have put a finger between them and the ground."[35]

The Japanese adversary was terrifying, although he was mostly invisible, or perhaps exactly for that particular reason. Striking from well-camouflaged defenses that seemed to grow out of the surrounding forest, he appeared as a creature of the jungle, even though he, too, was operating in an environment alien to him. Once tanks or artillery had been brought up, and they were forced into the open, the Japanese soldiers "fought like cornered rats," according to an American colonel.[36] A story was making the rounds among Australian and American officers about a Japanese soldier who had let himself be taken prisoner only because he was injured and too weakened by hunger to kill himself beforehand. When he was brought in for interrogation, he bit his own tongue off so he could not reveal any secrets to his captors. The self-inflicted injury caused him to bleed profusely, and he died a few hours later, having kept whatever secrets he might have known. "They were tough fanatics, with a psychology almost incomprehensible to us," Kenney wrote.[37]

Celebrating Christmas in a place like this would seem far-fetched, and yet the attempt was made. Clerics accepted great risks to make services possible on the frontline. In the jungle near Sanananda, Chaplain Clive Cox of Melbourne, in jungle green and with the cross inked on the sacking over his steel helmet, moved along a greasy track escorted by a single rifleman to reach an Australian unit dug in just a hundred yards from the Japanese. "The enemy still is on three sides of the unit," a war correspondent wrote.[38] Cox paid the ultimate price just a few days after Christmas. He was with his men when they came under rifle fire, was injured, and died shortly afterwards at a dressing station.[39]

In those conditions, staying alive became the main objective of most soldiers in the frontline. To the extent that anyone was pursuing objectives beyond that, it was to help injured comrades escape out of harm's way. During Christmas 1942, a group of Australian soldiers succeeded in evacuating their wounded from a forward perimeter back to the rear, carrying them on stretchers in single file through dense jungle, stopping every few minutes to rest and survey the surroundings for Japanese lying in wait.[40] Along the way, the group came across a Japanese camp that had been shot up several weeks earlier. It was a macabre spectacle of death. "There were mangled and rotting corpses scattered everywhere," wrote Reverend Frank Hartley, part of the Australian group. "Black-eyed skeletons stared with sightless eyes from beneath broken shelters. Bones of horses with their saddles and harness rotting around them shone white as the morning sun peering through the creepers caught them in her beams."[41]

When the group returned to the forward perimeter after having safely handed over the injured for medical attention, they brought mail from home and new provisions. "The small comforts (including sweets for men who were hungry for sugar) gave the soldiers new strength," the official history said, "and letters from home gave them new heart."[42] Those who had helped their injured buddies back to safety sensed a different kind of gratification, Reverend Hartley wrote, reproducing a talk he had with one of the infantrymen who had taken part. "You know, Padre," he said, "today when I knew that the men who had suffered here in silence so long had got safely through, I felt that it was the best Christmas present that I had ever had."[43]

Port Moresby, on the opposite, southern side of New Guinea, was a world away from the hellish conditions at the frontline. It was a beehive of military activity, as an influx of American and Australian personnel had turned the city into a major center of the emerging offensive against Japan's possessions in the South Pacific. It offered few attractions, as it was, in the words of one soldier, "a combination of ruins and dull war movements."[44] Another soldier described it as "a dry, dusty, dirty town consisting of a few houses, warehouses and docks," with most buildings "splintered after months of being subjected to enemy bombing."[45]

For Phil Sarno, a member of the 8th Photo Reconnaissance Squadron near Port Moresby, holidays meant nothing, and Thanksgiving Day had passed with hardly anyone noticing amid the hard daily work. "Our first Christmas arrived just like an ordinary working day. There was no time to repent in memories of home. It was still a crucial period here and the tasks were of a great and demanding variety," he wrote after the war.[46] A midnight mass was held in the evening of December 24 in the small bomb-battered Catholic church, but that was it as far as observance of the holiday went at Port Moresby.[47]

The food was mediocre. Most turkeys went up north to the frontline troops, and the troops posted at Port Moresby had to think creatively if they wanted to be served anything but the standard Army fare during Christmas. An American unit managed to catch a scrub turkey and penned it behind wire-netting for consumption during the holiday. In order to keep scroungers at bay, they also set up barbed wire and posted an armed guard 24 hours a day. The efforts paid off. The bird was still in the unit's possession when Christmas arrived, and each soldier was able to add a thin slice of turkey meat to the field rations.[48]

General Kenney did his best to raise morale, flying up two female volunteers and a six-man orchestra from Australia to put on a traveling show at Port Moresby. It "went over big," he claimed in his memoirs. "Two Red Cross girls, who came up with them, trimmed up a grass hut with colored paper and passed out candy, cigarettes, and trinkets all wrapped up just like Christmas back home," he wrote. "They even fixed up some scrub brush that the kids dragged out of the jungle for a Christmas tree and trimmed it with tinsel and candles. It was good to see all the youngsters hanging around getting buttons sewed on or using any old excuse to look at and talk to an American girl again."[49]

* * *

In his communique for December 25, General Douglas MacArthur, the commander of Allied forces in the Southwest Pacific, suggested all had been quiet in New Guinea during the past 24 hours. "On Christmas Day, our activities were limited to routine safety precautions," he said. "Divine services were held."[50] Robert L. Eichelberger, the commander of American forces at the town of Buna, disagreed. "On Christmas Day at Buna," he wrote later, "the fighting was desperate and the outcome of the whole miserable, tortured campaign was in doubt."[51] Combat in the area was brutal and grim, and acts of valor were deadly. The day before Christmas, Sergeant Elmer J. Burr, in an act that would earn him the Congressional Medal of Honor, saved his company commander by jumping on top of a grenade before it exploded.[52]

No quarter was given on either side. In the jungle conditions where lines of communication to the rear often passed along nearly invisible jungle tracks with ambush an ever-present risk, bringing captured enemy soldiers back to headquarters for interrogation was virtually impossible, and prisoners were rarely taken. Corporal Irvin Sheedy of the 32nd Infantry Division experienced first-hand what this meant when in a group of soldiers he was surprised by a Japanese attack. He was hit by a bullet behind the ear, and his body was penetrated by 57 pieces of shrapnel, making him unable to move. "I felt no pain. I played dead, watching the Japs bayoneting the wounded men around me. They killed 11 before they were driven off," Sheedy told a journalist more than a year later.[53]

Fighting during Christmas was concentrated around an airfield, running parallel with the coastline and known as the Old Strip. American and Australian troops attacked from each side of the strip but were unable to dislodge Japanese defenders positioned in a sturdy bunker at the end of the runway. On Christmas Eve, following a 20-minute artillery barrage. four Australian tanks attempted yet another assault on the Japanese positions. Although the tanks approached in cautious fashion, with 60-yard gaps between them, they were all hit by Japanese guns. "Next thing we knew there was a loud explosion, the tank shook and we knew we had been hit," one of the tank crew members recalled.[54] Another remembered trying to save a badly injured comrade while dodging fire from both the Japanese and advancing Australian infantry: "Reggie had lost both legs and he was bleeding very badly although conscious." He helped bandage his friend's terrible wounds and saw to it that he was given morphine before helping to carry him back to friendly lines.[55]

All of this was unknown to MacArthur, or he willfully chose to ignore it. His attitude towards Eichelberger was that of an aloof and arrogant boss with no interest in conditions on the ground. In a way, Eichelberger had been warned. When giving him his command, MacArthur had told him to "take Buna, or not come back alive." He had not been speaking figuratively. On

December 24, MacArthur had sent a letter to Eichelberger directing him to attack in force, "by regiments, not companies, by thousands, not hundreds." Eichelberger could only shake his head in disbelief, he told his wife later, saying "it indicated that he knew nothing of the jungle and how one fights there—that he had no detailed knowledge of how our forces were divided into many corridors by swamps."[56]

Australian General Edmund Herring, commanding operations in the Sanananda area near Buna, visited MacArthur on Christmas Day and found him in a terrible mood. "Well, we're not getting on very fast, are we?" he asked his Australian visitor. "If we do not clean this position up quickly, I will be finished and so will your General [Thomas] Blamey," he said, referring to the commander of the Australian Military Forces. "What will happen to you, young man," he added, addressing the 50-year-old Australian, "I just don't like to think."[57] Amid his despair, MacArthur remained relentless in his communication with Eichelberger. "Remember that your mission is to take Buna. All other things are subsidiary to this. No alchemy is going to produce this for you; it can only be done in battle and sooner or later this battle must be engaged," he had written in a letter shortly before Christmas.[58] Eichelberger was exasperated. "I think the low point of my life occurred yesterday," Eichelberger wrote to MacArthur the day after Christmas.[59]

Indeed, it was a low point for many. Conditions were wet and intensely unpleasant, and sarcastic remarks about Christmas abounded. "We hung out our socks and got water in them," one soldier wrote.[60] "There were no lights and no tinsel in the palm trees, and a chubby-cheeked Santa would have found himself sweating in his furs," Eichelberger added.[61] Instead of reindeers, captured Japanese horses were used to transport provisions to the troops. "Big tin cases of ham were packed on the horses and in many cases taken practically into the front lines," a correspondent reported.[62] Still, none of the packages made it further than the rear echelons. "The soldiers up front already had their hands full," Eichelberger remarked.[63] In a letter to his wife, he elaborated: "This afternoon I talked to a group of lads who were without cigarettes and whose clothes permitted various portions of their anatomies to stick out. They need a good sleep and some new clothes, cigarettes, etc."[64]

Since there were limits to what Eichelberger could communicate to MacArthur and still keep his job, the letters he wrote to his wife proved a safe outlet for his true thoughts about the situation he was in. "It is getting mighty close to Christmas and I am thinking about you this morning as I cogitate on life in general and my problems in particular," he wrote on December 22. "Our little palsy-walsies," he added, using the Hindi words for "friend" to describe the Japanese, "are hard to kill because they keep plenty of cover over their noggins. Therefore, while we make commendable progress, perhaps, it is nevertheless slow."[65]

He was awakened on Christmas morning by heavy Japanese bombing from the air, and his Christmas dinner was a cup of soup given to him by a thoughtful doctor at a trailside hospital, Eichelberger wrote in his memoirs.[66] "You'll never know how I missed you this Christmas season," he wrote to his wife on December 26. "Fortunately, we were busy night and day for the last three days, so by concentrating on our job here we managed to pass the holiday without feeling too low… The men are getting to know me now and I get a lot of greetings. I particularly like to talk to those who are going to meet our palsy-walsies for the first time. I can usually get them laughing. And then there is the American cemetery with its line of crosses, and I choke every time I pass it."[67]

CHAPTER 3

Behind the Bamboo Curtain

Japan and occupied Asia

Liemar Hennig, a 33-year-old Lutheran missionary from the cosmopolitan north German city of Hamburg, suggested a world that might have been. As the representative of a religion that fundamentally saw mankind as a brotherhood unified in faith irrespective of nation or race, he had spent the 1930s traveling around the globe to spread the Gospel, crossing borders at a time when governments were busy closing them. In the middle of the decade, he had ended up in Japan, and even as the nation's sons were sent to an increasingly brutal war in China, he had preached the Christian message of love, hope and redemption in cities such as Tokyo and Yokohama.[1]

In 1940, although tensions were growing between America on the one hand, and Japan and his native Germany on the other, he had decided to go to the United States to study at the Union Theological Seminary in New York for a year. "If you don't know the United States, you won't be able to understand Japan. All Christianity currently originates in the United States," he had told a colleague.[2] It was a remarkable admission of the central importance of America in world culture at a time when the Nazi leadership was dismissing the United States as decadent and racially inferior and no match for the rising German power.

Hennig had completed his studies in New York in late 1941, and he had only been back in Japan for a short period when it launched itself into its desperate war against the United States. A side effect of the new international situation was the sudden vacancy of the post of pastor at Union Church in Kobe, a large port city west of Osaka, as the incumbent, the American national Harry W. Myers, was detained and mistreated by the Japanese authorities. Due to his impressive credentials, Hennig was the obvious choice as his successor.[3]

Since Germany had followed suit after Pearl Harbor by declaring war on the slumbering American giant with what could almost be seen as suicidal fervor, Hennig might have been expected to mainly service Kobe's German community. But, despite the objections of the Japanese authorities, he decided to become the pastor of all foreigners. As a result, on Christmas Eve 1942, Hennig performed a service for the Germans first and then for a mixed group of people from both Allied and Axis nations. Russians, Americans, Englishmen, Indians, Danes and Dutch worshipped alongside citizens of Finland and Hungary, nations that had ended up throwing in their lot with Germany and Japan.[4]

The Japanese themselves mostly shied away. Many seemed to have forgotten that Christmas had actually grown in popularity in the decades leading up to the Pacific war. The religious meaning of the holiday had been of importance to Japan's Christians, and Christmas plays based on biblical themes had been shown at Sunday schools, but the celebrations had gradually become more mainstream among the general population as well. In particular, the practice of gift giving had struck a chord with newly prosperous urban dwellers.

Christmas exhibitions had been annual features in big Tokyo department stores such as Mitsukoshi and Matsusakaya. Christmas trees had lined the main streets, and Santas with obvious Asian features behind their fake white beards had greeted busy pedestrians.[5] Westerners had looked on, mostly amused. "You would be greatly impressed by the commercialization of Christmas in Japan," an anonymous letter writer said in correspondence from the remote and mysterious country. "Almost every store has special decorations and is trying to capitalize the Christmas spirit—tho many of them think it is just Santa Claus' birthday."[6]

By the early 1930s, Christmas had become a measure of how modernized and westernized Japan had become. It had turned into an occasion when even non-Christian Japanese would put on their holiday attire, invite friends over and exchange gifts. "This is especially so among young Japanese residing in the larger cities like Tokyo, Osaka and Seoul," lay missionary Paul Rusch had written, and he had made a bold prediction: "In Japan what the cities do today the country will imitate tomorrow, and I dare say it will not be surprising if before many years Christmas will have become quite one of the national holidays to be observed throughout the empire."[7]

It was a vision of a liberal Japan open to the outside world, and it was not to be. Even before war broke out with the United States, the celebration of Christmas was waning, not because of a lack of popularity among the population in general, but due to government interference. By December 1938, when Japan had already become bogged down in its seemingly endless war in China, Christmas celebrations were curbed. Restaurants were ordered not to serve champagne or make special Christmas dinner reservations. It worked. Sales of turkey were down by half.[8] As a substitute for the disappearing Christmas decorations, shopkeepers were told to display Japanese, German and Italian flags to celebrate the anti-communist fraternity among the three nations.[9]

By late 1942, Christmas had been all but wiped out. After a year at war, the authorities considered it inappropriate to celebrate what was essentially an imported Western holiday, not to mention that wartime shortages meant there was little room for festivities. To the extent that Japan did acknowledge the holiday, it was to accommodate its European allies, and in Kobe, the German Club Concordia was allowed to hold a Christmas party for the children of the German community. "The large number of German children, escorted by their parents or relatives, celebrated the Yuletide befittingly with games and other amusements," the *Japan Times Advertiser* reported.[10] Likewise, Japanese domestic radio, which otherwise ignored the holiday, made an exception by allowing the relay of a German short-wave transmission of a Christmas concert.[11]

Japanese radio's overseas service also took advantage of Christmas to broadcast into enemy homes. Radio Batavia, a Japanese station in the occupied East Indies, had started sending "Australian News Hour" in June 1942, featuring messages read by Australian and New Zealand prisoners to their families at home. The underlying motive was to attract listeners by appealing to their natural desire to hear news about loved ones locked up in Japanese prison camps, thus luring them into consuming Japanese propaganda. From December 21, the effort was stepped up, with prisoners reading special Christmas messages. One of them was a Group Captain Bish of the Royal Air Force, addressing British people in Australia. An official from the British Broadcasting Corporation monitoring the show believed he was not forced to speak: "Voice, delivery and manner seemed entirely genuine."[12]

Hori Tomokazu, the spokesman of Japan's Board of Information, also used Christmas Eve to send a message to Japan's enemies. "Many fathers, sons, husbands and brothers are not at home this Christmas to be with mothers, daughters, wives and sisters in a united family observance of this memorable day in the Christian world," he said. "They are far away, fighting in deserts, mountains, jungles, on the sea and in the air, many lost forever and resting in eternal sleep in foreign battlefields. It is a grim Christmas, not a merry Christmas. It is a Christmas faced with contradictions—a Christmas amid war and blind hatreds."

The spokesman blamed the US and British governments for this regrettable state of affairs, claiming that the two countries' leaders had betrayed the Christian spirit by turning their backs on a world guided by principles of fairness and equity. He concluded: "Only by eliminating, once and for all, the selfish American and British ambition of world domination... may the Christian peoples of the world celebrate a truly merry Christmas... in complete harmony with the Christmas message of 'peace on earth, good will to men'."[13]

The *Japan Times Advertiser* struck a similar note, claiming that the Axis was waging a war to create a new world order with "justice and fairness to all, regardless of race, creed or religion," whereas the American and British adversaries were pursuing selfish profit. "So as the world commemorates today this tragic travesty of Christmas," the paper said in an editorial, "it should have no difficulty in perceiving which side it is that has brought about this tragedy, and which side it is whose aims reach toward the real Christmas spirit."[14] It marked an astonishing level of hypocrisy, given the way Japan was treating its conquered enemies.

* * *

Large numbers of Allied prisoners of war were kept in camps throughout East and Southeast Asia, often in close proximity to the battlefields where they had laid down their arms after being overwhelmed by the Japanese offensives in late 1941 and the first months of 1942. In the Philippines, where US forces in conjunction with local units had kept fighting until late spring, thousands were incarcerated under abominable conditions. A mixture of malnutrition, disease, atrocious abuse and simple neglect caused death rates to soar among inmates who until a few months before had been strong and healthy young men.

At Cabanatuan, the largest prison camp in the Philippine islands, starvation was an everyday experience, and conversations inevitably revolved around the subject of food. In the daytime during work in the fields, at night in the bamboo barracks, small talk was about no other topic. "That's all we thought about," wrote one of the inmates, Joseph Quintero. "No women, no movies, just food."[15] Between June and November, 2,500 inmates perished in the camp. By December, no one paid any attention to the approaching holiday, as everyone was busy surviving. "The Christmas season slipped by unobserved and unnoticed," wrote Tony Bilek, an American prisoner.[16]

Unobserved and unnoticed but for one thing: the holiday brought food. Because of Christmas, the Japanese authorities allowed Red Cross packages to be distributed among the prisoners. It was a ticket to survival and ultimately a return to home, and the inmates knew it. "A hot sunny day set the stage appropriately [...] around noon, when a huge unnatural shout went up," former prisoner Ralph Emerson Hibbs wrote later, describing the mood when the packages arrived. "It was an American war whoop, a celebration like a touchdown cheer."[17] The packages contained evaporated milk, biscuits, cheese, instant cocoa, sardines, oleomargarine, corned beef, sweet chocolate, sugar, powdered orange concentrate, soup cubes, prunes, instant coffee, cigarettes and tobacco.[18] Colonel Irvin Alexander recalled the intense atmosphere. "No children anticipating Christmas, when they could actually gain possession of countless long-wished-for articles, ever suffered any more than we did while we were waiting for the distribution of our packages," he said in his memoirs.[19]

The packages worked miracles. "The first day in prison without a single death was Dec. 15, 1942—a reprieve granted solely by nourishment," said Calvin Ellsworth Chunn, a Marine captain who had been taken prisoner at the end of the battle for the island of Corregidor.[20] Colonel Eugene C. Jacobs, a medical officer, made the same observation. "After the package in 1942, the camp mortality fell miraculously from forty deaths daily to one or two a month," he said.[21] Part of the reason why the packages worked so well was that the prisoners knew better than to consume it all during the holiday and had the foresight to make it last. "This small amount of food sustained us until the latter part of February 1943," said Quintero.[22]

In addition to Red Cross packages, the Japanese were persuaded by a German priest, who was still active in the Philippines, to allow prisoners with family near the camp to receive food parcels during Christmas. In the capital of Manila, Gladys Savary, a 49-year-old American who had previously owned a restaurant and had escaped arrest, presumably because of her age, used this opportunity to help her nephew at Cabanatuan, whose vision had deteriorated because of malnutrition. She spent sleepless nights trying to fit as much nourishment as possible into the prescribed package size, including vitamins A and C. It paid off. Shortly afterwards, the nephew smuggled out a note, saying the vitamin supplements had helped him recover his vision. "Can't thank you enough," he wrote, "but will some day, somehow.", That day never came. The nephew was later transferred to a camp in Japanese-occupied Taiwan, where he died and was buried in a communal grave.[23]

Across the sprawling Japanese camp system, prisoners had the same obsession with food, and Christmas brought an unexpected glimmer of hope for many. Julian J. Gates, a second lieutenant with the Army Air Corps who had been taken prisoner during the battle of Bataan peninsula in the Philippines, described the first few months of incarceration with a few simple words: "sickness, H2O, food." He had been moved from one location to another, eventually shipping to the Japanese home islands, and by Christmas 1942 he was kept with other Allied officers at Yodogawa camp near the city of Osaka. On December 24, he wrote with a degree of sarcasm in his secret diary: "Jingle Bells, jingle bells, jingle all the way—Happy Xmas Eve! I am writing in bed with the cover up around my arms and head. I have a fever of 100 degrees."[24]

He remembered the situation a year earlier, when the Japanese had just made their main landing in the Philippines, and compared it with the situation now: "I thought last Xmas was tough, but at least I had food... Anyway, it is Xmas and I am going to try awfully hard to look up and see the brighter side of this bad situation. Xmas gift!"[25] The following day the situation improved dramatically, and it all had to do with food. The prisoners received the usual Japanese fare of rice, water and bread, but in addition, one of the prisoners had saved a small can of sardines, which was cooked up with the rice and other ingredients. "It had two tablespoons of lard (priceless), hot green pepper and black pepper, baked in a pot. It was wonderful!" Gates wrote in his diary. "There are two meals prior to this that I always remember, but today, if I live to be 100 years old, I'll never forget this Xmas dinner."[26]

Even the highest-ranking officers who had fallen into the hands of the Japanese were not exempt from demeaning and brutal treatment. Lieutenant General Jonathan M. Wainwright, the former commander of Allied forces in the Philippines, had been in captivity since May when he had surrendered with his remaining forces. Along with 178 other high-ranking officers, he had been transported in August on board the Japanese vessel *Nagaru Maru* to Takao, now Kaohsiung, in southern Taiwan, and then taken to Karenko prison camp near the island's rugged east coast.

The 400 prisoners in the camp were mostly senior officers, deliberately separated from their men so they could not exert an influence on them, and even though they were usually significantly older than the rank and file, they were forced to carry out hard work. Despite their seniority, the officers were also subject to regular beatings by their guards.[27] By December 1942, they had only been held captive for half a year, but they were already looking like walking skeletons, a fact brought home during the weekly bath when they saw each other naked. "Our labors had used up the inner muscles of our buttocks," Wainwright wrote in his post-war memoirs. "The skin of our buttocks just hung down the backs of our skeletonized legs like deep pockets."[28]

Making things even worse, mutual trust was at a low among many of the prisoners. "Not the least of our trouble came from ourselves—honesty was at a low ebb, clothes disappearing off drying lines, food from the kitchen; some squads very definitely got more than their share of food," wrote British Brigadier E. W. Goodman in his diary.[29] Some officers had fallen apart mentally, and had essentially turned into different people, Brigadier General Lewis Beebe remarked. "It is amazing how deprivation and anxiety will affect some persons. I would never have believed it of some of the officers here," he wrote in his diary. "They have become selfish and greedy, have no regard for the rights or comfort of others, are always whining or grumbling about one thing or another, and appear to have lost their self-respect completely. It is an eye-opener to me in many cases as well as being a revelation on character in general."[30]

Still, Christmas brought relief. At the Taiwanese camp, too, the Japanese relented somewhat over Christmas, and on Christmas Day they handed over 30 ducks to be shared among the prisoners, while each got an apple.[31] Major Thomas Dooley made a special point out of describing the Christmas Day menu in detail in his diary, emphasizing how much it meant to him: "Pork soup—noon—duck—supper. 2 bananas, 1 orange, peanuts, potato cake, piece of bread. Thoughts of home—hope they are happy + enjoy Xmas. Really good thoughts this date."[32] Wainwright noted how the sudden shift in the attitude of the Japanese captors raised the morale of the prisoners, while it also triggered quiet prayers that conditions would now improve permanently. "We ate our Christmas dinner together, were grateful for it, and hoped that it would mark a turning point in our treatment," Wainwright wrote, adding laconically, "But there was no change."[33]

* * *

Amid the general squalor of the camps, the prisoners were faced with a stark choice. Either they could give up and let themselves be carried away on a slow mental and physical decline that would likely end in death. Or alternatively they could find ways to lift morale just a tiny bit, even at a time when liberation, if it ever happened, was likely to be months or years in the future. It was a case of grasping for straws and struggling to discern a silver lining, even when there was none in sight. One method was through the medium of humor, or more often gallows humor.

At Changi prison on Singapore island, Major Burnett Clarke of the Australian Army created an "Xmas menu" card for the holiday in 1942, featuring an invitation to a sumptuous, imaginative meal in "the Officers Mess, Roberts Hospital." It kicked off with "savoury," followed by "pea soup, meat pie and baked vegetables." After that there would be "Christmas pudding with white sauce" and "ice cream with hot chocolate sauce and pineapple," and it would all be poured down with generous quantities of coffee at the end. It was a sarcastic comment on the real conditions in the camp, where malnutrition reigned.[34]

Theatrics and performances of various sorts also helped the mood, especially during Christmas. At Zentsuji camp in southern Japan, the prisoners performed the pantomime *Cinderella* for Christmas, putting maximum efforts into the show, even though they were suffering terribly from starvation diets and diseases. Frank Twiss, a former gunnery officer on board the cruiser HMS *Exeter*, was "a brilliant fairy queen, complete with wings and umbrella surmounted by one large star," according to the camp historian.[35]

The British prisoners, hailing from the isles that produced Shakespeare, were particularly fond of theater, but other nationalities among the prison population contributed, too, Twiss explained later: "Theatrics were also taken up by the Dutch, who were extremely clever at it, and the Australians joined us as well." There was, however, one exception, he admitted: "The Americans didn't go so much on theatre but they were very much better at a thing like barber shop singing."[36]

At Changi camp, British and Dutch prisoners also cooperated to make Christmas memorable. On Christmas Eve, 3,000 men assembled for a concert featuring a choir of one hundred, as well as a pianist and a violin player. "The standard of these performers was not amateur, for we have here many first rate professional musicians," wrote Eric Cordingly, a British chaplain. The highlight was, however, the midnight Eucharist, exceptionally allowed by the Japanese authorities. "Streaming back to the billets were men who had recaptured a glimpse of our Christian Christmas, an experience not easily forgotten," Cordingly wrote, describing how it affected the men. "Peace on earth to men of goodwill, that was the prayer in each person's mind."[37]

In Taiwan, too, Wainwright and his fellow officers saw Christmas as more than a holiday. They turned it into an attempt to lift the spirit and rekindle hope. "It became a hook on which to hang our very lives," he wrote later.[38] Since everything in the camps was in short supply, the Christmas preparations often required significant levels of ingenuity. "A number of the squads had gone to some pains to decorate their rooms with Christmas effects and there were some very clever arrangements, considering that there were no materials available. Paper of any kind is very scarce, but signs were made and Christmas Greetings were displayed. The Christmas cards were all made from cigarette boxes and similar pieces of cardboard. Some of them were very clever," Brigadier General Lewis Beebe wrote in his diary.[39]

Expectations were high, and Christmas began in a brilliant way at the Taiwanese camp. It was a bright, colorful sunrise in an area where the mornings were usually cloudy and mist-covered, and the sun shone throughout the day. The prisoners all went around after roll call to wish each other a Merry Christmas. "The spirit shown by everyone here today has been excellent. Everyone has been feeling good, and there was a noticeable feeling of Christmas atmosphere," Beebe wrote. He himself could not help but feel a bit of melancholy, as December 26 was his wedding anniversary. "Dorothy and I can't take our usual trip and dinner together this time," he wrote. "We have missed it for the past two years, and I hope we will be together on the next one."[40]

To take his mind off the sad thoughts, he had put himself in charge of Christmas entertainment. Part of this was a choir, which had rehearsed in the days leading up to the holiday and now moved from barrack to barrack singing one or two Christmas carols for each squad. Beebe noticed with satisfaction how it dispelled the sad atmosphere that was otherwise dominant. "Everyone seemed to enjoy the singing, and there was a noticeable pick up in morale, which continued to be good through the day today," he wrote in his journal.[41]

The choir even triggered an act of kindness where it was least expected.[42] "The camp commander came down and listened to part of the show, and left several bottles of rice wine for the performers," Beebe wrote. "We drank our share this morning and it was quite good. I noticed from the price tag that it cost .78 yen per bottle (78 sen) which would be about 10 cents at the last rate of exchange I heard quoted."[43] The choir was an undisputed success, but for some officers, the emotions triggered by the singing were almost overwhelming. Wainwright was sitting alone on a cot in his room when he heard "Hark! the Herald Angels Sing," an old favorite of his. "I could not help putting my head in my hands," he wrote later. "I was so glad they could not see me."[44]

* * *

The Dutch colonial government had built Bantjeuj prison in the city of Bandung in western Java in 1877 in order to imprison local Indonesians who had fallen foul of the law. In 1930, the pro-independence leader Sukarno had been incarcerated behind its white walls. Now, the Japanese army of occupation used the prison to lock up the former rulers, often for no obvious reason other than being Caucasian. This was why a group of Western women were being kept with their children in one of its damp, rat-infested cells shortly before

Christmas 1942. A single candle in a corner of the cell, provided by a guard as a "Christmas tree," spread light in the dark.

After a few days of confinement, one of the women, a mother in her early 30s accompanied by her three young children, began coughing blood. It appeared she had contracted tuberculosis from drinking contaminated water, and she was very worried for her children. The other women, who realized she only had a short time left, could offer no real comfort. On Christmas morning, the women in the cell were awakened by the sobbing of the children. Their mother had died during the night. A Japanese officer, alerted by the crying, slammed open the door, and one of the women rushed at him, shouting, "She is dead! She is dead and it is all your fault, because the water killed her!" The officer raised his whip as if to beat the woman, but as she continued yelling at him, he changed his mind, turned around and left the cell.

He returned shortly afterwards, dragging away the three children and the defiant woman. A mood of terror descended on the cell. Under the conditions prevailing with the volatile and unpredictable Japanese in power, anything could happen. The woman could very well have been taken to her death. In fact, the opposite turned out to be the case. The officer took the woman to his office and told her that he had decided to release the three children, asking if they had any relatives outside the prison. The woman informed him that their grandmother had so far escaped imprisonment, and soon after they were being transported on a horse-drawn cart to the elderly woman's home. They would stay there for the duration of the war.[45]

In December 1942, millions of civilians across East and Southeast Asia were preparing to pass Christmas under Japanese rule. Some were able to live in relative freedom. Among them was Ruth Barr, an American citizen in Shanghai's International Settlement, who was classified as an "enemy alien" along with her family but had not yet been interned. Yet, life in the huge Chinese city was hard, and the scarcity of products in the stores was a constant problem. News from the battlefields was difficult to come by, and the uncertainty about the outcome of the war made Japanese language lessons a necessity. Still, Christmas could almost be made to feel normal. "Children out at parties," Barr wrote in her diary on the 24th. "Quiet day at home for me. Dispensed cookies and enjoyed the tree and thought of many in USA."[46]

The urge to forget the war just for a short time was universal. In Manila, Gladys Savary, the former restaurant owner, was able to organize a Christmas party inside her walled courtyard for 22 mostly Western children and their parents, including the few British and Americans who had not yet been locked up. For the grown-ups, she had prepared fruit punch, and because it was spiked with Philippine rum, the party soon got boisterous. "Passing Japanese soldiers could hear the festivities, and several climbed the eight-foot wall to watch, but they did not interfere," she wrote later.[47]

Barr and Savary were lucky. Internment was a fact of life for a large number of civilians in the former Western colonies, and food was scarce. In one camp, the average daily calorie intake was 1800, significantly below the 2,400 calories recommended by the League of Nations. Red Cross supplies kept the prisoners going.[48] Help did materialize, occasionally. A British relief ship arrived in the Philippines in late 1942 with packages for civilian internees, provided by the South African Red Cross Society. "December 23, 1942—Comfort kits given out," Eunice Young, an interned nurse, wrote in her diary. "X-mas entertainment. 1st movie we had seen in a year. Toilet paper rationed 8 sheets per person. Soap 1 bar per week."[49]

Separation from family was a particularly painful part of the camp experience, adding mental strain to the physical challenges of survival. Some of the British soldiers who had been taken prisoner while defending their country's colonial possessions a year earlier had been stationed with their families and were unaware whether their relatives had been evacuated home or perhaps were locked up in camps of their own. Christmas 1942 was the first time some of the inmates in Sham Shui Po prison camp in Hong Kong realized that their wives had made it back to England. That was when they received letters from home, some dated back to July. "Hope my Chris is one of them, far happier for her," wrote Staff Sergeant James O'Toole from the Royal Army Ordnance Corps.[50]

At Manila's Santo Tomas internment camp, which held hundreds of US civilians, the Japanese commandant relented during Christmas and allowed the Philippine wives and families of interned Americans to visit.[51] The internees themselves began preparing for a week of Christmas festivities as early as October in a deliberate effort by leaders among them to prevent the holiday being passed in a brooding, pensive mood, with thoughts wasted on what might have been. Special attention was given to the camp's youngest detainees, and all children under the age of 12 received presents from an inmate dressed up as Santa Claus.[52] Nearly every family had a Christmas tree, mostly betel palms painted in bright colors and decorated with scraps of paper.[53] "It was all very beautiful, but also somewhat sad, as the internees thought of the contrast between this and their former Christmas celebrations," wrote Frederic H. Stevens, one of the internees, in an account published immediately after the war.[54]

Whenever possible, efforts were made to do something for the children of the camps. Sergeant David Griffin wrote a book for the 300 children at

Changi, *The Happiness Box*, to cheer them up for Christmas. It was about Winston the Lizard, Martin the Monkey and Wobbley the Frog and described their quest for the source and meaning of happiness. The secret was, Winston concluded at the end, to be "clever, industrious and kind." Written in just 36 hours and illustrated by a prisoner who used crushed chalk for his drawings, it never served its purpose. The Japanese commander, possibly believing that the book contained a coded message, ordered it destroyed, and only through quick thinking did Griffin manage to save it for posterity by burying it and recovering it after the war.[55]

Despite the attempts to make the Christmas as "normal" as possible for the children caught up in the war, the brutality universally in evidence bred hatred in young hearts. Eight-year-old Ernest Hillen, who passed Christmas with his mother in a camp for civilians in Java, was perplexed when he heard the Christmas message and its requirement to love every person, irrespective of nationality. He was not sure if it was to be taken literally: "What about the Japanese [...] They were the enemy! My mother had said so, again and again." He noted that Jesus had urged his adherents to also love their enemies, and wondered, "Had He ever been in a camp though? Had He seen the Japanese beating women and girls?"[56]

* * *

Louise Fillmore Blancaflor, an American woman born in Troy, upstate New York, and married to a Filipino doctor, had spent the days before Christmas 1942 in fear for her own life and those of her children. From her home on the island of Panay on the edge of the South China Sea, she had witnessed fierce clashes between Japanese soldiers and Filipino guerrillas. Japanese planes had flown overhead, and some had dropped bombs nearby, while long columns of Japanese infantry had marched by on their way into battle. The nights were filled with the sound of machine guns and trench mortars. It was clear that even though the US Army had been expelled from the Philippine islands several months earlier, the Japanese had not succeeded in quelling opposition from the indigenous resistance movement.[57]

Blancaflor described her fears and worries in her diary. "Our nerves seem to be affected with all this bombing and machine gunning—even the children feel it, but perhaps later on we will get used to it like the people in Europe," she wrote.[58] By Christmas, the fighting had subsided somewhat. The Blancaflor family turned their attention to the holiday. They had kept a small artificial Christmas tree and decorated it as best they could, the children picking bell-shaped flowers that substituted for real ornaments. On Christmas Eve, they gathered around the tree and sang "Silent Night, Holy Night." Still, even the smallest children were so influenced by the tumult around them that they instinctively knew it could not become a real Christmas.

The Blancaflors' nine-year-old son Millard reasoned in a way that sadly made it clear how much the business of war and killing had become part of their everyday lives. "I don't think Santa Claus can come. He may get shot," he said. His younger brother Roland, aged five, replied, "Of course, he can't come. The Japanese may bomb him."[59] Still, on Christmas morning, Roland got up before dawn and went straight to the Christmas tree, looking around for presents, in vain. "I just thought that maybe Santa Claus was able to reach us and left something," the disappointed boy said. Louise Blancaflor explained to her son how difficult it was for Santa Claus to come, and remarked in her diary, "I hope and pray that next year at this time we shall have peace."[60]

The Philippines had celebrated Christmas since the 16th century when Spanish explorers had first arrived and founded the longest-lasting Catholic community in East Asia, and 1942 was the first time in nearly 400 years that the birth of Christ was marked without the presence of a Western colonial power. This caused Christmas to be passed in an unusual manner. Jorge B. Vargas, a senior member of the pro-Japanese regime in Manila, sent season's greetings to his compatriots: "On this sacred day, it is my great privilege to greet the Filipino people wherever they may be and to wish them a Merry Christmas with the hope that the war will soon end in the complete victory of Japan and other Oriental peoples."

Manila-based newspaper *The Tribune*, working under strict censorship, contrasted the festivities with Christmas one year earlier, when the Philippines had been in the midst of war following the Japanese invasion. "The celebration this year has been made possible through the efforts of the Imperial Japanese Forces, which in the short time of twelve months have accomplished the task of maintaining peace and carrying out the program of reconstruction," it said. "By the gracious act of the Army, the curfew has been temporarily suspended during the season, making possible the holding of early morning mass in the Catholic churches and the midnight mass of the Nativity."[61]

American guerrilla Russell W. Volckmann noted in his diary the type of propaganda that was being disseminated by the Japanese in an attempt to pacify the population in the town of Kiangan, nested in the mountains north of Manila: "At the Christmas celebration in Kiangan, Jap Capt in his speech told the people there was no more war in the Orient; the Japs have superiority in the air, land, and water."[62] This was, of course, not true, not even in the Philippines, as the Christmas fighting on Panay showed.

Raymon Alcaraz, a former officer in the US-controlled Philippine Army who now served as a police officer on the nation's main island of Luzon, remembered how busy he had been during the previous Christmas, fighting alongside the American defenders to stave off the Japanese invasion. This Christmas, he had to mainly worry about material shortages. "Even prime commodities are getting scarcer and expensive as the Japanese occupation forces are living on the land, none coming from Japan or abroad. They get priority on supply of foodstuff and other prime commodities," he wrote in his diary.[63]

All of that was forgotten during midnight mass at Bayombong Cathedral, a picturesque 18th-century building, at a ceremony presided over by a Belgian cleric. Alcaraz was in an upbeat mood, and the solemn service had placed him in a state of renewed hope for the future. "Halleluyah, we are spending our first Christmas in two years quietly and frugally as dictated by the time," he wrote in his diary. "Christmas 1941 went unnoticed. At least we have Christmas 1942 and hope we will celebrate a better Christmas 1943. We can only hope and pray for better days to come."[64]

CHAPTER 4

Christmas with the Chiangs

China, Burma and India

It seemed as if it was going to be a bleak Christmas for Milton E. Miles, a US Navy observer and intelligence officer in China's wartime capital of Chongqing, deep inside the continent-sized country. Two cargo ships, the *LaSalle* and the *Reynolds*, had been on the way with much-needed supplies for waging war against Japan, and both had been sunk in the Indian Ocean. To lift the mood a little, Miles' closest Chinese partner, the sinister spy chief Dai Li, who could be charming if he wanted to, invited him and several other American officers to a Christmas party on December 24. The Chinese pulled out all the stops to make it a success. There were paper hats and fake moustaches, and a huge cake decorated with a rose made from three-inch-thick icing.

The American officers, all craving sweets after months in the austere Chinese hinterland, were eager to dig into the cake, and Miles managed to gulp down a large chunk before he realized the ugly truth: the Chinese cooks had not had the ingredients they needed, and the so-called icing was in fact colored lard. Daniel "Webb" Heagy, a US Navy officer, also had a taste and mischievously held back his knowledge, encouraging the man next to him, Marine Major John "Bud" Masters, to have a go. "Don't hold back, Bud," he said. "There is plenty." The American officers were all seated around Dai's table and had to eat the horrifying dessert with an assumed air of utter delight. "Webb, incidentally, played a trick on Bud by telling General Dai how much our Marine Corps major had enjoyed his piece, whereupon our genial host personally helped him to more," Miles wrote in his memoirs.[1]

There was a reason for the Chinese hospitality, even if it sometimes had the opposite effect to what was intended. The attack on Pearl Harbor had come as a godsend for China's leader Chiang Kai-shek. His country had been fighting alone against Japan since the summer of 1937, losing millions of men and being pushed back from the eastern seaboard, where most of the nation's factories and other modern economic assets were concentrated. Now, with the entry of the world's most powerful country into the war on its side, China's prospects had suddenly become brighter. Combining America's industrial might with China's vast manpower resources seemed a recipe for victory. A mood of optimism was in evidence in Chongqing, reflected on Christmas Eve, when Chinese Foreign Minister T. V. Soong met with US Colonel Frank Dorn. "We have a chance to do almost anything," an upbeat Soong said.[2]

Throughout 1942, thousands of American servicemen, and a good number of representatives of other English-speaking nations, had been swarming into China, considered a key ally in the war against the Axis, and by December as they were getting ready to mark Christmas, an awkward fact was making itself increasingly obvious. The Chinese and the westerners had known and interacted with each other for centuries, but at a fundamental level they were still strangers, groping in the dark in the hope of reaching common ground or just a modicum of mutual understanding. Often the cultural differences proved too formidable, and even when powerful forces pulled them together, such as the need to defeat Japan, the growing interface between the two cultures served as a reminder of their incompatibility. In some cases, familiarity also bred contempt.

For decades it had been the case that Christmas was when these differences became uncomfortably salient. What for many western sojourners in China was the most important holiday of the year was greeted with indifference or incomprehension by those surrounding them. It was with mixed feelings that Hannah Davies, a British missionary, remembered her first Chinese Christmas, spent in the city of Yangzhou in 1893, noting the contrast between the merry atmosphere in her own residence, and the sinister and alien world just beyond the doorway. "Outside," she wrote in an account after returning to Britain, "all was quiet except for the sound of a passing footstep on the rough road, or the sad ring of the temple gong, which every few moments broke the stillness that pervaded this great, heathen city."[3]

Little by little, some Chinese in the bigger cities developed an appreciation of Christmas, or at least an appreciation of how much it meant to their western counterparts. Just a few years after Davies' morose Christmas in Yangzhou, Sarah Conger, the wife of the US envoy to China, had a completely different and uplifting experience, waking up on December 25, 1898, to find presents placed by her Chinese hosts at the entrance of her residence in the imperial capital of Beijing: "We saw on either side of the steps a little evergreen tree in a pretty painted porcelain pot," she wrote in a letter home. "These trees were decorated with many styles of most intricately cut paper people, animals, birds, bats, and flowers in colors."[4]

The incongruous image of a bat being included among the paper figures on the trees presented to Sarah Conger reflected an undeniable fact: Western Christmas traditions remained something of a mystery to the Chinese, and even when they tried, they often got them wrong. On the other hand, the habit of exchanging presents was immediately appealing to the Chinese, as it was not unlike their own tradition of exchanging money gifts during the Lunar New Year, always falling a few weeks later, in the middle of winter. One figure in particular stood out to the Chinese, perhaps because his opulent obesity carried a message of plenty to a people who knew the ravages of famine only too well: "The Asiatics have adopted the Santa Claus feature of Christmas with great enthusiasm, and that is about the only feature of the holiday that interests the children," *The New York Times* reported in 1899.[5]

In the following decades, China was transformed from an empire into a republic, but it did little to change general attitudes towards Christmas. A huge step forward in understanding the exotic foreign habit was taken at the highest level of power after Chiang Kai-shek, the ruler of China since the late 1920s, converted to Christianity. He was first exposed to the Christian faith when in 1927 he married Song Meiling, the beautiful and well-educated daughter of a wealthy, heavily westernized and Christian family, but it did not stop there.

Chiang's Christianity, first adopted mainly out of convenience, became an intense personal affair after he was kidnapped by a maverick general in the northwest Chinese city of Xian in December 1936 and pressured to cooperate with the Chinese communists to resist the Japanese encroachment of his country. The days spent at the general's mercy were a tense period, culminating around Christmas, when Chiang faced a real risk of being executed. Death was breathing down his neck, and he credited his Christian faith with saving him.[6] Taking their cue from Chiang, members of his government would later explicitly associate Christmas with his escape from the kidnapping, as in Dai Li's invitation to Miles and the other American officers in 1942, which said, in broken English, that the party was to "celebrate the birthday of Christ and the escapement of Generalissimo from kidnapment."[7]

As tensions between Chiang's Chinese republic and the Japanese Empire heated up in the late 1930s, eventually erupting into full-scale war, he increasingly saw the conflict in Christian terms. In his diary he made it clear that he thought the fortune of war was mainly in divine hands: "I believe that God will not be false to my wife's and my piety, so that God would bless China, and would eventually spare the country from invasions and destruction."[8] Chiang believed that his own actions as a statesman and strategist only had a limited impact on how the conflict with Japan would end, suggesting that his chief contribution to eventual victory was to stay on good terms with God: "I only pray that God will soon forgive me for my sins, so that my nation will soon escape from oppression and realize independence," he wrote in his diary.[9]

The Christian outlook that permeated the elite around Chiang was in evidence in Chongqing in late 1942. On Christmas Day, all ranks of the foreign forces in the city were invited to a tea party in the auditorium of the National Military Council. For the occasion, life-sized images had been painted on the walls, offering a curious mix of ancient religious and modern political motifs. On one wall were the wise men riding towards Bethlehem on their camels, while another featured Churchill, Roosevelt and Stalin trampling on Hitler, Mussolini and Hirohito. The Chinese national anthem was played, followed by a Christmas carol, recalled Lieutenant Colonel John Monro, the assistant military attaché at the British embassy. "The Europeans and Americans sang in English and the Chinese in Chinese," he wrote in his memoirs. "This is not quite as bad as it sounds as the Chinese translation has the same metre and is sung to the same tune as the original."[10]

Paradoxically, Chiang's Christianity caused some unexpected friction with his western allies. One of his main pre-war political campaigns, inspired partly by his religious puritanism, had taken the form of the "New Life" movement, which sought to eradicate corrupting influences in Chinese society by eliminating practices such as smoking and gambling, while also getting rid of prostitution. The tenets of Confucianism were brought up to justify the measures, but with Chiang's intensified religious fervor, Christianity became a heavy influence as well.[11] Therefore, when a Red Cross nurse organized a dance for the enlisted westerners at the Victory Club in Chongqing during Christmas 1942, journalists quickly noted that it collided with the New Life movement's austere principles, which specifically targeted dancing, holding out the possibility that the lonely men would be unable to find any dance partners among local Chinese women. "Let us hope that the New Life movers won't be so cruel to their allies," a reporter stated.[12]

Meanwhile, Chiang invoked Christianity in his Christmas speeches, which were addressed to both a domestic and a foreign audience, and once again he revealed his belief in prayer as an actual, potent weapon that could be deployed in the struggle against the Axis. "At this Christmas, amidst the raging of a world conflict, I sincerely pray to Jesus Christ, the Prince of Peace, for the early arrival of our common victory," he said in his 1942 address, "so that the world may be delivered from the ruthless oppression of the three Axis countries, Germany, Italy and Japan, and that the conquered peoples now living under their domination may sooner obtain their liberation and freedom."[13]

The lofty rhetoric contrasted with the words used by his chief American advisor. US Army General Joseph Stilwell, known as "Vinegar Joe" because of his acerbic wit, sent out a separate Christmas message to men under his command, revealing his down-to-earth humor and understanding of life as it presented itself at the bottom of the military hierarchy: "Most of us will have large holes in the toes of our Christmas stockings this year, but, judging from your work over the past ten months, I know you can take it, that and a lot more."[14] At a deeper level, it reflected basic differences in the Chinese and American approach to war that were only going to become more obvious in the months and years ahead. The two allied nations were much more different than either of them cared to admit. "Anything" was not necessarily possible, despite the allegations of the Chinese foreign minister on Christmas Eve.

* * *

Chongqing was at the heart of what the Americans intended would become a major front in the battle to bring the Japanese Empire to its knees. It was called the China–Burma–India Theater, or CBI for short, and it was expected to be the scene of a massive land campaign in continuation of the titanic struggle that had pitted China against Japan since 1937. Just as in the Pacific, where the task was to bring huge quantities of materiel across vast expanses of water, the war in the CBI was a logistical challenge as much as a straightforward military one. The western powers had to haul their supplies halfway across the world, unload them in inhospitable terrain and transport them to where they were needed.

In late 1942, when the supply line to the unoccupied part of China known as the Burma Road was closed, the Allies shifted to airlifting materiel from northeast India across the Himalayas into southwest China. The operations area, nicknamed "the Hump" from the mountains that had to be passed, received far less attention than most other theaters involving Americans, mainly because on the face of it, there was less drama involved. The chief danger was the elements, not enemy fighter pilots. In the thin air at high altitudes, the aircraft crews had to struggle with dangerous, creeping sleepiness, as unconsciousness for more than a few moments implied the risk of death from anoxia, an absence of oxygen in the tissue.[15] "If its cold dogged heroism—a heroism that gets no reward, has no glamor—should be neglected or even forgotten for a day, the folks back home would be doing a great injustice to a great outfit doing a great job," war correspondent Herbert L. Matthews wrote in a dispatch published shortly before Christmas.[16]

While the patient and long-suffering pilots of the Himalayas plied their routes day in and day out, in a part of the world that even the Japanese sometimes seemed to have forgotten, the "Hump" crews' fellow airmen further south in Burma were confronting their foes head-on. On Christmas Eve, New Zealand pilot Charles Fergusson, better known as "Chook," was patrolling over Burma's jungle in his Hurricane when he met Japanese aircraft. In the dogfight that ensued "Chook" was shot down. "The airspeed indicator was virtually off the dial and the ground came rushing up. I pulled hard back on the stick but I realized I wasn't going to make it and I blacked out," he said, in a vivid post-war description of his crash. When he came to, he was standing in a shallow river with a terrible pain in his shoulder. Seeing his burning plane at some distance, he realized he had been thrown out just before impact. Moments later he was taken prisoner by a Japanese patrol and spent the rest of the war in captivity.[17]

In the skies over Burma, Christmas was business as usual. To William Joseph Alton, a fighter pilot from Oakland, California with Claire Chennault's famed Flying Tigers, the holiday hardly registered. "It's Christmas Eve, but I don't feel much in the mood for greetings," he wrote in his diary somewhere in the Burmese jungle. "Some missionaries are coming over for some kind of services, but we will be off raiding the Japs, so only the ground crews will be here." He noted that he and his unit had been on a number of successful raids recently. "I hope we hurry because every raid I go on puts me that much closer to Oakland again." In fact, he had already seen his home city for the last time, for he had less than a month to live. He was killed in action on January 12, 1943.[18]

Despite the feverish activity in the air, on the ground an uneasy quiet reigned in the Burma area in December 1942. In eastern India, British soldiers were streaming into camps and barracks in preparation for eventual deployment on the Burma front. Sergeant Sidney Shavin arrived in the city of Chittagong on Christmas Day and found a place inhospitable to newcomers. "The town was deserted and many of the shops were boarded up, but in a few places, you could buy a cup of tea and a handful of Burma cheroots," he said.[19] Frank Harrison, another British infantryman, also remembered an austere Christmas at Chittagong. "We had our Christmas dinner," he recalled. "Bully beef and biscuits, no beer."[20]

Some forces had already crossed from India into Burma and were waiting for the action that was bound to come in the future. This also was true for a group of young Canadian soldiers resting on a mountainside in the evening of December 24. "It was difficult to realize this was Christmas Eve," one of them later recalled, but suddenly the eerie darkness was filled with familiar notes. There was no mistake. It was the melody of "Silent Night," although the words were in an alien language. "Sung by a young child from one of the tribes in the area, it rang crystal clear, vibrating and echoing through the valley," he wrote. The singing ended as abruptly as it had begun, and there was a long period of silence among the young men. "Memories of that Christmas Eve, 1942," the young man reflected decades later, were not colored "by enemy, uncomfortable heat, snakes, mosquitoes or swamps, but by those spine-tingling notes heard 45 years ago, in a foreign land, sung by an unknown child."[21]

* * *

The British Empire in India was put on display in all its grandeur every Christmas when Viceroy Linlithgow left his official seat of government in Delhi and stepped onto his famous "white train" to embark on his traditional journey to Calcutta, not far from the colony's border with Burma. Traveling in style, as behooved the successor to the Mogul throne, he was accompanied by an entourage numbering 500 people, according to Harry Hodson, reforms commissioner for the government of India. "When you consider that His Excellency's entourage included official staff from private secretary to typists and cipher clerks, the Viceroy's Bodyguard of cavalry with all their [...] servants domestic and personal, together with servants of the servants in the caste-bound Indian tradition, five hundred begins to seem too few," Hodson remarked in his memoirs.[22]

When Linlithgow arrived in Calcutta in December 1942, he found a city much changed by war. Thousands of Commonwealth soldiers had put their stamp on the streets, as well as hundreds of newly arrived American GIs. A city of two million, Calcutta had one of the greatest concentrations of poverty in the world, but it also had much to offer for soldiers with filled wallets. There was entertainment ranging from *Mrs. Miniver*, a romantic Hollywood drama at the Metro Cinema, to Tchaikovsky's Fifth Symphony at the Globe Theater, and for those longing for American cuisine, there were two-inch-thick steaks. "Here tattoo artists ply a busy trade from morn to midnight, needling flags or nudes, portraits or monsters as you please," *The New York Times* reported. Beggars wailing "No mamma, no pappa, no baksheesh" were vying for the soldiers' attention with pimps asking, "Want nice girl?"[23]

India was literally on the other side of the world for many of the young western servicemen, and the geographical distance was often underlined by the impossibly long time it took for mail to reach its destination. Captain

Jack S. McGillivray, a doctor with the Canadian Medical Corps in Calcutta, received a Christmas cake from his parents in November 1942. It had been sent for consumption prior to Christmas 1941 and had been one year under way. "The package was battered and torn, but the cake was in good condition," he said, as he consumed it with a near 12-month delay.[24]

Christmas was an opportunity to forget the dreary reality of global conflict for a few precious days—or it would have been if not for the fact that the Japanese military picked the holiday to target the city. A three-hour-long air raid alert hit Calcutta on Christmas Eve. The Japanese bombers came in two waves with 90 minutes in between and dropped their loads seemingly at random over the sprawling city. Some detonated in the residential districts, causing thousands of windowpanes to shatter into the streets. Ian Stephens, the editor of the English-language newspaper *The Statesman*, took a break from work, climbing to the top of a nearby building to watch the events, and stepped onto the roof just when "a 'stick' of bombs started falling slap across the middle of the city, some of them pretty noisy and near."[25]

It was the fourth air raid in less than a week, and similar to the previous attacks, the planes mostly used anti-personnel bombs, suggesting that they were not primarily meant to cause material damage of any direct military significance. "It would appear therefore," *The Times of India* argued, "that the principal object of the attack was to cause the maximum number of casualties among the civilian population and to create nervousness among the citizens."[26] Stephens bicycled around the city on Christmas Day, inspecting the damage. "My mind's eye still sees the sullen faces staring down from blown-in glassless windows," he wrote in his memoirs.[27]

Despite the Japanese choice of ordnance, casualties were relatively light. During the first three raids on Calcutta, a total of 25 people were killed and about 100 injured, according to the authorities.[28] Life went on, the newspapers claimed, and the people of Calcutta were not much perturbed by the bombing. Linlithgow sent a congratulatory message to the residents of the city: "Yours is the first capital city in India to suffer in the war a baptism of fire and her citizens have provided an admirable example of steadiness and fortitude. Well done Calcutta."[29] The chief minister of Bengal, A. K. Fazlul Huq, also sounded an upbeat note. "Calcutta has taken its first experience of enemy night air attack without the morale of the people being shaken in the least," he said in a statement. "We are all prepared to face our fate with calm courage and robust optimism."[30]

Reality was somewhat less heroic. The people of Calcutta were scared, and they felt that not enough was being done to protect them from a possible

Asian blitz. To be sure, the wreckage of one Japanese aircraft shot down by British fighters during the Christmas Eve raid was later found outside Calcutta, but many felt the losses sustained by the attacker ought to be much bigger.[31] "There was no protection from air raids whatsoever," J. McKee Robertson, a British-American woman residing in Calcutta, said after the war, noting that there was a rumor circulating that only one plane had been deployed in defense of the city.[32] This was a gross understatement. More Allied planes were in the air to greet the Japanese bombers, but it was still not enough. "The military authorities are no doubt doing their best and we hope they will give a hotter reception to the raiders than what was possible to be done on the previous occasions," opined the *Amrita Bazar Patrika* newspaper, known for an editorial line critical of the British administration.[33]

A sense of resignation permeated much of the city, and it proved hard to enforce precautions among the population as long as it was unconvinced that the authorities had its interests at heart. Although a blackout had been ordered, authorities complained that instructions to cover windows had not been followed rigorously, and that many lights were visible from the outside.[34] Others voted with their feet, escaping a war they did not feel was theirs. Dock workers left in great numbers, accompanied even by members of the underpaid police force. Within just a few days at the end of December, altogether 350,000 people were estimated to have left, or about one-sixth of the city's population.[35] "Indian labor," Stephens wrote, "is mobile. If it doesn't like its surroundings it just rolls up its few possessions in a cloth-bundle and walks off."[36]

Ken Moses, a mechanic with the Royal Air Force, remembered a Christmas when it seemed almost all of Calcutta had departed, and basic functions were unattended to. "Even our Indian cooks disappeared leaving us to enjoy a dinner of billy-beef and 'dog biscuits'," he reminisced. "A trip into Calcutta for a meal proved a waste of time as staff had deserted hotels and restaurants."[37] It was now in some ways a ghost town. "Some of our street hawkers also disappeared—we never saw our bread delivery man again," recalled Katyun Randhawa, a young Indian girl.

The exodus out of Calcutta caused already fragile supply networks to virtually stop working. "The painful sight of long lines of people waiting for hours near the very few licensed shops for the supply of small quantities of rice, sugar or kerosene still assails the eye," a newspaper editorial lamented.[38] Representatives of the colonial government, or anyone associated with it by virtue of his or her pale skin color, often had an even harder time. Robertson, the British-American woman, ran a canteen for Allied soldiers but found it close to impossible to keep a steady supply of food items and other daily necessities. When she went to the bazaar to buy toothbrushes and toothpaste, the shopkeepers refused to sell the products to her. By Christmas, the situation deteriorated, and she was not even able to buy bread for the servicemen.[39]

The uncomfortable truth was that the Japanese bombers had achieved their goal. After dropping a handful of bombs and killing a couple of dozen people, they had managed to strike a blow at the heart of Calcutta. "Municipal 'sweepers' departed en masse, leaving dustbins overflowing and uncleared, and crows, kites and dogs squabbling over the debris amidst much smell," wrote Stephens, the editor.[40] In a figurative sense, it was the stench of a decaying system, coming apart as the exigencies of war had exposed deeply seated divisions between rulers and the ruled.

* * *

The British were a tired nation by late 1942, exhausted not just after more than three years of war, but also in a more general sense after carrying a global colonial burden for centuries. The Americans were a younger and more energetic people, bursting with boundless vigor onto the global scene by virtue of a conflict that demanded their worldwide presence. The differences between the two English-speaking peoples were in evidence wherever they came into contact. One of these places was India, and the contrasts were highlighted by the way Christmas was celebrated, or not celebrated.

Eric Holloway, a 21-year-old Royal Air Force pilot, had only just arrived in Karachi a few days before Christmas, trying to find a modicum of comfort despite washing and toilet facilities that were somewhere in between inadequate and non-existent. The British Empire was being stretched to the limit, and there were no resources to spare for the comfort of its soldiers. He praised himself lucky that at least it was winter, making the temperature somewhat bearable. "Christmas day was quite depressing as we were far away from home and hardly knew a soul there. No Christmas celebrations took place and the day passed like any other," he wrote after the war.[41]

At the same time, Karachi was seeing an influx of Americans, facing far fewer material constraints. The city was the initial main entry point of most US military personnel deploying in South Asia, and they soon left an indelible mark on their surroundings, not least with their voracious appetites, nurtured in their own land of plenty. "It was said [...] that a 'G.I' would sit down to a meal which included 10 or 12 eggs before starting on anything else," wrote George Molesworth, deputy chief of General Staff of Army Headquarters

India. Soon Karachi and adjacent areas were emptied of eggs, and prices of the hens that produced them soared, he explained, adding; "It was the old story of which came first? The egg or the chicken or the egg? It seemed that if the American rate of consumption continued for any length of time India would soon have none of either!"[42]

From Karachi, the Americans, loud and big, began fanning out into the rest of the Indian subcontinent. They had started to seep into Delhi in the autumn of 1942. While the officers wcrc installed at the Imperial Hotel and two other hotels,[43] the lower ranks were housed in what the author and civil servant Nirad Chaudhuri described as the "ugliest and meanest conceivable huts" that had been hastily put up along Queen's Way, one of the city's main thoroughfares. While the barracks failed to impress the Indians, they were in awe at the well-fed, healthy looks of the Americans themselves. "They were all strongly built, straight men," Chaudhuri remarked. "Their uniform was a shade of khaki which was almost cream, and in striking contrast to the green uniforms of the British soldiers."[44] They were big spenders, able to pay significantly more for local assistance than their British counterparts, who often were forced to watch their local servants abscond in order to work for the Americans instead.[45]

They celebrated Christmas in the boisterous American style. "Yankee soldiers festooned with bright necklaces of flowers snake-danced through New Delhi's streets behind an impromptu Indian band before they sat down to their Christmas dinner of goose and all the trimmings," the *Associated Press* reported.[46] The barracks at Queen's Way were decorated with red and green lights, and a huge "Merry Christmas" sign greeted visitors at the entrance. A public address system was rigged up, and Christmas carols were broadcast loudly to passersby on the road outside. Granted, the subtropical Indian climate was a far cry from the snow-covered wintry landscapes the soldiers knew at home, but it lent itself more easily to the biblical imagery of their childhoods: "The boys obtained two camels to symbolize the transportation of the Three Wise Men," the armed forces newspaper *CBI Roundup* said.[47]

The same issue of the *CBI Roundup* also carried a report from one of the most unusual parties anywhere in the world during that Christmas. At an Army base on the west coast of India, American servicemen hosted and entertained a group of 350 needy children and orphans. "Many of these were Polish refugee children who, dressed in their native costumes, danced Polish folk dances and sang songs of their tragic homeland to men who are supposed to be tough but can still get teary over things like that," the newspaper's correspondent wrote.[48]

The story of the Polish children's voyage to far India illustrated how the global conflict uprooted people and moved them across international borders in unpredictable ways. They had lived in eastern Poland at the time of the outbreak of the war in September 1939, when Soviet troops had occupied their part of the country, taking advantage of the Nazi invasion from the west. Subsequently the Soviet authorities had deported their families to distant places, mostly Siberia, as part of a plan to break the Polish will to resist by physically removing the most resourceful members of society. Many had died during the brutal deportation.

Three years on, the Soviet Union's unstable friendship with Germany was long gone, and Moscow had decided to release a large number of the Polish internees. The problem was what to do with the Poles, suddenly liberated but with no hope of returning to their unfree homeland. In this situation, help emerged from an unlikely source. The maharajah of Nawanagar, one of number of semi-autonomous states within British-controlled India, had decided to offer shelter to thousands of Polish children. Talking to reporters, he said he was motivated to make the unusual gesture out of affection for Polish culture, kindled by his own father's friendship with Ignace Jan Paderewski, a pianist and composer who had served as Poland's third prime minister after World War I.[49]

* * *

The Polish children in India were just a tiny fragment of the human flotsam washed up all across the Soviet empire, as well as on its fringes. For the few who found a new home in India, it was an excruciating journey. It took place via Iran, now under Allied control. Some had to walk most of the way, even though they were weakened after years in the Soviet prison camp system. "When we got out of Russia and reached Tehran, we looked like skeletons," said Feliks Scazighino, one of the Polish children who made the trek. "We all had to be deloused, our hair had to be shaved off, and our clothes burned."[50]

Each of them carried a personal story, almost always tragic. Kazimiera Grzywa was one of the involuntary actors in the vast, unfolding drama. She was a 19-year-old girl from the city of Lvov in what was then eastern Poland and had been deported to Central Asia in the spring of 1940 along with her parents. Ending up in concentration camp-like conditions, the small family had been put to hard work, exposed to a starvation diet and forced to endure a complete absence of hygiene. In the camp, which housed 45 Polish families, roughly half died within the first months.

By late 1942, as the Soviet government's attitude to the Poles had eased somewhat due to the common enmity against the Germans, the family was released and allowed to move to Uzbekistan, a Soviet republic in Central Asia. From there, it was their hope to reach other exiled Poles in India. It was too late for Grzywa's mother, and she died from the after-effects of the hardship during Christmas 1942 on the train station in the Uzbek city of Kitab. "The attitude of the Soviet authorities towards us was unwaveringly hostile. Medical and hospital care was very poor. There was no contact at all with Poland," Grzywa wrote in later testimony.[51]

The Polish children were not only often broken physically, but also traumatized mentally. Less than one in 10 arrived accompanied by a mother. Many did not know if their parents were still alive apart from a few who had vague notions of fathers serving with Allied forces in the Middle East. In their new Indian home, when they heard airplanes, they would run out of their buildings, seeking protection in the surrounding fields.[52] Franek Herzog, one of the Polish children, did not have fond memories even of the time after reaching safety in India. When Christmas came around in 1942, the harrowing experience of life in a Siberian camp was still too close. "It was supposed to be a festive season," he said after the war, "but in our hearts there was sadness, nostalgia and grief."[53]

Most East Europeans who had been sent to camps in the Soviet Union prior to the German attack in 1941 remained incarcerated one way or the other. Eleonora Carneckis was an American-born woman of Lithuanian ancestry who had returned to live in Lithuania, which had become an independent state at the end of World War I. After the Soviet invasion in 1940, her husband had been executed and she herself had been deported to Siberia with her five children. By late 1942, she lived in a barracks with 65 other people—mostly women and children—where the Lena River flowed into the Arctic Ocean. The windowpanes were made of blocks of ice, and at night there was no heating, forcing the inhabitants to huddle together and try to keep warm by the heat of each other's bodies.

Although they were barely surviving, the adults decided to make Christmas special for the children. Each family put aside a slice of bread or a teaspoon of flour every day to prepare for the Christmas meal. Meanwhile, the older children cut toys from wood they found nearby. Eleonora Carneckis' 14-year-old daughter Lucia was dressed up as Santa Claus with the help of an old sheepskin coat turned inside out, a fur cap and a piece of cotton serving as a beard. "The children trembled with delight on receiving their toys," Carneckis wrote nearly half a century later. "Of all the Christmas Eves of my life, I consider this one, spent in terror, hunger, cold, polar night, with dying […] on all sides, the most unforgettable, memorable and meaningful of all."[54]

In the atheist Soviet empire, Christmas was not officially observed, but it was celebrated discreetly in small pockets far apart, sometimes in great secrecy. The traditional Russian Christmas took place in early January, by which time the Orthodox Church, in a modest religious revival after years of suppression, would hold muted services, combining religious ceremonies with a call for greater contributions to the liberation of the motherland.[55]

At the time of Western Christmas, it was a day as any other in Moscow, apart from small parties held at the British and American embassies. For the group of foreign correspondents holed up in the vast city, the dinner at the reserved dining room at the Hotel Metropole was the same as on any other day. A foreign correspondent, walking through the eerie, dimly lit streets of the Soviet capital in search of signs of Christmas, did not expect to find much. After all, the communist giant was at war, in the middle of a life-and-death struggle with the Nazi invader and only the year before Moscow had seemed on the verge of falling. The journalist did, however, notice one person standing out: "He made his way across the open square," the correspondent wrote. "He had a huge Christmas tree over his shoulder destined to bring happiness to some houseful of children."[56]

Map of Europe

CHAPTER 5

Meeting an Angel

Eastern Front

It was only four days since Richard Jung, a young soldier in an armored engineering company of the German *Wehrmacht*, had been sun-bathing on the French Riviera and taken a swim in the warm Mediterranean, and now he was standing in the middle of the freezing Polish night, on his way to the Eastern Front. The train transporting the men to their destination was making a brief halt in the snow-covered countryside, and while they were waiting for it to move on, the company commander had spotted a small pine tree a little distance from the railway track. Now he was busy decorating it, hoping to cheer up the men. They called him *"der Alte,"* or "the Old Man." He was 25 years old.

The men gathered around the tree, now lit up by a few candles someone had produced from a crate inside the train. They considered themselves tough soldiers, but many eyes were shining with tears in the flickering light. Home was on the minds of most of the men. It was nothing like the richly decorated, brightly lit Christmas trees of their childhood, but the memory alone was almost overwhelming to some. At this moment, as they were lost in thoughts about a past now seeming impossibly remote and out of reach, they saw a lone figure emerging from the dark. It was an angel.

She had a white robe and long hair falling over her shoulders. She was wearing a headband with a star attached to it, and she had wings. In her hands was a basket filled with hard Polish peasant bread. The soldiers reached out, grabbing the bread and putting it in their pockets. Soon the young men started singing a traditional German carol. At first, only individual voices joined in, but soon the entire company was singing along. They knew they were on the way to the toughest front a German soldier, or *Landser*, could be sent to: immense, eternal Russia. Although no one said it out loud, this could very well be their last Christmas alive.

At the same time, while losing themselves in the choir, the men got a closer look at the angel. They noticed that her bare feet were stuck into rough men's shoes, and that her robe was dirty. The wings were made of cardboard and were drooping sadly. The soldiers had probably known all along, but now it was made painfully clear that she was a peasant girl in her late teens, trying to sell bread and make a little money desperately needed at home. Still, they wanted to keep the illusion of having met a messenger from God. "That night we believed in miracles," Jung wrote many years later, "that Christmas Eve in 1942 on an insignificant section of railroad in Poland."[1]

Christmas 1942 was a melancholy one for the *Landser* of the Eastern Front. The Russian foe had proved the German Army's most formidable enemy yet, and also the most implacable one. The Germans had been ordered to conduct a war of no mercy in the East, leaving their prisoners to die in mind-boggling numbers, and their adversary was now repaying in kind. For many German soldiers, the ultimate fear was not death or severe injury, but falling alive into the hands of the Russians. The mangled bodies of comrades recovered from the Soviet enemy bore testimony to the horrifying fate that might befall those who were taken prisoner. It was as if this fierce adversary had been formed by the land he inhabited: a brutal, rugged landscape visited by extremes of temperature, blistering in the summer, numbingly cold in winter.

Eighteen months earlier, the German soldiers had entered into the war against the Soviet Union with mixed feelings, contemporary testimony suggests. There was little outright zeal, but a certain widespread sentiment that it was a job that had to be done. Many resigned themselves to the idea that the invasion of the Soviet giant, foolhardy as it might seem from the outside, reflected reasoning beyond their grasp. The *Führer* knew best.

Soon, however, they were overwhelmed by the sheer size of the country they had invaded. "It almost seemed as if the same hill kept appearing in front of us, kilometer after kilometer. Everything seemed to blur into uniform grey because of the vastness and sameness of everything. We traversed treeless plateaus that extended as far as the eye could see, just one vast open field overgrown with tall grass," the young officer Siegfried Knappe wrote in his memoirs. "Nothing could have prepared us for the mental depression brought on by this realization of the utter physical vastness of Russia."[2]

The speedy advances of the first weeks had soon come to an abrupt halt, and the winter of 1941 and 1942 had seen the first major defeat of the *Wehrmacht*, robbing it of its aura of invincibility, as it was stopped at the gates of Moscow, within sight of the towers of the Kremlin. The year 1942 had brought new vigor to the German forces, and a summer offensive had revived some of the momentum that had characterized their operations in the early years of the war. In the end, however, that offensive, too, had bogged down, and now the Germans had entered their second Russian winter. They were slightly better prepared than they had been a year earlier. Many had warmer uniforms more suited for the inhuman temperatures, but this did only so much to boost morale, because now they knew what they were up against and what hardship lay ahead.

By Christmas 1942, the Eastern Front had become an endless source of pain and sorrow, extending all the way to the home front. Rudolf Häck, a 25-year-old former economics student from the southern German city of Stuttgart, spent the holiday in a military hospital. He had been shot through the lung during battles in the marshes of northern Russia in September. His spine had also been hit, and his lower body had been paralyzed. A military doctor had told him he should expect to stay in hospital for the next two years. Nevertheless, the day before Christmas he sent a letter full of hope to his parents. "My injuries are healing so marvelously that even the doctor is impressed. That is actually all I can offer you this Christmas: news that I am getting better, and my love for you." He died from his injuries one month later.[3]

* * *

At the airbase at Tatsinskaya, a village of 5,000 inhabitants on the southern Russian front, *Luftwaffe* pilot Kurt Streit was getting ready in the early hours of December 24 for what he thought would be an uneventful day. In front of him were rows of irreplaceable transport planes, not only the ubiquitous Junkers Ju 52, but also several ageing Junkers Ju 86s pulled from training schools in Germany to aid in the supply of the surrounded Sixth Army at Stalingrad. "At that moment Soviet tanks firing on the move broke into the village and aerodrome," Streit wrote later. "Combat planes immediately blazed up like torches. Flames were raging everywhere, shells bursting, ammunition blowing up. Lorries rushed about and desperately shouting men were running between them."[4]

The Soviet tanks were the spearhead of a large, armored column that had penetrated deep into German-held territory in the preceding days. The purpose was to compel the Germans to divert troops away from the vital mission of relieving the troops in Stalingrad, and also to take out airfields used to supply them. The Germans knew they were coming but had been ordered by the *Luftwaffe*'s commander-in-chief Hermann Göring to stand fast until Soviet tanks were firing directly at them. As the Germans rushed to organize a response, the attacking tanks were roaming almost at will, as they shot up the planes or rammed directly into their tails. One Soviet tank drove straight into the body of a Junkers Ju 52 transport plane with suicidal determination, and both disappeared in a huge ball of fire.

The Germans were seized by uncharacteristic confusion, bordering on panic. Pilots scrambling to get to their planes yelled out for orders about where to fly their aircraft and received only vague answers. The raging fires colored the sky an ominous crimson, as the snow-covered ground was littered with dead and injured soldiers trying to crawl to safety. "A Junkers and a Heinkel already in the air collided and dissolved into pieces," Streit wrote. "The roar of tanks and aircraft engines mingled with the explosions of the artillery and machine-gun bursts into a monstrous symphony."[5]

Amid the confusion, a majority of the German planes managed to get airborne. General Martin Fiebig, who was in overall charge of the effort to supply Stalingrad by air, was present at Tatsinskaya when the attack was let loose, and he was aboard one of the last Ju 52s to take off from the airfield. The pilot was able to fly it to the German-held city of Rostov. "At least it didn't ice up," Fiebig wrote in his diary. "What an absolutely lucky break!" As messages ticked in, it was clear that nearly three in four of the 170 operable aircraft at Tatsinskaya had succeeded in escaping. It was better than could have been hoped for, but Fiebig was exhausted. "I was at the end of my strength," he noted, adding that it forced him to commit a serious faux pas. "I went to bed early, even missing the Christmas visit of the Generaloberst."[6]

After the initial chaos, the Germans quickly organized a reaction to the Soviet incursion and managed to isolate the armored column, cutting it off from its supply lines. A large part of the Soviet tanks were lost along with their crews, and it was a severely reduced force that eventually was able to break through, partly with the help of captured fuel, and return to friendly territory. Still, the mission had succeeded in forcing the Germans to adjust their plans for a relief of Stalingrad, while also taking out a significant number of planes that could be used for supplying the beleaguered troops in the city. A German colonel who arrived at Stalingrad a few days later was straightforward in his assessment of the situation: "Worse than we have ever feared."[7]

Tatsinskaya airfield was far from the only place where the Soviets were active during Christmas 1942. Further up north, at the town of Velikiye Luki near the besieged city of Leningrad, they attacked a battalion of Danish *Waffen-SS* volunteers, organized in the so-called *Freikorps Danmark*. The battalion commander, Knud Børge Martinsen, had made the rounds earlier in the evening, talking to his men, and now the soldiers that could be spared

MEETING AN ANGEL • 73

got together for drunken revelry. As the bottles were passed among the men, one of them pointed out they had been warned that "Ivan" usually picked Christmas to attack. "There's no such thing as 'usually' around here," another replied with inebriated lack of concern.[8]

Shortly before midnight, the telephone rang at the battalion command. An officer picked it up and listened briefly and then turned toward Martinsen.

"They're actually attacking," the officer said.

Martinsen's reply was curt: "Damn it!"

The battalion's 1st Company reported that the village it occupied was swarming with hundreds of Soviet soldiers. The battle soon disintegrated into combat at close quarters, with bayonets and hand grenades being used as the main weapons. One soldier whose position inside the rubble of a house in the village was so well hidden the enemy had not noticed him called in by field telephone and was able to direct artillery fire with such precision that the attack was finally broken up.[9]

Before sunrise the Soviet attackers had been driven back, but it had come at great cost. The Christmas attack had been the bloodiest battle of the entire winter for the Danish volunteers, and as the Soviets renewed their attack on Christmas Day, more bloodshed was in store. No quarter was given. "With great difficulty I had a 5cm gun pulled up and shot up the whole village, causing a fire which forced them out of the houses (all made of wood), after which we took them out one by one. There must have been 50 or 60 of them," wrote Per Sørensen, commander of 1st Company, in a letter to his parents.[10]

The Russians, officially atheist, had shown the previous year that they picked Christmas for scattered attacks along the frontline, and 1942 saw a repetition of this pattern. Infantryman Hans Heintel was rudely awakened from his sleep on Christmas morning, lying on the floor in a heap of broken glass after having been blown out of his bed by the shock wave of a Soviet bomb. As he quickly realized, the city where he was doing occupation duty was being targeted in an air raid. "As usual, it had pleased the Russians to use a German holiday for an attack," he wrote later.[11]

The Germans knew well that Russian penchant for Christmas raids, and in many places, they took necessary precautions for Christmas 1942. It was "the most wonderful night of the year, but also one of the nights the soldiers feared the most," Harry Mielert, a young officer, wrote in a letter home on December 25. "We sprayed the Russian with so much fire from all our weapons right at dusk that he became quite nervous and probably feared us more throughout the night than we feared him. We sang our beautiful Christmas carols full of confidence, although we were clutching our rifles and our pockets were stuffed with hand grenades."[12]

Fernando Wassner, a soldier in a German reconnaissance unit, wrote home to his mother about a Christmas spent constantly on the run from pursuing Russians. Christmas Day his company was harassed incessantly by Soviet air strikes, and while on a patrol in front of his division the following day, his column of reconnaissance vehicles was spotted by a mass of advancing Soviet tanks and beat a hasty retreat to report to division headquarters. "When we returned the order had already been issued to pull out and withdraw at night," he wrote in his letter. "Our division no longer put up any resistance to major attacks. Every evening we blew up more vehicles that had broken down and could not be towed."[13]

Perhaps the Soviet soldiers felt a touch of envy that the German soldiers received more generous treatment during Christmas. Even though the Soviet Union had abandoned its Christian faith, Christmas did mean something to many of its soldiers. It was only a generation ago that Lenin's communists had seized power in what had until then been the deeply religious Russian empire. Traditional Russian Christmas was not observed until January, but once the holiday occurred, a few days after the German enemy had marked it, some of the very same thoughts occupied the men of the Soviet Army. "Frontline soldiers always connect New Year's Day with the sanctity of the birth of Christ, with the burning of ceremonial candles," wrote Boris Gorbachevsky, a junior officer in the 31st Army. "Remembrances of good traditions fill them with hope for the future."[14]

He noted how for Christmas 1942, each German soldier in his area, near the city of Rzhev, received a Christmas package consisting of "pies, cakes, chocolate, twenty grams of coffee, cigarettes, and alcohol." From afar, they could also glimpse Christmas trees glittering in all the German positions as reminders of more peaceful times. By contrast, the Soviet soldiers, the "fighters and commanders on the front lines for the Motherland," received only 100 grams of vodka to dull the worst fears of death in combat, as well as a piece of herring and a lump of bread, to be shared between two, Gorbachevsky noted with more than a little bitterness. In response, the soldiers sang a song full of gallows humor:

We're going into battle
For a herring's tail!
And we'll all die as one
For a hundred grams of vodka.[15]

* * *

Guy Sajer, a young Frenchman serving in the German forces near the city of Minsk, was standing guard on the outskirts of a small Russian village, trying to keep warm despite the freezing temperature. He was startled by the approach of a dark shadow and grabbed his rifle. Was it a Russian partisan? It turned out to be a German lieutenant doing the round among the guards.

"Everything all right?" the officer asked.

"Yes, *Leutnant*," Sajer replied.

"Fine. Well, Happy Christmas."

"What? Is it Christmas?"

"Yes," the lieutenant said and pointed him towards a building in the nearby village where German soldiers were celebrating the holiday. Now, Sajer heard the sound of sentimental German songs, and for the first time since becoming a soldier, he thought of his earliest youth. He would never have admitted it to any of his fellow soldiers, but at that moment he would have liked it more than anything else if someone had given him a mechanical toy as a Christmas present.[16]

War Christmases had been a firm part of German culture since the successful campaign against France in 1870 and 1871. For soldiers on the front in December 1870, it had been a profound experience mixing joy and sorrow with, in the words of one veteran, "memories of the sweet, bygone days of youth, that time when one snuggled up with heart's delight in childish love to one's dear parents."[17] Even though the physical hardship and the separation from family and home were felt keenly, it had also been a Christmas to remember. The special bond forged between men sharing the mortal danger of war had intensified the emotional nature of the holiday, and according to the same veteran, the soldiers had experienced "a Christmas celebration, a sweet celebration of youth, as never before, in an authentic comrade-like brotherly togetherness, which all participants will remember forever."[18]

In 1914, the Catholic chaplain Jakob Ebner had spent Christmas with troops near Verdun. Late at night on December 24, he had driven in a military automobile to a small wood near the frontline, allowing the soldiers to take turns to leave their positions briefly and participate in the midnight service. He had also noted the bond between home and front made more explicit by observance of the Christmas rituals: "Our thoughts rushed as if on a golden bridge from here to home, where they were also getting ready for Christmas in church and family."[19]

The two themes of bonding with one's comrades and bonding with the home front were salient for German soldiers on the Eastern Front during Christmas 1942 as well. Harry Mielert, the young officer, noticed it as he walked from position to position on Christmas Eve, speaking personally to each of his men, sitting down with them to drink a toast, share some pastry, and smoke a cigarette. "Everyone had photos [of family] and showed them to me with a mixture of embarrassment and pride," he wrote in a letter. He noted that the "old hands," normally tough and stoic, now revealed an unexpected tenderness. "They are not exactly weeping," he wrote, "but you can see how emotional they are on the inside, and they have to mobilize their men's humor in all its terseness and crudeness to get rid of this softness."[20]

The importance of maintaining a link with home was reflected in the massive amount of mail sent to and from the units on the Eastern Front. This went even for the encircled troops at Stalingrad, now only supplied with a slender air bridge. Around Christmas 1942, transport planes supplying the starving soldiers in the beleaguered city carried two tons of letters from home every day, taking up space that could have been used for food or ammunition, and tons of letters were also shipped out of the city, alongside the wounded. The officers planning the flights did not see this as wasteful. They knew that letters from home were invaluable for maintaining morale.[21]

Longing for home, a place that many of the soldiers would never see again, was a constant theme in the cold and strange immensity of Russia, and the feeling became especially painful during Christmas, when the soldiers were remined of earlier years when they had been able to celebrate the holiday with their loved ones. A 20-year-old lieutenant on a troop train passing through Germany shortly before Christmas on its way to the Eastern Front was left in a deep depressive mood when the train passed through his birthplace and he caught a quick glimpse of his parents' house, which he had not been able to visit for more than a year. He was thrown into a state of despair, and he spent the rest of the journey in an alcohol-induced stupor.[22]

Intriguingly, the German Army often seemed to worsen the mood with its propaganda. In a small booklet issued before Christmas 1942 to the soldiers of a division fighting near Lake Ilmen south of Leningrad, an anonymous writer described the Russian "steppes and marshes which will forever be alien to the soldiers' hearts." In contrast to this foreign world, he described the north German region of Schleswig-Holstein from which the soldiers hailed as "the beautiful land between the Baltic and the North Sea, with its expanses, as if inhabited with a soul of their own, its resplendent fields, and its light colors."

The writer readily acknowledged that not everyone would live to see this again: "Christmas 1942 requires of us all renewed willingness to do one's duty and, if need be, die." He also recognized homesickness was particularly bad during Christmas, and offered the scant consolation of seeing home in the mind's eye: "What time is more apt to stir longing and touch our hearts more than Christmas… Our hearts reach out far away to our loved ones at home, whom we are protecting here. Front and home bond in faith for the eternal good, the empire of love."[23]

* * *

Religion played a surprising role for the common German soldier, even though he served a regime that saw the Christian faith as an obstacle to the ideal, racially pure society it wanted to build. Lutherans from the north of Germany and Catholics from the south were united in their observance of Christmas. The feeling of living in extraordinary times that required extraordinary sacrifices was heightened in the charged religious atmosphere. In 1914, the Catholic chaplain Jakob Ebner had observed the same phenomenon. "With rifle in one hand and helmet in the other, they kneeled down on the hard, frozen ground in front of the altar, to receive the greatest gift of Christmas," he wrote in his diary. It was "a drama for angels and mankind, a great religious deed in a great and difficult time."[24]

Religion triggered a sense of magic associated with Christmas, recalling faint echoes of a past at home when old fairy tales had been told in the warm glow from the Christmas tree with its bright candles. A few German soldiers even waxed lyrical about the Russian countryside in front of them, imbuing the barren landscape with supernatural qualities. "Snow covers the devastation and transforms the bleak trees with their trunks and branches shot to pieces into an enchanted forest," the infantryman Friedrich Grupe wrote in his diary. "At night a marvelous full moon rises over the battlefield."[25]

Even though the German soldiers were surrounded by evidence of the death and devastation they had brought to Russia, they nevertheless managed to convince themselves that they were fighting for the right cause. Young men who had managed to retain their religious devotion despite Nazi efforts to roll back the influence of the Christian church, were made to believe that God was on their side, just as their belt buckles carried the inscription *Gott mit uns*—"God with us." The exhortation from a booklet published for Christmas 1942 was typical of this view: "Now, comrades, we will celebrate a German Christmas in enemy country! Make your hearts firm and pure! The Everlasting will bless our struggle if we keep the idea of love as a holy fire in our hearts. That way, the true, holy and great German Reich will emerge!"[26]

For some German soldiers, there was an experience akin to religious revival as the constant danger at the frontline left them desperate for some kind of consolation or spiritual refuge. "The value of religious care," a Protestant chaplain wrote in Stalingrad, "has probably seldom been so quickly recognized as now in the time of encirclement. This was especially apparent during the Advent and Christmas celebrations, when so many of the outward trappings [of the normal holiday] had to be renounced. Here the most inner meaning of Christmas came to have much more validity than in other years."[27]

Seeking comfort in religion was not always simple, and soldiers had to search deep in their memories for bits and pieces of the Christian faith that had survived the Nazi attempts to de-emphasize the subject in the schools. At a hastily arranged Christmas service near the front, a German soldier read the Gospel of Luke to his comrades, and a sergeant who had also fought in the previous world war exclaimed "Amen" and started singing "Sweeter the Bells Never Sounded," an old German carol. "Many were able to sing along. And then we sang on, all the carols we had sung at home," a younger soldier wrote in a letter to his mother. "The lyrics that some of us had forgotten, others remembered."[28]

* * *

When the Germans had arrived in the city of Rossosh on Russia's border with Ukraine in the fall of 1941, Natalya Grigorevna Krotova's husband had fled, but she had stayed behind. Since then, the middle-aged woman's apartment across from the train station had been taken over by the city's new masters, and eight members of the *Luftwaffe*, ground personnel dressed in trademark blue uniforms, had moved in. She used her local connections to make sure there was always enough food for the soldiers—chicken, potatoes and carrots—and she cooked for them. Over the months, a bond of affection had developed. The eight young men called her "Matka," "Little Mother."

Matka employed another Russian woman, Natasha, to do the cleaning and other manual tasks. Chubby and simple-minded, she laughed with childish embarrassment when the bored soldiers made her the target of harmless pranks. There was a warm and cozy atmosphere at Matka's house, like a little family. Both women might dislike the German occupation of their homeland intensely, but they managed not to make it personal. The eight *Luftwaffe* soldiers might be the enemy, but when they crossed the threshold into Matka's home, they became her boys.

It all came to an end during Christmas 1942. On Christmas Eve the eight soldiers had still been gathered around the table eating the goose that Matka, sweating and jolly as always, had spent the afternoon preparing. A few hours later, on Christmas Day, the soldiers were jolted out of their sleep by a Soviet air attack on Rossosh. Several bombs fell on the railway station just across from Matka's home, and ammunition trains blew up in huge explosions. By evening, large parts of the city center were in ruins. The eight German soldiers never saw Matka and Natasha again. They had been lost in the great maelstrom of war.[29]

Germany had embarked on a war of annihilation in the East, where, for racial reasons, friendship with the local population was considered out of the question from the outset. Still, the situation on the ground was often very different from the one foreseen by the Nazi planners of the bloody crusade in the Soviet Union. In one example out of perhaps thousands, a German unit trapped at Stalingrad developed a close relationship with a group of Russians who had sought shelter in their bunker. One of them was a prisoner, nicknamed "Pock-Faced Nikolai," who now worked for the Germans. He was killed on Christmas Eve trying to scavenge in the ruins for wood to be thrown on the bonfire, and there was genuine sadness among the soldiers. "Heat bought with blood," a one of them remarked laconically.[30]

Just as at least some Germans adopted a more nuanced perspective on the Russians once they came into closer contact with them, the same happened to the way that at least some Russians viewed the Germans, despite a genocidal war that cost the Soviet Union in excess of 20 million people, soldiers and civilians. "Look, there's the Gestapo, the authority. These were Nazis, Party members. But the simple soldiers, they're a people like us. Absolutely," said a Russian civilian in the city of Smolensk about his impression of the Germans. "Although I suffered under the Germans, I never met a subhuman... or sadistic type."[31]

Loyalties emerged which cut across political boundaries. Johannes Huebner, a theology student from northern Germany now involved in anti-partisan warfare in southern Russia apologized to his parents in a letter that he was unable to write often enough. "In the past few weeks, my battalion has been thrown from one forest to another, and now, shortly before Christmas, the war, the father of everything, also does not take a break." Four days after he wrote the letter, he was killed in action while clearing a partisan base, with a bullet to the neck and one to the chest. "The people of our area went to his grave and mourned the death of their 'father'," the battalion commander wrote in a letter to Huebner's parents. "That's what they called the young man with the big heart, who sang their songs, spoke their language and understood their soul better than any other German."[32]

There was still plenty of room for misunderstanding. The Germans believed, absurdly, that civilians in the occupied areas ought to be grateful to them for having saved them from the communists, even if the rule they themselves brought was far more brutal. An 18-year-old Russian woman was pressured by a female German official to agree to work in Germany, and when she hesitated was met with angry disbelief. "Greater Germany needs workers," the official shouted into her face. "There's a war going on. German soldiers are spilling blood for the future of Russia, our future with you! They must be helped. You don't want to refuse help to Greater Germany, do you?"[33]

The German Army emptied an asylum for the mentally ill in the village of Gedeonovka in the middle of winter to make room for its own wounded soldiers. As the patients were pulled out into temperatures of minus 35 degrees Celsius (minus 30 degrees Fahrenheit), abandoned to a certain death, a German officer mocked the onlookers: "You ungrateful Russians. At a time when German soldiers are liberating you from Bolsheviks, spilling their own blood in the battle for Moscow, to free you from Bolsheviks, your idiots are more valuable to you."[34]

This was the Eastern Front at its worst. However, in some parts of German-occupied Russia, conditions could seem almost quiet and quotidian. This was true for Elena Skrjabina, a Russian woman who had endured the starvation and random terror of the German siege of Leningrad and had managed to escape. By a circuitous route, by December 1942, she and her family found themselves in the German-held city of Pyatigorsk in the Caucasus, living in an apartment with a direct view of Mount Elbrus, Europe's highest peak. Christmas Eve was particularly peaceful. Some German soldiers had been allowed to go home for the holiday, and the rest held Christmas parties among themselves. It was almost as it they were not there any longer.

Skrjabina put up a Christmas tree and invited some friends over to pass the evening, exchanging memories about a life that had been lost. "Everything was forgotten: the darkness and starvation of the siege, the ruined city filled with corpses. All of us who had gathered in this comfortable little apartment around the elegantly decorated Christmas tree were transported in our thoughts back to the distant, beloved city during the days of its power and glory," Skrjabina wrote in her diary. "We did not wish to return to the present, to think about the Germans, about the battle for Stalingrad, about our so cloudy future. If only we could stretch out these moments of enjoyment of the past!"[35]

* * *

On Christmas Eve, Germany's encircled Sixth Army at Stalingrad was informed that the last hope of being relieved from the outside had been extinguished. For the past 12 days, the 4th Panzer Army under General Hermann Hoth had been carrying out Operation *Winter Storm* south of the river Don in an attempt to break through to the surrounded troops in the city bearing the Soviet leader's name, but even though the attacking units were equipped with state-of-the-art Tiger tanks, they had found that they were no match for the numerically superior Russians as they tried to cover the 75 miles to the beleaguered army. "[Soviet] tanks are being destroyed every day here on the Don, but [the enemy] keeps having new ones," a frustrated German soldier wrote in a letter home.[36]

Success was also impeded by Hitler's refusal to allow the Sixth Army under the command of General Friedrich Paulus to fight its way out of the Stalingrad cauldron and meet the 4th Panzer Army somewhere in the middle. The Sixth Army could theoretically have defied the *Führer*'s command, but practical circumstances made it impossible for the underequipped and exhausted troops to attempt a breakout. Estimates showed that there was only fuel for the Sixth Army's tanks to cover 20 miles of Russian steppe, not even half the distance to Hoth's vanguard. By December 24, the 4th Panzer Army was in full retreat, scrambling to return to its start position without losing irreplaceable men and armor.[37]

"It was a sad Christmas," recalled Wilhelm Adam, Paulus' adjutant, locked inside the Stalingrad cauldron with what was now the doomed Sixth Army.[38] Final confirmation that Hoth's tank column had been forced to retreat was radioed in at 6 pm on Christmas Eve, he wrote in his recollections. "We were as if paralyzed when shortly afterwards we gathered for dinner with General Paulus." The general described the strategic situation, essentially telling the officers seated around them that there would be no salvation, and that they might all die. "And so," Paulus added, addressing the most painful thoughts occupying them all, "we also have gathered here today in the light of burning candles to think of our families at home, just as at this very moment they are with us here in our thoughts."[39]

Paulus shared chocolate from a box he had been given by acquaintances in Romania. The officers passed it around in silence or exchanging just one-syllable words. In happier days, when the officers gathered around Paulus for festive occasions there would have been loud conversation and roaring laughter, but this evening there was an almost sepulchral quiet in the room, with only the muffled boom of shells and sharp noises of small-arms fire audible.

"The stark contrast between the brutal reality of war and the peaceful message of Christmas could not be erased with words," Adam wrote.[40]

It was a brief dinner, and shortly afterwards the officers dispersed to spend the rest of the evening with their respective staffs. It was hard for Adam to explain to his men just how hopeless the situation had become with the failure of Hoth's relief mission, but he saw no point in hiding it for them. "All were married, all had family," he said. "I told them truthfully about the events outside the cauldron." Then the talk turned to home. Letters and photos were passed around. The men shared two bottles of brandy. Shortly before midnight, Adam went to bed. "Thoughts were swirling around my head for a long time, until I fell asleep without having arrived at any clarity."[41]

Even in far-off Berlin, 1,300 miles away, doubts about the situation in Stalingrad were emerging. The self-assured propaganda minister Joseph Goebbels did not show any weakening of his certainty in public, and in his diary he remained full of scorn at the Soviet professions of victories, but he acknowledged that there was little room for optimism: "It is obvious that Bolsheviks would use Christmas to release pompous declarations of victory. That doesn't bother me at all. I am much more concerned about the situation in Stalingrad proper as well as on the Don front. It is downright tragic that out attempts to clean up the front there fail repeatedly due to a lack of manpower."[42]

The shortage of soldiers was felt keenly even though Germany was not fighting alone against the Soviet enemy. Italian and Romanian troops were also deployed as part of the campaign and saw heavy combat throughout Christmas. Battles within the battle were raging far from Stalingrad, but still connected to the titanic struggle for the city. Meanwhile, Soviet aircraft dropped leaflets over the Italian troops aiming to weaken their morale: "The Soviet Union possesses the greatest general – General Winter. We invite you to surrender individually, by platoons, by companies. Surrender before the end arrives for you."[43]

It was not an empty threat. In the valley of Arbuzovka, a combined force of Germans and Italians was surrounded by Soviet forces on all sides, unable to escape. Italian infantryman Francesco Stefanile was in that group of trapped soldiers, watching how automatic fire from the ridges around the valley created carnage in his column: "All those who were in the lead fell on top of each other without being able to defend themselves; those who tried in vain to get away from the line of fire were mercilessly mowed down." He thought about his family in the town of Nola near Naples, imagining that at this very moment, they would be carrying out Christmas shopping, buying clams, wine, sweets and fireworks. "Who knows if they are okay? I am sure that I am at the top of their thoughts," he said to himself. He felt tears streaming down his cheeks, immediately turning into hard ice.[44]

Inside the Stalingrad cauldron, similar thoughts occupied Hans Happe, a 19-year-old private in the 29th Division, as he spent Christmas in a blizzard, building a new bunker in minus 30 degrees Celsius (minus 22 degrees Fahrenheit), after his unit was ordered out of the old one. Even though they managed to complete the bunker in time for Christmas Eve, they were still freezing as their heater had not yet had time to warm the underground space. "At night I had guard duty at the exact time when you were getting ready for Christmas mass," he wrote in a letter home. "You look at the starry sky in the crystal-clear icy night, and you say to yourself: over there, 3000 kilometers northwest from here, our loved ones go to Christmas mass, happy, celebrating a merry holiday."[45]

Musings such as these were nearly universal. One letter from Stalingrad described it in straightforward, honest terms, far removed from the official image of the tough *Landser* ready to brave any hardship: "I don't know how many times the words 'Germany' and 'home' were uttered on Christmas Eve, but very often. I am in a bunker with someone who is 22 years old. On Christmas Eve he was weeping like a little child, but I must tell you all of us had tears in our eyes when we heard there was no mail from home."[46] Another letter, written by a young soldier to his aunt, reflected the despair felt in the trenches: "I would have liked to pass the wonderful Christmas celebration with my parents, but fate would otherwise, and I must pass Christmas in the frontline. What a Christmas."[47]

In that situation, it became even more crucial for the NCOs and officers to connect with their men. In Happe's unit, the captain walked from shelter to shelter, handing out cigarettes and chocolate and chatting with the men. It helped the mood, but the most important thing was the food: the soldiers fried meatballs from slaughtered horses, adding in ryebread that had been made chewable after soaking in water. "For me and for every one of my comrades, the most important thing is to be able to eat one's fill, and I was during this Christmas 1942," Happe wrote.[48]

Not everyone was that lucky. General Paulus reported that the first German soldier had starved to death on December 21, but the real situation was probably much more serious.[49] Only three days later, on Christmas Eve, the Sixth Army quartermaster counted 64 casualties from starvation.[50] The German *Luftwaffe* had proven increasingly inadequate in supplying the army, but still provided the only lifeline to the outside, however slender. "It has been established that troop morale is considerably improved when they simply hear the engine noise of the aircraft," the quartermaster noted in a report.[51]

Kurt Reuber, a 36-year-old priest and physician, was inspired by the overall mood of hopelessness and distress to draw a sketch of Virgin Mary with the newborn Christ with brown chalk on the back of a three-by-four-foot Russian map. He gave it the title "Christmas in the Cauldron" and added the words "Light, life, love" from the Gospel of John. "What else is there to say?" he wrote in a letter to his wife, describing the image to her. "Think about our situation, marked by darkness, death and hate—and our longing for light, life, love, which is so unfathomably large in each one of us!"[52]

He placed the drawing in his quarters, with a candle below to enhance the visual impact. Then he let soldiers enter in small groups, in the same way that German fathers would open the door of their living rooms to their children to unveil the magic, decorated Christmas tree. "An uncanny view, the flickering candlelight," a soldier who saw the image wrote later. "[We stood] silent, with eyes wide open. The picture emanated a ghostly calm… The picture wouldn't leave us alone. Many eyes were damp, there were tears."[53]

CHAPTER 6

"We're turning into wolves"

Eastern Europe

On Christmas Eve, 27-year-old Jewish resistance fighter Yitzhak Zuckerman was walking through the streets of the southern Polish city of Krakow while one of his boots was slowly filling with blood. He had nearly fallen into a trap and narrowly escaped an arrest attempt by the Germans, but while he had been able to run away, they had managed to put a bullet in his leg. He knew he was going to die if he did not receive medical attention, but in order not to attract attention he strolled along the sidewalk as casually as he could despite the intensifying pain and the sickening feeling of warm, sticky blood flowing down his ankle. He mixed with the crowd, stopping every now and then with feigned interest to read an announcement put up on the wall. It was past 5 pm, and curfew was at 6. He had only minutes left.

He entered into a Catholic church and sat down near the entrance. The building was empty, except for the priest and a person who was confessing his sins. After a short while, the other visitor left, and Zuckerman went up to the priest. He explained the situation. He needed first aid and water, and he asked to stay in the church until dawn. The alternative seemed to be almost certain death. Of all nights during the year, this would be the one when Christians would show compassion, he figured, but the priest turned him away. He couldn't take the risk, he told Zuckerman, and ordered him to leave the church.

Zuckerman was back in the streets, which were now nearly empty because of the impending curfew. With growing desperation, and sensing with alarm that he was growing progressively weaker from his untreated wound, he spotted a doctor's sign at the entrance of an apartment building. It was in Polish, with no German translation. This was good news as it suggested that the physician was a patriot who preferred not to treat members of the occupying power. He rang the bell, and the residents of a neighboring apartment came out and opened the door for him. They told him the doctor was not in, but he made his way into the corridor and collapsed on the stairway.

The rest of the night proceeded in a haze. Zuckerman slipped in and out of consciousness, with moments of intense fever making way for periods of shivering chill. At one point, two men came out and quickly bandaged his leg, while children brought him cakes and bread before disappearing back into the relative safety of their apartments. He picked up random sentences in the dark. One voice said they had to do something about the injured man. Another answered, "Let him stay till morning. He's lost a lot of blood and isn't getting medical aid. He'll die anyway." Shortly before dawn, the concierge approached him, and after realizing he had not died yet, she motioned him to her apartment, asking him to be quiet, so no one heard. "Hard times, we're turning into wolves," she said.

She gave him food and a place to sleep, and he did not wake up until the next evening. The woman talked to him again. She wept and told him he had to move on. Her son was due to visit, and he would be upset to see her risk her life for a stranger. She gave him a stick to support him and enable him to walk despite the injured leg, and in much pain he managed to get to Krakow railway station. From there he caught a train to Warsaw, and finally was able to make his way past the guards into the Jewish ghetto.[1]

It was no coincidence that Krakow was tense over Christmas, and that the Germans were more alert and aggressive than in normal times. The city was generally known to be a relatively peaceful part of occupied Poland, but two days before the holiday, Jewish fighters had thrown grenades into Cyganeria, a coffee shop catering to members of the German military. Several Germans had been killed. In the massive search carried out after the attacks, even more Germans lost their lives in shoot-outs. On December 22, as they tried to seize a member of the Jewish resistance, Adolf Liebeskind, he fought back. "He had lived like a hero and died like a hero," according to a post-war Polish account. "When the Gestapo came to Lutawskiego Street to pick him up, he killed two Germans and wounded two more before being taken down by a German bullet."[2]

* * *

Two days before Christmas, German soldier Hans Pietzcker sat down in Warsaw and wrote a letter to a friend. Put in a pensive mood by the approaching holiday, the 22-year-old former university student reflected on how war had changed him, and how it had caused an unbridgeable gulf to open up between him and people at home who only knew about the conflict from the overenthusiastic narratives of sanitized news reels. He had come to terms with the fact that he would very likely be killed in action, and in a way, he preferred such an end. He no longer feared death and considered it a more attractive option than having to go home after the war and trying to pass on his harrowing experiences to those who had not themselves been through them. Those returning from the war "won't have an easy time," he remarked in his letter. "The routine of everyday life has a crushing power on us all."[3]

There was indeed a chasm between Germany's home front and the alien and horrifying new world that its victorious armies had created in the countries to the East. By Christmas 1942, Poland had been occupied by Germany for more than three terrible years. The Nazi reign had been characterized by mass terror from the earliest days. In February 1940, the head of the General Government in Poland, Hans Frank, had bragged about the harshness of his rule in an inebriated conversation with a correspondent for Nazi party organ *Völkischer Beobachter*, making sure to emphasize the difference with Czechoslovakia, also under German rule. "In Prague, large red posters were put up to announce that seven Czechs had been shot. I said to myself, if I were to put up a poster for every seven Poles shot to death, all the forests of Poland would not be enough to produce all the pulp needed for those posters."[4]

Of course, Frank's callous remark never made it into the party mouthpiece. Nazi propaganda only allowed the public in Germany to know so much about what was going on, but bits and pieces of information seeped back into the country, especially brought home by soldiers on leave. Their message was often: Germany has better win this war, or we will be doomed by the thirst for revenge among the peoples in the East. This was no exaggeration, as events in Poland during Christmas 1942 demonstrated.

Radom, a city of about 80,000 residents roughly 60 miles from Warsaw, was an example of how the everyday business of killing continued throughout the holiday. Among the buildings run by the German authorities was the construction management office on Słowackiego Street, where a number of Jewish slave laborers were employed in the daytime. One of the workers, surnamed Ickowicz, had owned a candle factory before the war, and one morning he had brought Christmas candles to work, hoping to sell them through the fence to Poles passing by outside. That was to prove his death sentence.

A German SS officer saw the trade going on and immediately reported it to his superior, Herbert Böttcher, the head of the police in Radom. Böttcher had Ickowicz arrested and locked up in a cell in the building, where he spent half a day. An eyewitness later described how he saw a car drive up, and how Ickowicz emerged from the building carrying a shovel and a sack of lime. The eyewitness asked the driver of the car, whom he was somewhat acquainted with, what would happen next. He replied that on Böttcher's orders they were to take him to the Gestapo headquarters at a housing estate named Planty. "The car returned later without Ickowicz," the eyewitness said. "Everybody said that he had been forced to dig his own grave, and he was shot at Planty."[5]

Jews had made up more than a quarter of Radom's pre-war population, but everyone was at risk of becoming a victim of casual German brutality. Several civilians had been rounded up throughout the city in December on suspicions of being members of the resistance movement and were tortured mercilessly over Christmas by SS-Oberscharführer Ferdinand Koch, the head of a *Sonderabteilung* or "special unit" charged with fighting partisans. "On the very day of Christmas Eve more than a dozen people [...] were brought to the *Sonderabteilung*," one of the detainees, the banker Antoni Brynski, said after the war. "They were let in by Koch, who first beat them up mercilessly, and then, on Christmas Day, beat them with a bull whip and forced their cell mates to beat them in the face."[6]

Radom was not special at all. It was just one of thousands of Polish cities, towns and villages that were being forced into submission with terror applied across the board. Civilians, regardless of gender and age, were devoured by the Nazi monster. A few days before the holiday, German police arrived in the village of Tymienica near Lodz, looking for a suspected member of the resistance. When they did not find him, they shot his 71-year-old father, 14-year-old daughter and 12-year-old son instead.[7]

In another operation five days later, German police, assisted by Ukrainian auxiliaries, surrounded the village of Mszadla Nowa, also searching for partisans. The people they were after turned out to have left the village and were nowhere to be found. In order not to have to walk away empty-handed, and to signal that merely being related to a partisan could lead to death, the Germans seized their family members, altogether 11 people, and forced them to lie down facing the ground. Then they shot them one after the other. The youngest victim was a nine-month-old girl.[8]

* * *

Colonel Stanley William Bailey of the British Special Operations Executive parachuted into Yugoslavia on Christmas Eve 1942.[9] His objective was to establish contact with the Chetniks, one of the main partisan movements, and he arrived at Chetnik leader Dragoljub Michailovic's headquarters the day after. The Chetniks were under suspicion of doing little to fight the Germans, and part of his mission was to ascertain the extent to which the Chetniks had been sabotaging the railway network, thus making it harder for the Axis forces to transport troops and supplies to the Mediterranean. He was to discover that very little sabotage had taken place. The Allies were beginning to realize that everything was murky and played out in shades of gray in occupied Yugoslavia.[10]

There was one constant, however. Very often innocent civilians had to pay. At about the same time as Bailey jumped out of his transport airplane, a 20-year-old woman opened fire and injured two German officers in the town of Mladenovac. She also killed a local collaborator who tried to arrest her, before taking her own life with a bullet. In retaliation, soldiers of the German Army's 704th Infantry Division surrounded the town and arrested 72 men and 52 women, all innocent apart from happening to live where the attack had taken place. "The division applies for authorization to shoot in reprisal 50 hostages and/or people detained as retaliation prisoners," the division wrote in its war diary.

Permission was apparently given on Christmas Day, as the diary entry shows: "Forty-nine men and one woman shot to death in Mladenovac for the attack on two officers of the 2d Battalion, 724th Grenadier Regiment. 2d Lieutenant Dr. Engelhardt died in the military hospital in Belgrade. The division applies for authorization to shoot an additional 25 hostages and/or all people detained as retaliation prisoners from the district of Mladenovac. The execution will be carried out by the SD [security service] in Belgrade."[11]

Yugoslavia was a key part in the East European empire which Germany had established little by little since the late 1930s. Nazi power had expanded from one country to the next, until most countries between the Baltic and the Adriatic were in the German sphere of influence one way or the other. This was either through outright military subjugation and occupation, as had been the case with Poland, or through alliance, as with Hungary and Romania. In many cases, it was a mixture of both, where formerly sovereign states were emasculated and divided into smaller vassals and puppets that could formally consider themselves friends of Germany but could also rest assured that any attempts at deviation from Berlin's wishes would be stamped out with an iron heel.

A case in point, demonstrating how Germany's East European suzerainties were employed in the service of its ultimate goal of creating a racially pure continent with no Jews, was Czechoslovakia. Devoured in pieces by the German

Reich in 1938 and 1939, it was now reduced to a number of smaller entities, including the puppet government of Slovakia, which was doing its part in segregating the unwanted from the rest. The forced labor camp at Bystré, 200 miles northeast of the Slovak capital of Bratislava, had a mixed population of Roma and inmates referred to as "Aryan asocials." It had been set up in the summer of 1942, and now, half a year later, the population suffered a variety of illnesses. During Christmas, work was suspended, and instead the laborers attended training classes and reeducation carried out by the local priest or the camp command.[12]

This could seem mild by comparison with the harsh conditions in German camps, but the Slovak government also toed the line when it came to the most sinister aspects of anti-Jewish persecution. Anton Vašek was the head of Department 14 in Slovakia's Central Economic Office, making him the key official in charge of transporting Jewish citizens to their deaths in German camps. On Christmas Day 1942 he wrote in the introduction to his own book *Die Lösung der Judenfrage in der Slowakei* or *The Solution of the Jewish Question in Slovakia* that "it is generally known, that through the measures of the Slovak Republic, four fifths of Slovak Jews have been deported."[13]

Meanwhile, in what had once been the western part of Czechoslovakia but had now become the German-ruled protectorate of Bohemia and Moravia, the Germans had established Theresienstadt Concentration Camp. It was a transit camp to the much more sinister camps in the East, a last stop before death. It was also a "model camp," meant to serve as concrete proof of the humane treatment of the Jews when for example delegates from the Red Cross visited, but even here there were insufficient supplies to keep starvation at bay. "The food isn't so bad now, especially for the workers. The aged who do not work do not have enough food," the young Jewish inmate Gonda Redlich wrote about the conditions in Theresienstadt in December.[14]

Many of the Jews in Theresienstadt were from families who had tried their best in the pre-war years to assimilate into the European societies where they had settled, keeping their Judaic faith but engaging in the economic and political life of the nations where they lived along with all other citizens. Christmas highlighted how it was common among them to take over traditions from their Christian neighbors, and even now, as the Nazis openly carried out a campaign to erase them from European memory, debates raged if this was the right thing to do.

As a Zionist activist pursuing the ideal of a Jewish homeland in Israel, Redlich was part of such a discussion, as in Theresienstadt, the Christian inmates were allowed to carry out Christmas services.[15] "My position isn't simple. I am ashamed of the celebration of Christian festivals, not only from a Zionist perspective, but in my opinion, it is a great shame to celebrate any holiday without feeling the sanctity which is the basis of that holiday," he wrote in his diary on December 24.[16] As he wrote these words, elsewhere in the East, a travesty was made of that very sanctity of Christmas.

* * *

Heinrich Himmler, the Reichsführer or supreme leader of the German SS, had started thinking about Christmas as early as in October. In a letter to Oswald Pohl, head of the SS Main Economic and Administrative Office, he ordered that preparations should be made to hand out the belongings of murdered Jews to ethnic Germans in the occupied Soviet Union. For each adult of German descent in Transnistria, a region along the Dniestr river on the border between Ukraine and Moldova, the following should be prepared: "a dress or suit and, as far as available, with a coat and hat, 3 shirts, appropriate underclothing, and other items of daily use as well as a suitcase." The poor should get special attention, Himmler stressed in the letter: "Needy persons are also to be given feather beds, blankets, and bed linen."[17]

The top-secret letter also instructed that clothes and other belongings of freshly killed Jews were to be given as Christmas presents to ethnic Germans in Zhitomir, Halbstadt and Nikolaev, all cities in occupied Ukraine. Altogether a quarter million people, members of the sprawling German diaspora that had spread across Eastern Europe since the Middle Ages, were to benefit. It was a tall order, but Pohl, whose somewhat bureaucratic-sounding title covered a function of managing the vast concentration camp system as something akin to a business, knew exactly where to source the items: warehouses at Auschwitz and elsewhere that held enormous quantities of objects that had been stripped from Jews shortly before they had been put to death. Himmler emphasized the importance of the task at the end of the letter, and stressed a not-to-be-ignored deadline: "The matter is very urgent, the things must be at our disposal by Christmas!"[18]

The task of distributing the spoils of the most infamous genocide in the history of mankind was an ongoing process in Himmler's sprawling empire, and it usually intensified around Christmas. Watches and fountain pens taken from slain Jews were shipped to Sachsenhausen concentration camp, where special repair shops had been set up, staffed with prisoners who had repaired the items in their former lives.[19] "I intend to make a Yuletide gift to the units of the *Waffen-SS* as indicated on the attached list from the watches, wristwatches, and fountain pens as listed on the same," Pohl said in one letter filed to SS headquarters in Berlin. Himmler liked the idea so much that he added that 15,000 ladies' watches should also be sent through the Sachsenhausen repair shops before being shipped to women among the ethnic German groups in the East.[20]

The linkage of Christmas with mass killing was one of the most perverse outcomes of Nazi rule. It was one that particularly baffled those who, a few years later, were charged with meting out justice over the individuals found responsible for the enormous crimes taking place in Europe in the war years. When Nuremberg judges, in quiet disbelief, wrote their verdict on a participant in a massacre of Jews and Roma that had taken place at Simferopol on the Eastern Front during the preceding Christmas, they added: "On the mystic chords of memory, no echo sounded of the Christmas carols he had heard in childhood, nor did he recall the message of Peace on Earth and Good Will Toward Men."[21]

Sobibor camp in eastern Poland was a killing factory to an even larger extent than Auschwitz. It was officially designated an "extermination camp"; in other words, whereas Auschwitz was meant not only for murdering people, but also extracting labor out of them, Sobibor served no other purpose than extinguishing life. With a few exceptions, every person was gassed and cremated within minutes of arrival by train. Among the newcomers, only a few young men deemed fit for work were allowed to stay alive, perhaps just for days, to assist in the killing. For them, Christmas Eve was terrible. The guards, angry at the news of setbacks on the fronts in Russia and Africa, got themselves into a drunken frenzy and decided to take out their frustrations on the Jewish prisoners. Stumbling out of the canteen, they fetched them from their barracks and forced them to do pushups in the snow, beating them viciously in the process.[22]

Like Sobibor, Treblinka was for extermination only, and Christmas was busy. Jews in the transit camp of Kielbasin near Bialystok in northeastern Poland were initially to have been sent to Auschwitz to be murdered there but were redirected at the last moment to Treblinka extermination camp, which was closer. It ensured that German soldiers were home in time for Christmas. It made no difference to the Jews themselves, who were dead a few days later either way.[23] None of the victims left any testimony but many, perhaps most, only understood at the last moment what awaited them. This was the result of their executioners' deliberate attempt to conceal the terrible truth until it was too late.

For the SS administrators at Treblinka, for example, it was important to disguise the true purpose of the camp, to prevent panic when the trains reached their destination. Shortly before Christmas, Franz Stangl, the commandant of the camp, ordered a fake railway station to be built to lull those condemned to die into a false sense of security. There was a painted clock, ticket counters, timetables and signs saying "To Warsaw," "To Wolwonoce" and "To Bialystok."[24] The deception worked. "When persons descended from the trains, they really had the impression that they were at a very good station from where they could go to Suwalki, Vienna, Grodno and other cities," said Samuel Rajzman, a survivor.[25]

Stangl was not present at the camp during Christmas to see how the new system of deception worked. He was away on home leave in Austria. His wife Theresa had visited him in Poland the preceding summer, and she had found out about his deep involvement in the murder of the Jews, even though he had tried to tell her lies about working only on "construction." Now five months had passed, and the intervening period had mitigated some of the shock that she had initially felt about knowing the truth. "It was so wonderful to see him, and at Christmas, too. In Austria, at home, what with Christmas and everything, what I knew was happening in Poland seemed utterly unreal," she said after the war. Stangl kept up his lies about staying aloof from the killings, even telling his wife he was pulling strings to seek a transfer away from the Polish killing fields. She felt he was becoming more relaxed as a result. "We had a good Christmas after all: I can still see his happy, relieved face," Theresa Stangl recalled later.[26]

* * *

The SS doctor in charge of the Auschwitz hospital was in a rush to leave for the Christmas holiday on December 24, and he had completed his morning round before 9 am. It was a routine much feared by the patients, since it often took the form of clearing hospital beds by winnowing down the weakest, who usually would be disposed of with injections of lethal doses of phenol. Once the doctor had left the building, all prisoners drew a sigh of relief, certain that they would at least live to see another day. They soon realized their joy was premature.

Late that same afternoon, Oberscharführer Josef Klehr, a medical orderly with no training as a doctor, entered into the hospital. "Today I'm the camp physician," he proclaimed self-assuredly and started selecting patients for execution. He picked about 200, who were killed immediately afterwards with phenol injections. "Everything was already in the Christmas spirit, and everyone had somehow prepared himself for this day and wanted to have a little Christmas celebration. In this atmosphere Klehr burst in and murdered the prisoners," Tadeusz Pazcula, a former inmate, said during Klehr's trial after the war. "I don't think I need to describe what kind of poverty of feeling and coldness is needed to carry out this activity on such a day."[27]

The camp hospital was the scene of death on a daily basis. Dr. Stefan Muczkowski, a 48-year-old curator at the National Museum in Krakow, was bought there on Christmas Day, hardly breathing. His body was covered in bruises, the victim of horrific punishment. "He was so battered and beaten up that he died on the same day as a result of the injuries," said Stanislaw Glowa, a prisoner who worked as an orderly in the hospital block, when providing testimony after the war. He added: "I do not know who had beaten him." The curator had arrived at Auschwitz little more than a month before, on November 14, 1942. Like many other prisoners who were no longer young, he lasted only a short time.[28]

The fact that no one seemed to know why Dr. Muczkowski had been maltreated, and no one seemed to care either, was typical. When a prisoner was punched, kicked or whipped to death, it hardly mattered why, since the flimsiest of excuses could be used by the sadistic guards. The prisoners at the camp knew they could lose their lives at any time, for tiny reasons, or for no reason at all. Auschwitz was the dark heart of Hitler's empire. Or, in the words of Heinz Thilo, an SS doctor at the camp, it was the "*anus mundi*," Latin for "the anus of the world."[29] It constituted a concentration of slave labor from across Europe, bringing together people from all corners of the continent with nothing in common other than having fallen foul of the Nazi regime.

Just before Christmas, a large number of Norwegian Jews arrived in the camp. Among them was 21-year-old Kai Feinberg, who had previously been locked up in the concentration camp Berg south of Oslo along with his 46-year-old father and his two brothers. Straight from the train at Auschwitz, the four were marched for over four hours with a group of prisoners to the Buna factory outside the main camp area and directly exposed to a cruel routine of back-breaking work, accompanied by relentless physical beatings. "I have marks left by the Germans all over my body," he told a tribunal after the war. "They would beat us with anything they had around: a whip, rifle butt, stick." There was no letup because of the holiday, he explained: "On Christmas Eve we worked all day until 3.00 a.m."[30] Kai Feinberg's father lasted only a few days before dying from the brutal treatment, and shortly afterwards, his two brothers succumbed, too.[31]

Despite the inhuman discipline and the threat of fierce punishment, some prisoners managed to carry out Christmas rituals in secrecy. A group of female Polish prisoners in the staff building marked Christmas Eve by singing traditional carols and lighting candles on a fir bough they had smuggled in.[32] At the same time, a Catholic priest among the prisoners completed a religious service in Block 18, using a piece of bread for the Eucharist.[33] In one uncharacteristic case, the Christmas spirit even touched a member of the SS, who was inspired to a rare humane gesture. The SS officer, Dr. Roland Quästl, felt pity for the inmates, and during Christmas he arranged to have some of them detailed for duty in his apartment. When they arrived, he had a Christmas tree and presents prepared for them. It later transpired that the inhumanity at Auschwitz had overwhelmed him, and he had applied to be sent to the front.[34]

Quästl was an exception from the rule. Most camp guards never relaxed their brutal treatment of the inmates, but they did grow sentimental over Christmas. Rudolf Vrba, a Slovak prisoner at Auschwitz during Christmas 1942, described how the mass murderers who were running the camp would exhibit a childlike infatuation with the holiday. "They would burn without scruples, indeed with patriotic fervor, one thousand children," he wrote in his memoirs. "But their eyes would grow misty when they swapped pictures of their loved ones at home."[35] This was a recurring theme in concentration camps throughout the war. The French illustrator Bernard Aldebert, who was locked up in Mauthausen, noted how the worst *kapos*, prisoners turned guards, often were the most sentimental ones: "We saw how Maryan and Yanouch, the two Polish monsters, spent entire days to cut out golden stars, stick them together, paint them and decorate them with red strips of paper with the word 'Gloria'."[36]

SS staff and those of their families who lived within the camp perimeter could obtain Christmas trees from Hauptsturmführer Hans Aumeier, in charge of the economic operation of Auschwitz, the camp's commander Rudolf Höss wrote in a message to his staff a week before Christmas. In the same message, Höss explained the rules that would be in place during the holiday. Each unit would be allowed to let one in 10 of its personnel return home for Christmas on a six-day leave. "Family fathers are to be given priority," the commandant emphasized. For SS guards that were not permitted to go home for Christmas, special allowances were being made. The camp's "SS kitchen" was ordered to prepare crackers and cookies for the personnel, to be consumed during the holiday, which Höss referred to by the Old Norse name of *Jul*, not the traditional German term *Weihnachten*.

Christmas trees were central to the German celebration of the holiday, and they were placed in many concentration camps. According to the Austrian professor Peter Kuon, "the monumental Christmas tree in the roll-call area served no religious purpose, but rather had a political dimension. It was meant to exhibit the superior culture of the master race and mock the feeling of the slave laborers."[37] The French officer Georges Loustaunau-Lacau, who was incarcerated in Wiener Neustadt, found the provocation almost unbearable. "By way of mockery, the commandant has erected a Christmas tree in the middle of the square, full of colorful lightbulbs. The contrast between the routine horror and the traditional symbol of peace and charity is so stark that we would like to tear the damn tree to pieces and smash the bulbs. The entire German hypocrisy is on display, with its fake coziness and appeal to neighborly love."[38]

The hypocrisy reached a high at Auschwitz during Christmas 1942, after a Christmas tree had been erected at Auschwitz II-Birkenau. On December 25, SS-Oberscharführer Gerhard Palitzsch, one of the most notorious camp guards, had prisoners from a special penal unit lined up, ordering them to carry sand to the women's camp using the bottoms of their trench coats. This had to take place on the double, and *kapos* and SS men were standing along the route beating the prisoners with sticks as they passed. "Blows were raining everywhere. Some had swollen faces, torn noses, slit mouths, perforated cheeks, all were bleeding. And the more visible the wounds, the more they excited the savagery of the assassins," according to one account.[39]

It lasted for three hours. Those who collapsed from exhaustion were pushed into a ditch full of nearly freezing water. "When it was over, the dead bodies were pulled out of the water and laid out on the square in the men's camp, under the Christmas tree. This was done while the orchestra played, and the Germans said that they were Christmas gifts for the Poles," a former inmate, Leszek Turkiewicz, said in post-war testimony.[40] The survivors were marked for life. "After this, I have never been able to see Christmas as a beautiful holiday. I can no longer celebrate Christmas the way others do," one of the prisoners, Hermann Reineck, said many years after the war. "It's simply not possible."[41]

* * *

Some prisoners tried to use Christmas to escape from the concentration camp hell. Some succeeded but most did not. On December 24, Polish political prisoner Wasyl Bolszakow was handed over to the infamous Block 11 in the Auschwitz compound, a building designed to punish prisoners for various infractions. Bolszakow had managed to get beyond the barbed wire and enjoyed about 24 hours in freedom before being captured again. No one was surprised this happened. The immediate area outside Auschwitz was nearly impossible to get past, not least because the local population knew any kind of assistance to escaped prisoners was punishable by death.[42]

One rare escape from Auschwitz did take place during Christmas 1942. It was a better time than any other, since camp guard was understaffed due to the holiday. The escape involved four inmates—three Poles and one German. The German, Otto Küsel, had a privileged position due to his nationality and a winning personality, and managed to get hold of an SS uniform and a horse-drawn wagon. The three Poles hid inside chests loaded onto the wagon, and Küsel drove it out of the camp. Before the first checkpoint, one of the Poles emerged from the chest and put on the SS uniform, succeeding in impressing the guards with his stern demeanor. This way they managed to leave the Auschwitz area and eventually made their way to Warsaw.[43]

Küsel ran a huge risk, and he was arrested again several months later and sent back to Auschwitz, where he was tortured but narrowly avoided execution. His motives for taking part in the flight were complex. "I didn't want to escape, for I had a good life in Auschwitz," he said after the war. As the prisoner in charge of the work detail with the three Poles that escaped, he faced a stark choice: "My only options were to inform on them or escape with them, for if they had escaped without me, no one would have believed that I had not noticed their preparations. And then it would have been my turn. But I did not want to report them."[44]

The camp of Sobibor, too, saw a rare escape during Christmas 1942.[45] Three Jewish men, two Jewish women and two Ukrainian guards managed to sneak out of Camp 3, the extermination area which housed the gas chambers and mass graves, apparently having decided beforehand to utilize the time when the guards were most inattentive because of the heavy drinking that would predictably take place. The fact that two Ukrainian guards took part in the escape is significant. The entire endeavor probably would have been impossible without their knowledge about camp routines, and it demonstrated that the Ukrainians, often among the most inhumane guard personnel, themselves were treated brutally by their German masters and often only stayed on for fear of the severe punishment meted out to deserters.[46]

The exact circumstances of the escape are unknown and will probably never come to light, since most witnesses, primarily prisoners at Sobibor, were murdered later in the war. However, it appeared to have been well planned, and the escapees made away with two rifles and a significant amount of ammunition.[47] They quickly separated into at least two groups. One group consisted of one of the young women, Pesia Lieberman, as well as the two Ukrainians. They found shelter at a Polish farm near a village 30 miles southwest of Sobibor, but the farmer turned them in, and the three were surrounded and killed in a firefight with Polish auxiliary police. The four others in the second group also did not survive the war, although their exact fate is not described in any of the extant sources.[48]

Back in Sobibor, the German reaction was fierce. Collective punishment was a routine matter, designed to break down solidarity among prisoners and encourage them to block escape attempts before they happened. "The next evening, the workers from camps nos. 1 and 2 were assembled and an evening of musical entertainment was organized, with dancing and singing (loud)," Hersz Cukierman, who worked in the Sobibor camp kitchen, said after the war. "In camp no. 3 about 300 Jews (permanent workers) were shot in retaliation for the escape."[49]

* * *

Outside of the camp system, Poland's Jewish population, or what was left of it, lived on in scattered places. One of them was 18-year-old David Sierakowiak in the ghetto in the Polish city of Lodz. For him, Christmas came in the form of ration coupons allowing him to buy a new pair of shoes. He was not able to use the coupon, however, since he did not have cash. The general gloom was mitigated by news from the front suggesting the Germans were coming under pressure, but there was little tangible information. "In politics there's nothing new. Huge battles are reportedly going on, but we know nothing specific," he wrote in his notebook on December 25. "Too bad no food can be bought for an affordable price. At home, we are eating the last bits of our rations. But who cares! Just to hold out until spring!"[50]

Others had given up waiting for Allied victory and had taken their fates into their own hands, trying to evade the Nazis by hiding. The Parczew forests near the city of Lublin had concealed both Polish partisans and Jews for months, and in late autumn, the Germans had carried out comprehensive sweeps of the area, killing large numbers of people, not just armed fighters but also entire families. Those who had escaped detection during these operations believed that the Germans would be too busy celebrating Christmas to continue the campaign over the holiday, but they were wrong. The "hunt," as it was called, went on for several days, and hundreds of Jews lost their lives. Husbands got separated from their wives, children from their parents in the chaos and wandered around aimlessly in the woods.[51]

A small number of Jews were able to escape the horrors of the Holocaust by finding refuge among Polish gentiles. Christmas was particularly perilous, because religious practices were highlighted, and anyone showing a degree of hesitation about how to carry out the rituals of the season could suddenly stand out in a dangerous way. An example was Cyna Glatstein, a 14-year-old Jewish girl, who had escaped the Warsaw ghetto and now worked on a farm in the countryside, posing as Polish peasant Lucinka.

As a good Catholic, she attended Christmas mass and went from house to house in her village to sing Christmas carols. She was also invited to the village Christmas party at the mayor's home. As the beer and wine started flowing more freely, the suspicions that many had harbored surfaced. Cyna spoke beautiful Polish, but her nose seemed Jewish to her peers, and now she was showered with questions: "Where were you born? Where was your farm? Where did you go to school? What church did you attend?" Cyna was dizzy from the alcohol, and she knew one wrong word could be fatal. Whenever possible she stepped outside and retched, and she was able to keep clear-headed enough to answer all questions to the satisfaction of the other partygoers. She survived that Christmas.[52]

Some Polish Jews had given up any hopes for themselves and merely wanted their family to live on, focusing all their efforts on the next generation. Felicja Braun, a five-year-old Jewish girl from Warsaw, was placed by her parents with a gentile Polish couple in the summer of 1942. During Christmas the same year, she saw her father for the last time. He visited her and told her to be a good Christian. Then, before departing, he sang a song for her: "This is the last Sunday. Today we part forever."[53] Abraham Hofman, one of the last survivors of the Jewish ghetto in the Polish town of Wawolnica, 30 miles northwest of Lublin, was in the same situation and left his daughter, who was not yet one year old, on the doorstep of a Polish home on Christmas Eve. The little girl survived the war. He did not.[54]

CHAPTER 7

Family Man

Germany

As 12-year-old Karl Epstein was walking through the busy streets of Berlin a few hours before Christmas Eve, no one could tell he was a Jew. Wearing a simple jacket, knickerbockers and knee-length socks, he looked like any German boy of his age. The only thing that might set him apart was the confused look in his face. After all, he had just passed through the gates of the camp where he had spent the past weeks as a laborer in prison-like circumstances, and now he was accompanying a middle-aged German to his home in a working-class neighborhood in the Nazi capital. Here, he would be celebrating Christmas as the guest of a family of full-blooded Aryans.[1]

It was a twisted road that had brought Karl to Germany in the midst of winter. He was not yet in his teens, but he had seen enough tragedy and carnage to last him a lifetime. Born into a Jewish family southeast of the Ukrainian capital of Kiev, a part of the Soviet Union now under German control, he had miraculously survived several rounds of slaughter directed at the Jews. In October, he had managed to escape from the Jewish ghetto in the city of Dunayevtsy, also in Ukraine, just before the Germans marched in and killed all its inhabitants. He had left behind what remained of his family. His 35-year-old mother had been dragged outside the city and machinegunned before being tossed into a mass grave along with his 15-year-old sister Rosa, and his younger sister Shenya, aged four.

He had hidden his Jewish identity and managed to be recruited for labor in Germany, also lying about how old he was and saying he was the minimum age of 14. Soon he had found himself on a train heading west, along with hundreds of other young Ukrainians who had signed up for work in agriculture and industry in Germany. In early November, he had started at the Riedel chemical plant in Berlin. He was the youngest member of a small work gang where everyone else was German. None of them suspected he was Jewish. He received the same food as the others—potato soup thickened with flour—and he suffered no abuse. For the first time in months, he was treated as a human being, not a hunted animal.

And now, it was Christmas. His German supervisor, believing he was an ethnic Ukrainian, and thus strictly speaking of an inferior racial stock according to Nazi ideology, but still infinitely preferable to the hated Jews, invited him to his home for the holiday. He wanted him to experience what he called a "German Christmas." When he picked Karl up at the labor camp, the man brought clothes that would make him look like a German. They did not have to travel far to get to his home. It was only a few stops on the tram from the camp to the big apartment complex where the German lived, in his own flat on the second floor. His wife was standing ready to receive them, immediately showering Karl with motherly affection: "What a nice boy. He is still only a child. How can you let children work? Oh, the war, the war!"

She fed him cookies, and he was allowed to walk around in the apartment. He was in a state of awe. They had faucets with cold and hot water. They had a toilet you could sit on. They even had an oven that worked, like magic, when you pushed a button. In the living room there was a small mechanical Christmas tree, with a Santa underneath, which turned round and round when you flipped a switch. It was luxury so extreme that he did not even know that it existed. And yet it was all here, in the home of a common German worker. It left one big question. Karl could not understand why the Germans, who had everything, would feel so threatened by the Jews that they wanted to exterminate them down to the last man, woman and child.

Little by little, the other guests arrived. The middle-aged couple's children were already grown up and had families of their own. Their son was an officer in the *Wehrmacht* and arrived in full uniform, complete with a peaked cap and a greatcoat against the cold temperatures. It was men looking just like him who had killed Karl's family. He brought his two children, aged five and six, just a little older than Karl's own sister, who had lost her life at the edge of a mass grave two months earlier.

Karl could not show any unease, but the sense of magic he had felt gradually evaporated as the apartment filled with people, all consumed by arrogance and disdain for Germany's enemies. As they sat down around the table, the uniformed son declared himself full of confidence that Stalingrad would soon be securely in German hands. It made no difference that Moscow had not been taken, he said, since the Soviet enemy would disintegrate by itself. England was not a serious challenge, and never had been. A new wonder weapon would soon be rolled out, and Germany would prevail on all fronts. They drank a toast for the *Endsieg*, final victory.

Karl was sitting among the men and was the object of great curiosity. He was an actual living specimen from the mysterious East on the border of European civilization, a place which most Germans talked about with a slight feeling of dread. Still, he noticed that he was spoken about more than spoken to. He could not help the feeling that he was present as a piece of exotic war booty. Later, everyone was given presents, including Karl, who received a used jacket from the mother of the house. He was happy, but as the children sat by the small Christmas tree playing with their presents with beaming faces, he inevitably was reminded of the many Jewish children he had seen killed by Germans in Ukraine.

The party ended early, and all the guests departed after having been treated to real coffee, but Karl stayed during the night. The German couple prepared a bed for him on the couch, but it took a long time for him to fall asleep. Thoughts were swirling through his head. He had seen a level of material plenty that was beyond even the wildest imagination of people like him, from poverty-stricken Ukraine. It was a family that had everything. And yet, the Germans as a nation, consisting of fundamentally decent people like this Berlin couple, wanted more, and they planned to take it from those who had little or nothing. The only, unanswerable question was: Why?

The following morning, Karl was fed one last time before returning to the camp, taking the tram through the wintry streets of the capital with his German host. He shook hands with him at the gate and then walked back to his barracks. He was immediately surrounded by the other laborers who wanted to know all about his trip. He told them about the food, the faucets with the hot water, and the modern oven. They listened with great interest, but when he described the mechanical Christmas tree that turned round and round at the flip of a switch, they dismissed him with a shrug. That was too crazy. A thing like that didn't even exist. Obviously, they thought, he was lying to them.

* * *

Five miles from the Riedel chemical plant complex where Karl Epstein was toiling away, trying to hide his Jewish identity with the knowledge that he would die if anyone found out, Propaganda Minister Joseph Goebbels was also busy at work, even though he would much rather be elsewhere. Goebbels, 45 years old and one of the most powerful figures of the Third Reich, considered himself a family man. The proud father of five daughters and one son—Helga, 10, Hildegard, 8, Helmut, 7, Holdine, 5, Hedwig, 4, and Heidrun, just two years of age—he had perpetual bad conscience about not being able to spend more time with his children.

Still, his responsibilities at the head of what was officially referred to as the ministry of "the people's enlightenment" located inside a palatial building in the Wilhelmstrasse kept him desk-bound for most of the time. Christmas only made the situation even more painful, intensifying his desire to be with his family while adding exponentially to his workload. He was trying to arrange his duties and do as much as possible of it in advance, so that he would not have a pile of uncompleted work staring at him during Christmas.

Even so, two days before Christmas, Goebbels had a full schedule, and he felt it as if his "brain was completely emptied." To a great extent, this was a problem of his own making, as he had a micromanaging boss' inclination of meddling in even the tiniest details. Thus, a major part of the day was spent picking the right music for the most recent *Wochenschau*, the weekly newsreel shown in all German movie theaters, forming the regime's most important interface with the public. "This damned Christmas has given me so many additional responsibilities that I will be genuinely happy when the so-called holiday is over," he wrote in his diary. "I am not able to rest until late into the night. I don't feel physically fit enough to just shoulder any burden. Thank God work will probably be somewhat less once Christmas is over."[2]

In the days leading up to Christmas, he returned repeatedly in his diary to the subject of his family, and especially his children. He was not sure he would be able to see them at all. "That depends entirely on the development of the military situation. If we once again end up in a difficult situation in the East, just like last year, I will probably be unable to excuse myself from my duties, not even during the holidays and not even for a brief moment."[3] He knew that the time not spent with the children was time lost forever and that he was to some extent failing as a father. "They grow up practically without my supervision, and I am always amazed after a certain time has passed to learn how much they have developed intellectually and emotionally. Once when the war is over, I will be able to devote more time than I have so far on their education. I can't think of or wish for anything better to happen when peace arrives."[4]

The frustrating thing was that the children were only a short drive away, waiting for him in the large manor named Lanke, built especially for Goebbels near the shore of Lake Bogen 10 miles north of the Berlin city limits. It was a luxurious place, erected at great expense in the mid-1930s. It had 70 rooms and even a private cinema where Goebbels himself would watch new movies for a final stamp of approval before allowing them to be released to the public. It had attracted some of Nazi Germany's most glamorous movie stars, including Emil Jannings, Heinz Rühmann, and Swedish-born Zarah Leander with the dreaming eyes and a voice so deep she could be mistaken for a man.

Goebbels' wife, Magda, was not with the children. She suffered from a range of ailments, including depression, a heart condition and a slight facial paralysis, and she had been admitted to a clinic in Berlin. "Things are unfortunately not going as well for Magda as I had actually hoped," he wrote in his diary. "The second blood transfusion has not been entirely successful. But one can assume that the crisis will be over in a few more days."[5] Whether concerning himself with the moral welfare of the German people or looking after his own family, Goebbels had more than enough on his plate.

On December 22, he noted in his diary that the German high command had been forced to report on setbacks along the middle Don river in Russia. "It's good that our people are reminded of the seriousness of the situation. Illusions are no good for the conduct of war. Even if it brings no joy to report this kind of unpleasant news, especially just before Christmas, truth must be respected," he reasoned. The day after, he remarked that secret service reports suggested a Christmas atmosphere spreading in the population, despite the less than stellar news from the fronts. "They do acknowledge that the situation in the East is serious, but do not understand the full gravity of the defensive battles there. The situation in Africa is also seen as increasingly serious," he wrote.[6]

The German people, shielded from full knowledge of the situation of the Reich, were entitled to some rest, he thought. "Everything is about Christmas at the moment. I also do not have the intention to disturb the festive atmosphere in the last days before Christmas," he wrote. "We haven't done too much to build up the Christmas mood in the papers and on the radio, but of course it more or less happens by itself. I hope the German people will be allowed to enjoy some peace during Christmas. There will be plenty of opportunity to be concerned again once the holiday is over."[7]

Even so, for the regime itself, the holiday meant no letup in the incessant struggle against the enemies of the Reich, external or internal. In his diary on December 24, he described how a number of trials for treason had been concluded, resulting, he added with a degree of righteous satisfaction, "almost exclusively in the death penalty."[8] And then there were the Jews. They were the real adversary, a sinister and only partly visible force hiding behind the powers battling Germany. Goebbels launched attacks on them nearly every day in his diary, venting an irrational hatred that had animated him for years.

"The Jews rage on. They try to stir up world public opinion against us," he wrote in one entry.[9] In another, he added: "The English are the Jews among the Aryans."[10]

One evening shortly before Christmas, Goebbels had the chance to make a brief visit to Lanke. "I am able to spend some time with the children, which they are very happy about. It is such a pity that one cannot spend more time in this way," he wrote.[11] The following day, they came to see him in downtown Berlin. Together, they visited a traditional Christmas market where members of the Hitler Youth were selling home-made presents for the benefit of the poor. "The war doesn't give us much time for private activities," he noted, "but every now and then one must simply try to take that time for oneself."[12]

Christmas Eve was the big question. Would he be able to make it home? It turned out that he did have a few brief minutes for family. Late in the afternoon, he drove to Lanke for a short break from work. "All the children are together in Lanke. Helga and Hilde already wear long dresses and look like real ladies. They recite a poem and sing a song, and it's almost as if there is peace. If it wasn't because one had to constantly think about one's responsibilities and was overburdened with concerns of all kinds, one could almost fool oneself into believing that the war was far away. But it is much closer than we normally want to think about. The children are very happy that I have found time to visit them after all. Unfortunately, I can only spare half an hour, before I have to return to Berlin."[13]

Meanwhile, his wife Magda was lingering in the background, prevented from being more than a passing presence due to her illness. One of the days when the children came to see him at the ministry, they visited her together at the clinic. On December 19, she was in his thoughts again, and for a very good reason. "Today is our 11th wedding anniversary, and we celebrate it with a small family party in her room. We hope that Magda can come to Lanke for at least a couple of days during Christmas," he wrote in his diary.[14] It turned out that she was actually allowed to leave the clinic during the holiday, and on Christmas Day he had her driven to Lanke. The family was together.

It was family bliss, or at least as much family bliss as the war permitted. The duties at the ministry could take a backseat temporarily. "Now I will try to take some time off from work for the next two or three days in order to gather energy for the great burdens waiting in the future. I will very much need the virtues of mental strength in the time that lies ahead of us."[15] He pondered the cost of war, even to someone like him, who was spared the dangers of the front: "One runs the risk of completely growing apart from one's family. This has become a burning issue for countless people today. One can only imagine what it means for a father if he is away at war for years on end, but it also has a profound impact for the family at home. War is not just the father of all things. It is also the greatest abnormality in the life of man."[16]

The image of Goebbels the family man, who struggled to have time for his wife and children despite pressures at work, the father in the old German patriarchal mold who worried intensely about the welfare of his children even if he was often somewhat aloof—it looked appealing on paper, as put into writing in Goebbels' effortless and wordy prose, but it was all built on a lie. A dark secret lurked behind the façade. Goebbels was an almost pathological adulterer, whose conquests included a long list of names: Agnes and Anneliese, Charlotte, Erika and Hannah, Julia, Tamara and Xenia.[17]

None of it meant much to him. It was all mainly just play, and perhaps he justified his indiscretions with the fact that his wife Magda, too, was known to sleep with male acquaintances.[18] Still, in the 1930s it had suddenly become more serious as he had developed an infatuation with the beautiful and exotic-looking Czech-born actress Lida Baarova, who had become a frequent visitor to his spacious bed at Lanke. Taking advantage of his own immense privilege, he had even for some time entertained the thought of a formalized ménage à trois that would unite himself, Magda and Lida in a semi-official marriage, until Hitler abruptly put an end to what would have been an outrageous affront to German family values.[19]

One would never have guessed Goebbels' reckless promiscuity from reading his diaries written around Christmas 1942. It amounted to an oversized conceit about who he was as a man. Maybe he had even come to believe in it himself. As he was rumored to have said—although the remark was almost certainly apocryphal—if you tell a big lie often enough, eventually it will be believed. In his voluminous diaries, he had told lies about himself and his family so frequently that he had gradually fallen victim to his own private deception. The man who had helped lead an entire nation astray ended up seducing himself with his own words.

* * *

One of the many tasks that kept Goebbels busy was a Christmas broadcast, *Ringsendung*, taking the German public on a virtual tour to the furthest corners of the vast territory ruled, mostly with an iron fist, from Berlin. For 90 minutes beginning at 6 pm, it claimed to showcase real-time interviews with German soldiers from the eternal ice of northern Finland to the blistering sun of the Sahara.[20] The program was the third of its kind. The first time it had been carried out, in December 1940, the broadcasters had lured listeners with the words: "German Christmas. Ninety million celebrate. Forty microphones link front and home." It was not an exaggeration. With 15 million registered radio receivers, the regime had pretty much the entire population covered with its state-of-the-art technology.

The program served several purposes. It was, as Goebbels himself had argued in 1940, a way of making soldiers forget that they were separated from their families by vast distances and give them the illusion that they were somehow part of a communal celebration of the holiday.[21] It also highlighted the geographical extent of the territories under German control, on a scale not seen since Napoleon. Finally, it demonstrated the technological prowess of the regime, enabling it to broadcast live with the participation of stations thousands of miles apart.

In one location after the other, Berlin was in touch with soldiers from all corners of Europe. Two submarines in the Atlantic were also taken out of the crucial campaign against Allied convoys so they could participate.[22] "*Achtung*, calling the port on the Arctic Ocean, Liinahamari," the anchor said in a clear voice. "This is Liinahamari, a port on the Arctic Ocean," went the muffled answer from nearly 2,000 miles away. There were greetings, too, from Crete and Russia, Poland and France.[23] The anchor in Berlin grew excited when at the end a group of sailors from the Kriegsmarine in the port city of Kerch on the Black Sea suggested singing "Silent Night" together: "All stations follow the wish of our comrades far away down on the Black Sea. Now they are singing on the Arctic Ocean and in Finland, and now they are joining in from the Rzhevsk operation area, and now we join them up with the stations in Leningrad and Stalingrad, and now France is here, and Catania. Africa sings too. Now everyone has joined up, in this very minute, singing the old German folk song."

The quality of some of the broadcasts was clearly affected by the long distances. The radio operator from Stalingrad could hardly be heard over the atmospherics: "This is Stalingrad. This is the front on the Volga." For other parts of the broadcast, however, the sound was so good that some listeners allegedly felt betrayed and quietly voiced the view that this could not be real. In fact, it was actually a deception, to some extent at least. The *Ringsendung* did indeed feature communication with German servicemen from all corners of Europe and deep into the Atlantic, but the recordings had been made beforehand in a production process that had stretched over the entire period from December 18 to 23. Each participating unit had also been required to send pre-recorded security copies of their contributions to

Berlin by "no later than December 22" in case there was a technical glitch that prevented a connection from being made.[24]

Goebbels spoke on the radio at 9 pm after the broadcast had come to an end, quoting the German Romantic poet Friedrich Hölderlin: "Live on high, O Fatherland. And count not the dead! For you, Beloved, not one too many has fallen!" It was meant to get people used to the idea of dying for the Reich, reflecting, as he said, one of the "harsh but courageous lessons of war, a lesson that offers comfort and strength, only in a loftier sense."[25] His words went out on all radio stations, addressing the entire people, he wrote in his diary with a mixture of pride and awe at what modern technology was capable of. "I take pains in this speech to summarize in simple words what the German people is thinking this evening. I believe I hit the exact right note [...] Sometimes you have to be on the same wavelength as the people, even if I don't allow any sentimentality in my speech. In reality, this Christmas is the Christmas of the firm heart."[26]

The Nazis believed they had learned much from the previous world war, which in their view had been lost mainly because of weakness at home. The army at the front had never been beaten, they asserted. The logic was straightforward. It was important to involve the home front completely and never disconnect it from events in the various theaters of war. Large-scale media events such as the Christmas *Ringsendung* were designed to serve that need, linking up all areas under Reich control, at home and abroad.

Goebbels was satisfied. It was a "wonderful and gripping broadcast, which brought the war front and the home front together."[27] He saw signs everywhere that he was winning the hearts and minds of his own people. Amid the busy work around Christmas, he left his ministry for a brief moment to visit a military hospital in the Barbarossa Strasse. He made a speech to the injured soldiers and was impressed by their spirit and morale. "What a difference compared with the [First] World War. Christmas 1917 was more or less the saddest and most depressing in the history of Berlin. This time around we can truly talk about a common Christmas despite the war."[28]

* * *

In fact, Goebbels had good reason to be happy about his work. The *Ringsendung* made a deep impression on Wolfhilde von König, a 17-year-old girl from the south German city of Munich. "Home front and war front were intimately connected," she wrote in her diary. "Dr. Goebbels sent his greetings, especially to Germans abroad and overseas. They are in a constant struggle for the people, but on this night their thoughts about home, about Germany, are even more fervent. Thus, we are united in our common faith. We are Germans of one mind."[29]

One of the dominant themes in Goebbels' war propaganda was the "safety of the home front" but in the western city of Düsseldorf, which had experienced several massive air raids in the past months, including one that severely damaged major parts of the inner city, people were sarcastic about the propaganda minister's words, secret reports testified.[30] Other major cities, too, had been damaged, and thousands of civilians had already lost their lives, as the western Allies intensified their strategic air campaign meant to bring Germany to its knees by breaking the country's industrial backbone and destroying its people's willingness to fight.

A German soldier at Stalingrad wrote home about Christmas at the front: "This year, we had a sad Christmas. No letters from home, no Christmas tree, no candles, no nothing. We haven't had anything that would remind you of Christmas. But I am happy that you at home could at least celebrate Christmas in peace."[31] In fact, his happiness was misplaced. German civilians were no longer assured a life in peace. No part of the Reich was beyond the reach of bombers taking off from bases in England.

This also meant that official announcements that had been accepted at face value by the people in the past were now the subject of considerable skepticism. Not all Germans believed the propaganda they were fed any longer. The weekly newsreels shown in the cinemas, which Goebbels himself was involved in at a detailed level, triggered suspicions when during Christmas 1942 German soldiers were seen well-equipped and well-fed on the Russian front. Some moviegoers openly expressed the view that the footage was probably taken in earlier, happier years when the war was proceeding more to Germany's liking.[32]

Still, the Germans were determined to celebrate Christmas as they always had, without being bothered excessively by the war news. "Interest in events at the front has decreased somewhat. People are more concerned with Christmas," Goebbels wrote in his diary as early as December 18, nearly a week before Christmas Eve. This went for the lower rungs of society, but it also went for the very top. Marga Himmler, married to Heinrich Himmler, the head of the SS, was thinking as little as possible about the war. "There is a lot to do with Xmas approaching, but it also pleases me," she wrote in her diary. "If only things would not always be so rushed."[33]

At the same time, while some Germans were losing faith in their leadership, and many chose simply to ignore the growing signs of defeat, others were as loyal and trusting as always. A middle-aged German, identified only as Max R. and living in the Bavarian city of Pfaffenhofen an der Ilm, wrote to his son-in-law in Stalingrad: "We celebrated Christmas in a simple and cozy way. My brother was also there. Of course, we opened a few bottles and toasted you. If only you could have been here! We hope and believe that this will be the case next year." By Christmas 1943, everything would be turned around, he predicted. "The Russians will continue to rush against us and suffer horrifying losses, so that during the coming year they will be completely annihilated. I believe just as firmly that Rommel will once again push the English east, and that the English, the Americans and of course the French will be thrown out of North Africa. What else stands between us and victory, once our aircraft fly through the stratosphere and attack America. Indeed, we Germans can achieve anything."[34]

* * *

While in some parts of the world Christmas was seen as an opportunity to highlight the basic unity of humankind, pointing out that the ongoing global conflict was an unnatural state of things, in Nazi Germany, the emphasis was on the peculiarities of the German Christmas, and it was described as yet another example of Germany's inherent cultural superiority over all other nations. "Let us," the popular publication *German War Christmas* exhorted its readers, "spend a moment in front of our Christmas tree to consider how Bolshevism has wiped out every last remnant of Christmas, and that Americanism has let it degenerate into a noisy chaos of jazz and bar business. Then we know that even in times of war—no, actually especially in times of war—we must celebrate Christmas in the cozy community of the family."[35]

There was one fundamental problem with Christmas, and all Christian traditions in Germany more generally; it had a foreign origin, with roots undeniably located in Israel, homeland of the Jews. Moreover, for the Catholic church, which claimed the allegiance of millions of Germans in the south of the country and in former Austria, there was the added problem of a hierarchical religious organization with a leadership residing in the Vatican, outside the immediate control of the German government. As long as the Catholic church remained in its present form in Germany, it was by its very existence a challenge to the undisputed rule of the Nazis.

In line with their ultimate aim of removing the Christian church as a factor in German society, the Nazis sought back in history for a pre-Christian celebration of solstice as a model to be imitated. The objective was a kind of pagan Christmas, where the annual cycle of life in nature—birth, bloom, and death—was in focus. As the *Book of Celebrations for the German Kin*, published in 1942, explains, "Christmas is a celebration of young light! It is a celebration of young life! Since times immemorial, all customs that the Germans have ever developed for this day of magnificent wonder tell us about the light that lies like a little child in a golden cradle. The cycle of the year comes to an end, and a new year begins."[36]

The Nazi Party had celebrated Christmas the first time in 1920, 10 months after its founding. From the outset, the Christian character of the festival was downplayed markedly, while its pagan roots were at the forefront. Rather than commemorating the birth of Christ, the members of the fledgling political movement marked the winter solstice on December 22, to highlight the link to Germany's pre-Christian past, as well as its association with Nordic or Aryan culture. Eschewing the tradition of honoring events happening in the Near East almost 2,000 years earlier, it was, in the words of party newspaper *Völkischer Beobachter*, an opportunity to bring together "the loyal and worthy core of a movement to which the German future must belong."[37]

After Hitler assumed political power in 1933, the attempt to "Nazify" Christmas entered into the mainstream of German culture. Swastika-shaped lights adorned Christmas trees, and children were given chocolate men shaped like members of the SS and the paramilitary SA. New carols were composed, such as "Exalted Night of the Clear Stars," toning down the Christian aspect of the holiday, and alluding heavily to the Nazi understanding of its roots in an ancient, mystical worship of light.[38] The same purpose was behind the introduction of new Christmas symbols such as a "sun wheel" associated with the ancient Norse god Odin, or cookies shaped as loops, a symbol of fertility.[39]

The Nazis knew they could not rush things. Especially as the war progressed and ever larger sacrifices were asked of the German people, it was important to let the public keep their most beloved traditions, of which Christmas was the prime example. The secret service reports, which constituted the most reliable testimony of the general mood in the absence of actual opinion surveys, suggested widespread predilection for old Christmas carols such as "Silent Night" and "Lo, How a Rose E'er Blooming" written for Christians, by Christians with a clear Christian subject matter. "The frequent broadcasting of these Christian Christmas carols reflects the opinion that without them, apparently it would be impossible for major parts of the people to enter into a real Christmas mood," the author of a confidential report wrote in a commentary, with a certain level of frustration at the intransigent German public.[40]

* * *

Alex David and Frieda Grüneberg were an elderly Jewish couple who had made their way by a circuitous route from their Berlin home to the Swiss border. The journey had taken several days and they had spent nights in strangers' homes, taking advantage of an underground escape network that existed despite the tight controls imposed by the Nazi state. On Christmas Eve they planned to carry out the last dangerous move into freedom in Switzerland. Weighed down by their heavy luggage, they walked through the snow from an abandoned train station. For a brief moment, they were both saved.

Alex David Grüneberg later explained what happened then: "I did not notice that my wife had returned to German soil to look after a handbag that she had lost. At this moment, a guard appeared and arrested her, and we lost sight of her." Frieda Grüneberg was taken to a nearby customs building and interrogated before being locked up. Shortly afterwards she hanged herself in a string she had made from handkerchiefs tied together. All that was left was evidence of a last act of defiance, described in the official German documents: "Mrs. Grüneberg refused to sign the interrogation report, saying that she would rather be shot."[41]

Despite the enormous risk associated with trying to flee, the Grünebergs knew they hardly had a choice. By Christmas 1942, there were only 51,257 Jews left in Germany, down from as many as 1.5 million at the beginning of Nazi rule. During the decade that Hitler's regime had lasted, a large number had emigrated, forced out by intensifying discrimination, but at the onset of the war, that avenue to safety had been closed. As late as December 1941, altogether 131,828 Jews had remained in Germany, but in the course of 1942, tens of thousands had been deported to the East. No one knew for sure what happened to the Jews once they arrived at their destination, but there were speculation and rumors.[42]

Victor Klemperer, a Jewish university professor in the East Germany city of Dresden who had escaped deportation mainly by virtue of being married to an Aryan woman, described in his secret diary the dreary reality of Christmas in a society in the throes of war, detailing how he had to use pages from an old telephone directory to wrap the modest presents he was able to prepare for acquaintances. This was only the smallest of Klemperer's worries, since he faced the daily risk of being sent to the concentration camps despite his status as a World War I veteran. Against this sinister backdrop, Klemperer and his wife engaged in hopeful conversation, depressingly similar to the conversations they had had during earlier Christmases:

"This will be our last Christmas in the Third Reich."

"But that's what we were thinking even last year, and we were fooling ourselves."

"Now it's different."[43]

In the Schwabach area in northern Bavaria, informants told security police that there was growing concern, not least among people with strong religious beliefs, triggered by rumors of mass shootings of Jews in Russia. Some even talked about "annihilation." The author and literary critic Hermann Stresau, who had lost his job as a librarian because of his lack of support for the government, was aware of the genocide taking place, noting in his diary in December 1942 that an American newspaper had called for the execution of all members of the SS, cited in the German press: "Over the story, the headline goes, 'An Infernal Plan.' Then what about our plan to liquidate the Poles and the Jews?"[44]

Combined with fears that the military situation on the Eastern Front was turning against Germany, the citizens of the Reich spent a Christmas of lingering worry about the future, according to a report prepared by an unnamed police official on December 23. "It is the view in wide parts of the rural population that Germany's victory in the war is still not a done deal, and that the Jews will exact a terrible revenge when they return," he wrote.[45]

It was widely understood among the Germans that Jews and other enemies of the Reich were being dealt with sternly. The fact that in the northern city of Bremen, for example, they had a slang word for concentration camp prisoners—"Zebras" due to their striped uniforms[46]—indicates that the system of incarceration, and the deplorable physical state that the inmates were in, was common knowledge. Still the raw reality of terror and sadism that existed behind the barbed wire inside the camps was a secret to most.

Germans employed in the concentration camp system were often careful to shield their families from what they saw. An example is Hans Grieben, an SS soldier who was undergoing training at Dachau, one of the oldest concentration camps in Germany. "At night I prepare a decent Christmas tree for our barrack room," he wrote in a letter home, giving the prisoners in the camp no mention. "For decorations we use cigarette paper cut in smaller pieces, cottonwool from the medical services, and small wooden figurines."[47]

The true extent of the Nazi system, with hundreds of camps and subcamps dotted across the map of Germany, was only realized by a few in the know. It ran the gamut from relatively livable camps for western prisoners-of-war to camps designed to be hell on earth. Among those experiencing the German camp system in its most lenient form was Jack Griss, a private in the Canadian Army who had been taken prisoner during the Dieppe raid the previous summer and spent Christmas in the Stalag VIIB prison camp in easternmost Germany. "The boys are trying to decorate the hut for Xmas and they are putting on a pantomime 'Aladdin'," he wrote in a letter to his wife, sent via the Red Cross. He asked her to send needles, thread, shoe polish and toothpaste, hoping he would be free before the items arrived. "Keep smiling honey," he wrote at the end of his letter, "this can't last forever."[48]

Captured members of the Polish armed forces, defeated in the brief war in 1939, were treated with varying degrees of severity. Polish officers in general were accorded the same treatment as their British and French counterparts. Stanislaw Mikosz, a cavalry captain kept prisoner for more than three years, had never given up hope that he would soon be reunited with his family. Thinking that the war might be over before the end of 1942, he had paid another inmate also held at Woldenberg camp a few cigarettes to carve a relief plaque that he could give his eight-year-old daughter for Christmas.[49]

Krystyna Wituska, a 22-year-old former member of the Polish resistance who had been deported to Germany and now was locked up in Berlin's Alt-Moabit prison, spent the days before Christmas thinking about home. "I send you all my best wishes," she wrote in a letter to her parents in Poland on December 22. "I am sure that we all have the same great wish—that someday we will be together again."[50] Wituska shared a cell with a German woman, the dissident Rosemarie Terwiel, who received a parcel from home on Christmas Eve. "We simply didn't know what to eat first," she wrote to her parents. "What's more, we had candlelight and two cigarettes. I must say, things haven't been that good in a long time."[51]

It was no coincidence that she shared her cell with a German. Citizens of the Reich were everywere in the concentration camps. Willi Schlagintweit, a Bavarian petty criminal sentenced to years of confinement over fraud, was sent to Mauthausen-Gusen concentration camp in Austria shortly before Christmas. He quickly realized that he and his fellow inmates were literally being worked to death. They were fed a soup of rotten fodder beets and potatoes, boiled in a cauldron that emitted an unbearable stink. "On such a diet, we often worked day and night, for example during the Christmas of 1942, when I worked for 12 hours in the quarry, and then I peeled potatoes for the whole night," he said. "The cycle was repeated for five days and nights, followed by one night off, and then we worked again and again for four consecutive days and nights. The majority of my fellow inmates died of hunger and exhaustion."[52]

* * *

Where was Hitler in all this? The sources suggest he was fully aware of the crimes taking place in his name in the society he had created. A single surviving document handed to him a few days after Christmas 1942 shows that he was being informed in minute detail about the lives expended to make his vision of a German-dominated Europe come true. On December 29, Himmler presented him with a statistical overview of the result of the campaign against "bandits" behind the frontline in southern Russia and Ukraine. "Bandits" was a broad term, covering both partisans and Jews, as the document demonstrated. It reported the deaths of a total of 374,570 people in the period from August to November.

They included 1,337 individuals who were "confirmed dead after skirmishes," as well as 737 executed "immediately upon capture" and another 7,828 "prisoners executed after prolonged, thorough interrogation." In another category, consisting of "people assisting bandits or suspected of being bandits," 1,457 had been executed, and a much larger group, consisting of 363,211 Jews, had also been put to death. In other words, the document made clear that Jews had been killed in the hundreds of thousands within the span of a few months. A short note in the margin of the document, by Hitler's adjutant, confirmed that it had been brought to the *Führer's* attention.[53]

For a brutal dictatorship such as Germany, opposition of varying degrees appeared in a surprising large number of cases. Sometimes, the opposition was perhaps not even intended as such. One example was as early as December 1939. A group of nuns running a girls' school in the town of Heinsberg near the Dutch border had ended up in a report prepared by the SS security service after they had led their students in a performance of "Silent Night" in the English language.[54]

Three years later, acts of defiance were in evidence throughout the Reich. In Munich, a circle of university students organized in the White Rose group spent Christmas 1942 preparing a new leaflet criticizing the inhumanity of the Hitler regime, to be distributed early in 1943. Also during Christmas 1942, three leading members of the German resistance, the Social Democrats Carlo Mierendorff, Theodor Haubach and Emil Henk, met in the skiing town of Oberstdorf in the Bavarian Alps to discuss the right time to carry out an assassination of Hitler. They agreed that timing was essential. If the dictator was killed too early in the war, before the western Allies had succeeded in establishing a foothold on the European continent, the risk was too great that Germany would be devoured in a Soviet avalanche. Patience was called for.[55]

A significant part of the active and passive opposition to Nazi rule came from the Christian church, which remained strong in Germany, especially in the countryside. Dietrich Bohnhoeffer, a 36-year-old Lutheran pastor who worked for the German secret service *Abwehr* but was in fact a member of the resistance movement, wrote an essay during Christmas, marking the 10 years that had almost passed since Hitler had gained power in January 1933. Watching the injustice all around him, he felt he had no choice but to work for change. To be sure, Bohnhoeffer was fully aware that his activities for the underground were intensely dangerous. He expressed his wish to die only after having lived a full life but acknowledged this was a luxury that one could not afford in the middle of a war where news of deaths at the front had become commonplace and barely caused anyone to raise an eyebrow. "Basically, we probably all feel that we belong [to death] and that every new day is a miracle."[56]

Some Germans found themselves in opposition to the regime without actually meaning to, simply by following their basic human impulses to help those in need. Helmut Simmet was a young schoolboy and a member of the Hitler Youth in the Saarland in westernmost Germany, enjoying his time off from school at Christmas when he was suddenly confronted with the harsh realities of the war that was going on. On his way to a frozen pond where he planned to skate with his classmates, he came across a construction site where a number of Russian slave laborers were forced to work. One of them was a young woman dressed in rags, shifting dirt with a shovel while carrying her newborn baby in a sling over her shoulder. Their eyes met, and Simmet thought he saw an expression in her face as if she begged him for something edible for herself and her child. He shrugged briefly and patted his pockets to show that they were empty, and he had nothing to give her.

The rest of the day he could not get the sight out of his mind, comparing it to the Virgin Mary cradling the newborn Christ in the warmth of a stable in Bethlehem. "She had been much better off than this homeless woman and her child, born abroad in a camp barrack," he thought. "It had been placed on top of straw in a manger, instead of dangling in a piece of cloth tied to its mother, while she had to carry out hard work." The following day he returned to the construction site with a few raw potatoes and a sandwich but could not find the woman. Instead, he saw a male Russian laborer that had also been there the other day, and guessing it was the child's father, he passed the food on to him. He hurriedly walked away but was stopped by a German worker, who had watched the entire scene. "Get lost and never come back," the man shouted. "As a member of the Hitler Youth, you should know that it is prohibited to give the Russians anything to eat. They get fed well enough in the camp." Simmet passed the rest of the Christmas in a quiet state of shock, never finding out what happened to the Russian mother and her small child.[57]

American soldiers at an advance dressing station in New Guinea with a makeshift Christmas tree decorated with surgical cotton wool and cigarette cartons. (Australian War Memorial)

Corporal Frank Abrashinsky, from Sheboygan, Wisconsin, serving with the 127th Infantry Regiment, enjoys a Red Cross Christmas package near Buna, New Guinea. (US Army Signal Corps)

Australian girls decorate "Austerity Christmas Tree". (Australian War Memorial)

GIs learning Maori dancing during a Christmas visit to the city of Gisborne, New Zealand. (National Library of New Zealand)

Men of the US Army Air Force 38th Bomb Group attend a Catholic mass held on Christmas Day, 1942 in New Guinea. (National Archives photo no. 342-FH-3A-32915-67763AC)

Christmas card prepared by Dutch prisoners at Changi camp near Singapore. (Private collection)

Mock Changi prison menu card, prepared by Major Burnett Clarke of the Australian Army. (From the collection of the Marks-Hirschfeld Museum of Medical History, The University of Queensland)

While still on alert duty, pilots of the US Army Air Force 51st Fighter Group consume their Christmas dinner near their aircraft at a base in China on December 25, 1942. (National Archives photo no. 342-FH-3A-2359-74184AC)

Polish orphans released from prison camps in the Soviet Union upon their arrival in India. (Imperial War Museum)

A German soldier with a Christmas tree. From the publication *Deutsche Kriegsweihnacht*, or *German War Christmas*, 1942 edition. (Private collection)

A German soldier writes a letter home, full of homesickness. Illustration from Christmas booklet issued by German unit on the Eastern Front in December 1942. (Private collection)

Leise flehen meine Lieder
hin zu Dir beim Kerzenschein.
Lieber läg' an Deinem Mieder
ich und wär' bei Dir daheim.

Freezing German soldiers try to get a traditional Russian stove working. Cartoon from Christmas booklet issued by German unit on the Eastern Front in December 1942. (Private collection)

A Finnish soldier brings a Christmas tree to his outfit. (SA Kuva)

A German soldier disguised as Santa Claus arrives on skis south of Lake Ilmen, near Leningrad. (Institute for War, Holocaust and Genocide Studies, Netherlands)

The Stalingrad Madonna. (Wikimedia)

One of the buildings at Auschwitz concentration camp is adorned with a Christmas tree. (Memorial and Museum Auschwitz-Birkenau)

Portrait of Hitler in the 1942 edition of the publication *Deutsche Kriegsweihnacht*, or *German War Christmas*. (Private collection)

Luftwaffe officers at night fighter school mark Christmas 1942. (Private collection)

German Christmas postcard 1942.
(Private collection)

A *Wehrmacht* soldier dressed as
Santa Claus visits members of
the German *Luftwaffe* in what
appears to be a posed photo.
(Institute for War, Holocaust and
Genocide Studies, Netherlands)

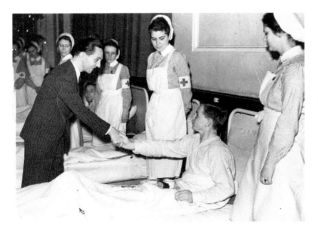

German Propaganda Minister
Joseph Goebbels visits injured
soldiers in Berlin, Christmas
1942. (Institute for War,
Holocaust and Genocide
Studies, Netherlands)

A box with cookie molds, for German families with husbands and fathers at the front. (Private collection)

Cartoon in a German magazine, December 1942: "Don't be sad, Oskar. He has definitely been hoarding snow." (Private collection)

In den Jahren des Krieges wie des Friedens darfst du niemals mehr den stillen Dank und das verpflichtende Gedenken an jene vergessen, deren Opfer dir die geborgene Weihnachtsruhe der Heimat ermöglichten; deshalb brenne am Fest in jedem Hause ein Licht für alle die Getreuesten, die an den weiten Fronten des Großdeutschen Krieges ewige Wache halten.

A page in a German Christmas calendar from December 1942. The place names around the edge list areas occupied by German soldiers in the course of three years of war. (Private collection)

A Christmas party in December 1942 at the camp in Westerbork, the last station for Dutch Jews before being transported to their deaths in the East. Seated to the left is camp commandant SS-Obersturmführer Albert Konrad Gemmeker. Seated to the right is SS-Hauptsturmführer Ferdinand Hugo aus der Fünten, who was responsible for the deportation of Jews. (Institute for War, Holocaust and Genocide Studies, Netherlands)

Sergeant Hiram Prouty of the US Army's 175th Infantry Regiment dressed as Santa Claus during the Christmas season, arriving on a M3 medium tank, at Perham Down, England, December 1942. (US Army Signal Corps)

Staff Sergeant William Steinbeck of New York passes out cigars to members of Company C, 56th Signal Battalion, V Corps, stationed at Bristol, England, December 24, 1942. (National Archives photo no. 111-SC-176868)

A Christmas party at the British Admiralty for children of Allied nation staff. A group of Chinese children can be seen in the center. (Royal Navy)

A member of the German Afrika Korps marks Christmas at a time when Axis forces found themselves within a shrinking perimeter in Tunisia. (Private collection)

Patients crowd around a Christmas tree at the 2nd New Zealand General Hospital at Kantara, Egypt in December 1942. (National Library of New Zealand)

Men of the 49th Fighter Squadron of the US Army Air Force in the North African desert get their Christmas Day dinner on December 25, 1942: turkey, cigarettes, oranges and candy. (National Archives photo no. 111-SC-164149)

A German submarine crew celebrate Christmas 1942 somewhere in the southern Atlantic. (Private collection)

President Franklin D. Roosevelt with an oversized globe given to him by the US Army as a Christmas present in December 1942. (Library of Congress)

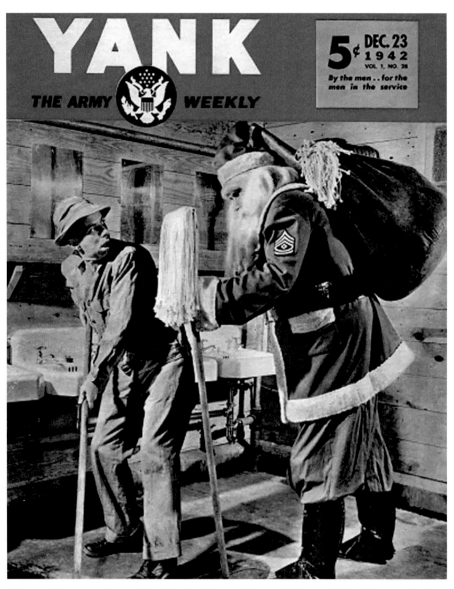

Cover of *Yank*, a weekly published for the US armed forces, Christmas 1942. (Private collection)

CHAPTER 8

"Christmas Action"

Western Europe

Jean-Pierre Lévy, a 31-year-old Jewish member of the French resistance, was arrested by three police officers on Rue Mercière in the city of Lyon on December 24. Two officers grabbed him by the arms, and a third officer pressed his revolver against his back as a warning against attempting to escape. He was brought to the police station on Place des Célestins for questioning. It was a bad situation. Lyon had become a much more dangerous place overnight little more than a month earlier, after the German Army had moved in and occupied the southern part of France in reaction to the Allied invasion of northwest Africa.[1]

For two years prior to that, the entire area had nominally counted as the unoccupied part of France, but as it was ruled by the pro-German Vichy regime, it was always a sham. Deportation of the region's Jews to camps in Eastern Europe had already begun long before the German troops moved in. The police force to a large extent did the work of the Nazis, and now with the last pretenses of any independence gone, being caught as a member of the resistance movement could be deadly. Lévy knew his life was at stake as he entered the gate of the police station. He was carrying a handgun concealed inside a roll of toilet paper. His heart skipped a beat when one of the officers put the toilet paper in the windowsill without noticing that the end of the gun barrel was protruding slightly.

It was not clear why Lévy had been brought to the police station, and the questions the officers asked were oddly random. "Why are you wearing a moustache?" one of them asked, knowing full well that it was a common way for members of the resistance and ordinary criminals to alter their appearance and escape recognition. "That's my right, and I've been wearing it for several months already," Lévy replied, trying to appear slightly annoyed without being obnoxious. The officer went on, undeterred: "You're sweating, it seems you don't have a completely clear conscience." It was true. Lévy could feel the droplets forming on his scalp. Quick thinking was called for. "Well, put yourself in my place," he answered. "I am questioned by the police even though I have done nothing wrong. Besides, when your last name is Lévy, and you are Jewish, you're in a constant state of apprehension."

It gradually occurred to Lévy why he had been arrested. It was not on suspicions of being a member of the resistance, but as part of an investigation into a burglary case dating back to spring of the same year. Yet, he could not relax. One wrong word, and his true identity as a resistance leader could be exposed. He dutifully answered the officers' probing questions, warily observing the toilet paper through the corner of his eyes, until suddenly they told him to collect his things. He picked up the toilet paper, trying to seem as casual as possible, and was now led out of the building and driven in a car to his apartment. More questions followed, until the police officers understood they had no excuse to keep him. "We'll let you go, but if we find out that you have fooled us, we'll bring you in again," one of them said.

With his heart pumping, Lévy walked away, knowing immediately that he could not stay for one minute longer in Lyon. He got on a tram, then got off after a few stops, shifting to a line that went in a different direction, all in order to make sure he would throw off any agents following him. Eventually he met up with friends at a restaurant where he knew he would find them. "How are you?" he was asked. "Like someone who has just been arrested less than an hour ago and has had enough," he replied. He soon learned that the police had discovered his true identity and were now on the lookout for him again, and this time they would not let him go. For every minute he stayed in the city, he was risking his life.

Later the same day contacts in the resistance movement saw to it that he was transported by car to Miribel, a suburb of Lyon, to seek temporary shelter at the home of a man known to be sympathetic, Henri Deschamps. He was a schoolteacher who had lost his job after participating in a demonstration against the Vichy regime, and so he was reliable. It was risky to house a leading member of the resistance, but the teacher was unperturbed. Rather than hiding Lévy in a corner of his house where no one would see him, Deschamps invited him to participate in the family's big traditional Christmas dinner. The table was a spectacle of culinary plenty despite the war. One of Deschamps' daughters was a doctor and was paid by her patients in kind, mostly in the form of agricultural produce.

Lévy later managed to move on from the Deschamps' home and remain undetected by the security forces who wanted to catch him and eventually kill him. In hindsight, it had been foolish to embark on dinner with complete strangers at a time when he was being sought by the police and they could be hot on his heels, Lévy wrote, but "the atmosphere was amazing." As society was thrown into a devastating war, where death could come at any moment, people were prepared to take greater risks even if only for the sake of experiencing a moment of joy, such as the simple pleasure of sitting around a well-decked Christmas table.

* * *

In neutral Sweden, Astrid Lindgren, who was later to become a world-famous writer of children's books, was also enjoying a plentiful holiday spread, spending her fourth war Christmas in a state of relative material comfort. In her apartment in the capital Stockholm, she and her children could enjoy a ham, pickled pork, calf kidney, pâté, herring and smoked eel. She was privileged, and she knew it. As an avid newspaper reader, she was only too well informed about the situation beyond Sweden's borders. "Out in the world it's pure misery," she noted in her diary on Christmas Day, but added: "The Germans are faring badly in Russia and Africa. Large-scale military setbacks. I guess it must be the beginning of the end."[2]

Through an acquaintance, she was informed during the Christmas holiday about the conditions in neighboring Norway, which had been occupied by the Germans since April 1940. One telling story was about a Norwegian count who had been sent to labor camp through no fault of his own, while German soldiers had ransacked his manor and hauled away 2,000 bottles of wine before drinking themselves senseless and forcing the countess to cook tea for them at 3 am. Meanwhile, in the notorious camp Grini, prisoners were being beaten up. Lindgren was full of anger, as she completed the day's entry: "They will have to pay on the day of reckoning."[3]

The rumors about the maltreatment at Grini, a former women's prison outside the Norwegian capital of Oslo, were not exaggerated. New prisoners were routinely exposed to the same violent welcome at the moment of their arrival. "They get their baptism of fire immediately after they have walked through the door. They are slapped and beaten with canes," an inmate, the architect Odd Nansen, wrote in his diary. "They don't know yet that they have arrived in a hell governed by a bunch of insane devils."[4] Altogether, close to

20,000 Norwegians were incarcerated in Grini during the war years, many only transiting on their way to camps in Germany.

Christmas marked a pleasant change in the dreary daily life at Grini. The prisoners were exempt from work and received an extra portion of porridge, with cinnamon and butter added. The prison commandant banned the reading of the Bible during Christmas, but in Nansen's barracks, one of the prisoners instead told an old Norwegian folk tale about Johannes Blessom, a man who made it home to his remote parish just in time for Christmas. "He made it, to the object of his desires, the heart of Norway, where we all want to go, but we probably have to endure much hardship yet before we get there," he wrote in his diary.[5]

Another inmate, the 32-year-old resistance member Trygve Bratteli, also received better food than usual. It was meatballs. On Christmas Day, his building was visited by Germans. He could hear them from afar, walking with heavy boots and smashing open doors to signal their arrival. When they got to the cell where he was locked up, they could not help but notice how clean and neat everything was. "Look," one of the Germans said, "what a primitive people is capable of once it comes under the guidance of a civilized nation."[6]

Throughout Western Europe, from France to Norway, people that had been subdued by the Nazis for years were beginning to rise in opposition to the occupation by December 1942. In every country, it was still a small minority, and young men of fighting age were disproportionately represented. The population in general, ordinary people, were more concerned with staying alive and making it to the end of the war, ensuring that they and their families would at least not starve or freeze. It was possible in most cases, but it became ever more challenging due to the predatory nature of the Nazi rulers.

* * *

Many of the presents that ended up under German Christmas trees in 1942 were loot from the rest of Europe. The Nazi rulers spent their years in control of the continent sucking assets out of its economies with staggering ruthlessness, and in the period around Christmas, the effort was intensified. The commander-in-chief of the *Luftwaffe*, Hermann Göring, who had his hands in many things other than the air war, was the mastermind behind that endeavor. He had laid out his plans as early as August at a meeting for senior officials in charge of the administration of the countries of occupied Europe. It was called the "Christmas action."[7]

Göring, never afraid of coming across as too pompous, held the meeting at the Ministry of Aviation in Berlin, inside a grand room named after himself. On the agenda was the need to exploit the conquered territories more comprehensively than had been done so far, and the "Christmas action" was but a little part of that, albeit a telling one. "I intend to send a number of purchasing agents with extraordinary powers first to the Netherlands and Belgium, and then to France," Göring told his audience, "and I will give them until Christmas to buy more or less everything they can find in the best shops and warehouses, and all that I will hang in the shop windows for the German people, and the German people can buy it."[8]

Priority was given to shoes, cosmetics, toys and other items that typically could serve as Christmas presents. On the face of it, everything was done properly, and all was being paid for, but the money came out of budgets which the occupied countries were made to finance themselves. In essence, therefore, it was theft by other means. Granted, it was not unheard of. Bringing the spoils of war home was a tradition harking back to antiquity. The emperors of Rome had done it, and the rulers of all the other empires Europe had seen had done it too. "It was called looting. You were allowed to drag away what you conquered. Now, we have become more humane," Göring told his audience with a slight tone of regret, before adding mischievously: "Still, I plan to loot, and I plan to do so thoroughly."[9]

There was a rowdy atmosphere that day in the Hermann Göring Hall as the plunder of Europe was being planned, and the stenographic record at one point notes "bursts of laughter" from the audience of ranking Nazi officials, but the scheme reflected a challenge that the German leadership considered with extreme seriousness and could only ignore at its own peril. In their view of history, the German Army had remained unbeaten at the front in 1918 but was stabbed in the back by traitors at home. Germany had lost the previous world war due to a home front whose will to fight on had been weakened by hunger. The Nazis would not allow this to happen again.

Partly this could be achieved through an extensive security apparatus. But even more efficiently, it could be done by ensuring that the German people did not suffer any material want. Hitler himself made a reference to this on Christmas Day. Keeping the people happy was important, he told his confidante Martin Bormann. "The *Führer* emphasized repeatedly that the greatest impact could be achieved if we can inform the German people about higher food rations and other subsidies," Bormann wrote in a note. A few days later, Hitler made clear how the Germans were to be kept fed and satisfied. It was to be done, he said, "through greater contributions from the occupied areas."[10]

This was exactly what happened after Göring laid out the plan for the "Christmas action" in August. At the end of that month, an order went out to spend 300 million Reichsmarks on the specific aim of providing Christmas presents for the German people. The task of organizing this huge effort was given to Colonel Josef Veltjens, who had become friends with Göring when they both served as combat pilots in World War I. He enjoyed the impressive title of Plenipotentiary for Special Tasks, although his real job was partly to comb Europe's black markets, which were the only places to find most of the needed products.[11]

Veltjens and his colleagues had less than four months to complete the task, and transportation back to Germany proved especially challenging. Although by December 20, goods valued at a total of 244 million Reichsmarks had been purchased in the occupied countries, only a portion of this total ended up fulfilling its purpose of sweetening the German Christmas. "It was impossible to bring all of these goods to Germany and to make them available for sale on time. 2,306 boxcars with 11,138,229 kg; and further, by ship, 6,335 bales of goods with over 100,000 kg, arrived in Germany," Veltjens wrote in a report the following January.[12]

The list of places that were primarily to benefit from the "Christmas action" once again underlined the Nazi concern with keeping public opinion at bay with the help of material incentives. Distribution was primarily made in bomb-damaged regions, where morale was most likely to falter, as well as in big cities such as Berlin, Vienna, Hamburg, Breslau, and Königsberg, where support for the regime mattered the most because of the large populations.[13] It seemed to work. Initial reports from the security service suggested that the people were happy with the extra availability of goods.

It was not just Christmas presents that flowed in a steady stream to the Reich. Food did, too, and the Nazi government was in no doubt about the potential consequences for the people who were deprived of their means of survival. Göring had made that perfectly clear in his August meeting with the administrators: "The *Führer* has said so repeatedly, and I concur: if starving is necessary, the starving must not be done by Germans, but by others."[14]

Even though this showed how far the German leadership was prepared to go, by late 1942, few people in occupied Western Europe did actually starve. Elsewhere in the continent was a different matter. The occupied areas of the Soviet Union were undersupplied, and Greece was faced with a regular hunger disaster. In the area of the capital Athens and the adjacent port city of Piraeus alone, hunger had cost the lives of an estimated 40,000 people between late 1941 and late 1942.[15] The situation was so desperate that the Allies relented on their naval blockade of continental Europe, and since August 1942, regular shipments of Canadian wheat had been arriving in Greece under the auspices of a Swiss-Swedish committee.[16]

Among the occupied people further west, the occupation did not yet have such disastrous consequences. Mass starvation was to become a fact two years later in the Netherlands, but in 1942, material want manifested itself mostly in empty shop windows. "Noel to be frugal in drained France," *The New York Times* reported about conditions in France, noting that candy, flowers and rare vintage wines were out of the question as presents. "People prefer postage stamps, pearls or anything with a value disproportionate to its volume that a prospective fugitive may carry in his vest pocket or handbag."[17] Life was hard but still bearable for most people in Western Europe, with significant exceptions. By Christmas 1942, the full weight of Nazi wrath was already being brought to bear on one group of people—the Jews.

* * *

SS-Obersturmführer Albert Konrad Gemmeker, the 35-year-old commandant of Westerbork transit camp in the Netherlands, was known for his urbane and gentlemanly manners, and he was eager to please. In December 1942, he had been in his position as head of the camp for two months, and he felt it was time to mark his arrival in a formal fashion. A celebration of Christmas—or in the usual SS lingo, *Jul*, to de-emphasize the holiday's Christian origins—was just the occasion. He knew exactly how he was going to spoil his guests, who were all ranking members of the German administration in the Netherlands. There would be plenty of good food, as well as drinks ad libitum. And there would be entertainment, a variety show organized by the camp's Jews. "He wanted to show what 'his' Jews were capable of," said Louis de Wijze, then a 20-year-old inmate.[18]

The actors and singers performing in front of the guests that Christmas were all destined to die, as were the orchestra, the people backstage and the technicians—and most of their audience of uniformed officers with their shiny jackboots and their expensively dressed wives and girlfriends knew it. Crowded Westerbork was the last station for virtually all Jews of the Netherlands before they were forced on trains and sent east for extermination. One of the guests at the Christmas party, SS-Hauptsturmführer Ferdinand Hugo aus der Fünten, who was responsible for the deportation of Jews to the camps in the East, had admitted as much on an earlier occasion: "All roads lead through Westerbork."[19]

Westerbork, which saw nearly 100,000 Jews pass through on their way to the murder factories in Poland, showed the evil of the Holocaust in all its absurdity, putting on display how the industrial killing of people, put to death merely because of their ethnicity, could be merged seamlessly with the routines of everyday life. The perimeters of the camp were guarded by SS soldiers, but internally everything was run by the Jews themselves. This meant, for example, that the camp had a good school system for the children and excellent medical care, including a hospital with 1,725 beds, 120 doctors and other staff, and facilities stretching from X-ray to dental surgery. People who would be killed a few months in the future could still get their teeth fixed.[20]

The only thing that stood out in the general atmosphere of civility was the unit in charge of internal security, also organized by the prisoners themselves. The individuals picked for this duty were reputed for their propensity for brutality and violence and soon got the nickname "the Jewish SS."[21] Despite the Jewish guards, the physician Elie Cohen, who arrived at the camp in December 1942, was surprised at how normal it all seemed. "As a Jew, you enjoyed more freedom inside Westerbork than outside it," he wrote after the war, adding, "The curse of Westerbork was always that transport train, of course."[22]

It departed on Tuesdays. The night before, the names of those selected for deportation East were being read out in each barracks. While those not on the list often threw themselves into mad dances because they were allowed to live at least for another week, those who were to embark on the dreaded transport started packing their things, mostly in the quiet resignation of the condemned. "Husbands were powerless to protect their wives, parents had to watch helplessly while their children were torn away from them forever. The sick, the blind, the hurt, the mentally disturbed, pregnant women, the dying, orphans, new-born babies—none was spared," the lawyer Abel Herzberg wrote.[23] A mother was overheard pushing her children to eat, the way mothers do, but with chilling words, showing how callousness and cruelty had become normal and a part of everyday life: "If you don't eat your pudding up straightaway, then Mummy won't be with you on the transport!"[24]

During Christmas, the transports were suspended, and the general atmosphere in Westerbork camp was somewhat more relaxed than usual, as preparations went ahead for the camp commandant's party. "There was delicious cooking in the central kitchen and a lot of cleaning. Tables and chairs were also being hauled through the camp to the large hall right at the center," said Louis de Wijze, the 20-year-old inmate.[25] Dozens of young prisoners were enrolled to do the menial work during the party, and all were ordered to scrub themselves clean and pass by the camp's hairdresser to look tidy.[26]

At half past seven on the big day, as snow was falling gently over the camp, one Mercedes after the other rolled up in front of the hall where the Christmas party was to be held. Prisoners were lined up to escort the female guests inside the building, where other prisoners were ready to take their furs and coats. The hall itself was staffed with girls from the camp, wearing black dresses, starched aprons and white caps that made them look like waitresses in an expensive restaurant. Boys, including 13-year-old Gerhard Durlacher, carried beer and warm dishes from the kitchen.

As the party got underway, the hall filled with the sounds of boisterous laughter and clinking beer mugs. Every once in a while, an important guest rose to deliver a speech. When this happened, all Jews were ordered to leave, and the girls were made to shiver outside in the cold in their thin outfits. A singer performed popular German hits. One of them went, "Yes, his name is Waldemar, and he is no star." Durlacher, hearing the merry notes through the walls of the building, remembered it from before the war, when he had been sitting at home in front of the radio listening to it with his mother.

A group of SS men staggered out the door and found a spot at a hedge. There they opened their flies and, Durlacher later wrote, started "pissing like horses." While the Germans were still busy relieving themselves, he and the other young assistants kept carrying more beer past them. Out of earshot, one of the Jewish servants whispered: "I hope they burst." Durlacher was disgusted by the situation. They are the barbarians who have enslaved us, and look how they behave, he thought. He saw their sidearms and quietly scolded himself for not being daring enough to grab the arms and finish off his tormentors. "If only," he thought, "I had the courage and the strength."[27]

Most of the Jews commandeered for service during the party escaped trouble, at least that one night. The Germans were too drunk to even notice them, which was good. However, a group of young Jewish men on duty outside the building had the bad fortune of coming across a soldier surnamed Hanitz. He had only one arm and was known to possess a mean streak. He had clearly had too much to drink and had drifted out for fresh air. When he caught sight of the Jews, he decided he wanted to top off an inebriated night by commanding them around. He made them stand in a long line, barking orders at them. "He let us march," said de Wijze, who was in the group. "Purely for his own fun. In the meantime, the party went on for quite some time."[28]

* * *

The doomed prisoners at Westerbork were enjoying what was termed a "Christmas break" when the weekly trains to Auschwitz and other camps were briefly halted. Still, it was abundantly clear that the German authorities were in the process of making the Netherlands "Jew-free." By the end of 1942, a total of 38,000 people had already been funneled through Westerbork to their final destination.[29] Likewise, across Western Europe deportations to the camps in Poland had been picking up in the course of 1942, as the implementation of the Final Solution, which had initially been concentrated in the conquered territories in the East, was gradually made to encompass the entire continent.

As elsewhere the Nazis did their best to conceal from the Jews the fate that awaited them. By mid-December 1942, the Jewish Council in the Netherlands purportedly received postcards from Dutch Jews who had already arrived at camps in the East. "The food is good, with hot lunches, cheese and jam sandwiches in the evenings," according to a postcard allegedly sent from Monowitz, a concentration camp in Poland. "We have central heating and sleep under two blankets. There are magnificent shower arrangements with hot and cold water." The Theresienstadt camp was described as "a friendly town with broad streets and lovely gardens." It was, a postcard claimed, possible to get help with hard work, and "those who wished could take a nap in the afternoon."[30]

The extent to which the lies were believed by the Jews and their non-Jewish neighbors is hard to establish at a distance of eight decades. Few could imagine the full horror of what happened in the East, but the majority probably guessed that the conditions there were not better than what the Jews left behind. Still, a surprising number of Europeans were active participants in expelling the Jews, and even more looked the other way. There was much cruelty in the way the Europeans treated their Jewish compatriots as they were hunted down by the Germans, but there was also kindness and willingness to sacrifice. Scattered across the continent were havens where heroic individuals risked their lives to help persecuted Jews.

At a French château near Switzerland, a group of Jewish children and adolescents, escapees from the roundups earlier in the year, were spending the Christmas in tense anticipation of escaping into safety across the Swiss border. They were being sheltered by members of the Swiss Red Cross under the leadership of the resourceful nurse Rösli Naf.[31] While she was preoccupied planning for the rescue of the young Jews, she had no way of making the holiday cozier for her young charges. "The ever-tightening supplies made it impossible for her to put aside new treats—there just wasn't enough to eat day-to-day. This must have been painful to Rösli and other Swiss Red Cross representatives, since Christmas was so very important to them," one of adolescents, the German-Jewish girl Inge Joseph, wrote in her memoirs.[32]

Peter Feigl, a 13-year-old German-born Jew on the run with his family from the Nazis, had already lived in a number of different countries by the time he found himself in a Catholic school at the Château de Montéléone in southern France in December 1942. His parents, assimilated Jews who had decided to give Peter a Catholic upbringing to protect him from anti-Semitism, had placed him at the château in the summer when the French authorities had started rounding up the Jews. Shortly afterwards, they themselves had been detained, and now Peter Feigl was alone, at the mercy of strangers.[33]

Having never seen himself as Jewish, Peter felt that the preparations for Christmas came natural to him, and in his diary, he wrote how on December 23, the students at the château set up a manger of clay. Still, he missed his parents too much to be truly happy. "This will be a very sad Christmas for you as well as for me," he wrote in his diary, addressing the entry to his parents. On Christmas Day, he added: "Noël, Noël, Noël, this is the day that is normally so joyous. But you are far from me; where? If we could only celebrate our Christmas quietly around a very modest Christmas tree […] Oh well, perhaps next year we will be together again?"[34] He did not know, but when he wrote these words, his parents had already been dead for nearly three months. They had been on a transport train that arrived in Auschwitz on September 6 and were gassed within minutes of stepping onto the camp platform.[35]

* * *

Towards the end of his 5,000-word Christmas message broadcast by radio to millions of devout Catholics around the world, Pope Pius XII finally mentioned the Jews. It was while speaking of a Christian vow to bring about a society more in line with the fundamental ideas of the faith: "Mankind owes that vow to the hundreds of thousands of persons who, without any fault on their part, sometimes only because of their nationality or race, have been consigned to death or to a slow decline."[36] The message was cautious in the extreme, failing to identify both the Jewish victims and their Nazi executioners, but to those able to read between the lines, it was clear who was being targeted.

Italian dictator Benito Mussolini was listening in on the radio, and he was among those who immediately understood what the Pope was trying to say. Appreciating how it would strain his alliance with Hitler, he was furious at this interference in politics. "The Vicar of God, that is the representative of the Ruler of the Universe on Earth, should never speak; he should remain in the clouds," he told his foreign minister, Count Galeazzo Ciano, with scorn and sarcasm in his voice. "This is a speech of platitudes, which might better be made by the parish priest of Predappio," the autocrat said, referring to the north Italian village where he was born.[37]

In Berlin, Goebbels tried to brush it off. "The Pope's Christmas speech is without any depth or significance," he wrote in his diary. "It's all kept in a general tone, which will meet with a complete lack of interest among the governments of the belligerent nations."[38] As usual, the propaganda minister was insincere, and the Nazi leadership was probably more concerned than he let on. A confidential document from the German security service analyzing the Pope's speech carried an angry reaction to the thinly veiled condemnation of the killing of the Jews. "With those words, the German people is practically blamed for committing an injustice against the Poles and the Jews, and the Pope makes himself the advocate and champion for the actual war criminals," the document said.[39]

The Pope's words of admonition did not come out of the blue. In his Christmas speech one year earlier in December 1941, he had launched a veiled attack on Nazi Germany, saying among other things that in a world order based on ethical principles, there is "no room for the violation of the freedom, integrity and security of other states" and also "no place for open or occult oppression of the cultural and linguistic characteristics of national minorities."[40] His statement had prompted *The New York Times* to praise him as "a lonely voice in the silence and darkness enveloping Europe."[41]

At the same time, there were also other signs that parts of the Catholic church increasingly prioritized general humanitarian principles above the need to accommodate the wishes of the political power in Rome. This became obvious at the Bagno a Ripoli camp set up about four miles southeast of Florence for Jews and enemy aliens. It had been established inside a formerly Jewish-owned mansion with 40 rooms, but despite the luxurious surroundings, overcrowding had soon made life precarious. The Catholic church provided some help. Prior to Christmas 1942, the archbishop of Florence donated 360 lire to the camp, asking for the rations of all inmates to be improved during the holiday.[42]

Even the Pope himself made a similar gesture, seeing to it that all POWs in Italy received a pocket calendar, with a special papal blessing, as a Christmas present the same year.[43] More worrying to Pierre Daye, a Belgian collaborator who visited Rome around Christmas, an atmosphere of what he termed "Anglophilia" permeated certain circles in the Italian capital. He especially recalled a dinner hosted by the Duchess of Villarosa, a well-known socialite. "I didn't hear anyone speak anything but English even though no English guests had been invited," he wrote, in disgust.[44]

Even so, Pius had long been criticized for not being outspoken enough in his criticism of the Nazis despite mounting evidence that they were committing crimes on an unprecedented scale throughout Europe. The reticence was not for lack of personal courage. Ciano had complained about the intransigence of the Catholic church and especially the Pope for years, writing in his diary as early as in May 1940 that "he is even ready to be deported to a concentration camp, but will do nothing against his conscience."[45]

Rather, the Pope was guided by ideology. He was of the conviction that for all its atrocities, Nazism could be a bulwark against the advance of atheist Soviet communism. "Stalin is the new Attila the Hun, not Hitler," he told the German ambassador to the Vatican.[46] In conversations with Daye, the Belgian collaborator, he argued that he had to be opaque and ambivalent in his public statements to maintain a measure of diplomatic flexibility in the dangerous world of European great power politics. "The Church, you see, dear sir," the Pope explained, "is like a cat wishing to cross a table covered in precious crystal without knocking over or smashing anything. It is obliged to be extremely supple and slither with the utmost prudence."[47]

It was not possible to remain Janus-faced in the long run, and as 1942 wore on, Allied diplomats were increasingly frustrated by Pius' reluctance to openly denounce Nazi barbarity targeting especially Jews and Poles. "The Holy Father seemed to occupy himself with spiritual matters, charitable acts, and rhetoric while adopting at the same time an ostrichlike policy toward atrocities that were obvious to everyone," Harold Tittmann, a senior US representative at the Vatican, wrote in his memoirs.[48]

In England, Victor Gollancz, a writer and publisher from a family of Jewish-Polish immigrants, expressed similar views, suggesting in his pamphlet *Let My People Go* that the Pope had it in his power to effect great change. "A great deal could be done by the Vatican in this matter of informing the German people," he wrote in the conclusion. "If the Pope would broadcast to the many millions of German Catholics, not once but repeatedly; if he would give the plain facts, and describe them for what they are, an outrage against the God of Mercy and Compassion; then the effect would be as unquestionable as his authority is unique. Have we approached him at all? If so, have we exhausted all the possibilities of persuasion?"[49]

Western representatives at the Holy See argued that the Pope had a special obligation to speak out. When the Pope on one occasion remarked that he had to stay neutral between the belligerent nations, the British envoy Francis d'Arcy Osborne remarked, "Is there not a moral issue at stake, which does not admit of neutrality?"[50] The Vatican's Undersecretary of State Domenico Tardini secretly condoned this view, writing in his diary: "I could not but agree."[51] Tardini was hardly alone, and pressure inside the Vatican for a firmer stance also built up. Among the most vocal advocates was the Polish-born head of the Jesuit order, Wladimir Ledochowksi, who shortly before his death in December 1942 called on Pius to end his silence.[52]

Once Pius had delivered his remarks, the reactions were mixed. The Polish government-in-exile in London had wanted him to excommunicate German Catholics who participated in atrocities against civilians, and it was displeased.[53] Germany was also not happy, for the opposite reasons, and showed this by barring its diplomats from attending the Pope's Christmas liturgy.[54] Tittmann, the US diplomat, met with Pius shortly after the Christmas message and left with the impression that the Pope believed he had been able to make his case as clearly as possible. "Taken as a whole he thought his message should be welcomed by the American people and I agreed with [him]," Tittmann wrote in a dispatch to his superiors.[55]

CHAPTER 9

Blitzmas No More

Britain

The war had hit the royal family hard, throwing it into a permanent state of disarray and confusion, as it had virtually any other family in the United Kingdom and throughout the Commonwealth. Separation had become a sad fact of life. At the start of the hostilities, Princess Elizabeth and her younger sister Margaret had been moved to Windsor Castle, 20 miles from the center of London, whereas their parents, King George VI and Queen Elizabeth, had stayed on in the capital. The king was keenly aware that he was absent from a large part of his daughters' lives during some of their most formative years, and under the difficult circumstances, he seized any opportunity to spend brief, precious moments with them.[1]

One such opportunity was the annual Christmas play performed by the two princesses and other Windsor children every year since 1940, when, the king admitted, he had "wept through most of it."[2] Two years on, Princess Elizabeth, now 16, was taking her first steps into adulthood, pursuing grown-up royal pleasures such as the hunt. That autumn, she had killed her first stag near Balmoral Castle,[3] and during the Christmas holiday she visited a unit of the Grenadier Guards, where she was already a colonel.[4] Even so, when the annual Christmas play premiered, this time featuring the fairy tale of "Sleeping Beauty," she was a child again. Performing in front of an audience of 400, mostly Guardsmen and girls from the Auxiliary Territorial Service, the women's branch of the British Army, Elizabeth was a roaring success. "When she took the arms of the two 'sailors' and sang 'Mind Your Sisters,' she brought the house down," Lisa Sheridan, a photographer and frequent visitor to Windsor Castle, wrote in a letter to a friend.[5]

The American First Lady Eleanor Roosevelt visited Britain in late 1942 and was confirmed in her view of the king and queen as "simply a young and charming couple, who would have to undergo some very difficult experiences."

When she was put up at Buckingham Palace, she understood that the hardship of war was to some extent shared by the royals. The window in her room was boarded up after having been shattered by the shock wave of a German bomb, and due to fuel shortages she could only have a small fire in her sitting-room, as well as one in the outer waiting-room. "They hoped I would not be too cold," the American visitor noted.[6]

The royal hospitality extended beyond members of the US presidential family and other VIPs. Charles Badley, a captain with an American engineer regiment, experienced a special honor that few other servicemen shared. Along with another American and three British officers, he was invited for Christmas dinner with the 75-year-old Queen Mary, widow of George V who had passed away in 1936. Badley was received at the entrance by a doorman whose quiet dignity made him feel like "an unshod hillbilly in town for the very first time." Ushered into the room where the Queen Mother was receiving her guests, he found himself sitting next to her. Badley sent a letter home about the experience: "We spent some little time, Mother, talking of you," he wrote. "The Queen told me how she wished it were possible for you to have been there."[7]

The British–American brotherhood, strengthened by war against a common enemy, was one of the main points in the king's Royal Christmas Message, a tradition that had only been introduced a decade earlier, but that by now already had become a fixed part of Christmas for many Britons. The American alliance inserted a measure of optimism into the speech which had been lacking before. True, one year earlier, the United States had already been a formal member of the grand coalition arraigned against the forces of aggression, but it was in name only. Now, the application of American manpower and industrial might was beginning to pay dividends, from the tropical islands of the Pacific to the deserts of North Africa.

"This year," King George said in his broadcast, which aired at 3 pm sharp on Christmas Day, "it adds to our happiness that we are sharing it with so many of our comrades-in-arms from the United States of America. We welcome them in our homes, and their sojourn here will not only be a happy memory for us, but, I hope, a basis of enduring understanding between our two peoples." The king, who was speaking from a study in a country house while the queen and the two princesses were listening through loudspeakers in another room of the building,[8] recalled a story told by President Abraham Lincoln about a boy who was carrying a child up a hill and was asked by a bystander if the burden was not too much for him: "The boy answered,

'It's not a burden, it's my brother!' So let us welcome the future in a spirit of brotherhood, and thus make a world in which, please God, all may dwell together in justice and peace."[9]

The king spoke slowly and deliberately and without faltering for 12 minutes, carefully suppressing a stutter that had troubled him since boyhood. Touching on a topic of intense personal concern due to the daily separation from his daughters, the king turned to the ways in which the war had split families apart: "Our Christmas festival today must lack many of the happy, familiar features that it has had from our childhood. We miss the actual presence of some of those nearest and dearest, without whom our family gatherings cannot be complete. But though its outward observances may be limited, the message of Christmas remains eternal and unchanged. It is a message of thankfulness and of hope—of thankfulness to the Almighty for His great mercies, of hope for the return to this earth of peace and goodwill. In this spirit I wish all of you a happy Christmas."[10]

King George had spoken not just to Britain but to the entire Commonwealth, from New Zealand to South Africa and the West Indies, and his words had been translated simultaneously into French, Afrikaans and Hindustani.[11] Lionel George Logue, an Australian speech therapist who had successfully helped the king get his speech impediment under control and enabled him to address his people with confidence, was the first person to congratulate him.

"Splendid," he said.

"I think that's the best we've done, Logue," the king replied with a smile.[12]

The newspapers agreed. "The king's message put 'confidence' into Christmas," the *Sunday Dispatch* stated.[13] The king had done his job. He had fulfilled his function as a crucial element in the long, never-ceasing campaign to keep morale high, or rather prevent it from plummeting. It was something of an inner struggle for him since he was better informed than the vast majority of his subjects about the strategic situation. British and American soldiers were fighting in Africa. The Mediterranean was slowly being brought under Allied control. The battle of the Atlantic was going better. Still, victory remained a long way off. More death and suffering were to be endured by his people before they could entertain any hope of peace. He knew, but he could not say so in public. "Outwardly one has to be optimistic about the future in 1943, but inwardly I am depressed at the present prospect," he wrote in his diary in late December.[14]

* * *

General Alan Brooke, the chief of the Imperial General Staff, had hoped to get home early on December 24 to pass the holiday with his family, but a note from Winston Churchill abruptly thwarted these plans. The prime minister wanted to see him and James Grigg, the secretary of state for war, on an urgent matter. It was not unusual to draw on Brooke's expertise at any time, no matter how inconvenient. Churchill's famous ability for work rubbed off on his surroundings. That was the price for fighting a world war, including during Christmas.

It turned out that Churchill wanted to discuss the provision of additional six-pounder tanks to the 11th Armored Division in North Africa. "He was peevish and troublesome, but more or less satisfied by increasing troops by an additional 6 pdr tank," Brooke wrote in his diary. He was finally able to leave work, and his entry for Christmas Day, in all its content brevity, spoke volumes about a man who finally had the opportunity to take time off from a crushing workload: "Happily and peacefully spent at home."[15]

Just as the British nation was exhausted by Christmas 1942 after three years of war, its leaders were fatigued as well. "Tired," Foreign Secretary Anthony Eden wrote in his diary on Boxing Day, describing his dominant mood with a single word. "There is always a reaction after these long periods of work and strain, and the spring seems to uncoil more and more."[16] It was a cold day, and he spent part of it on walks, but was reluctantly forced to carry out long phone conversations for work. "I was not alone in feeling the physical and mental burden," he wrote in his memoirs. "As the months passed we were all to show it, even the Prime Minister, and sometimes we would express it in impatience or intolerance of each other."[17]

They were driven to do their utmost partly by the realization that this was more than a traditional European great-power conflict. The war had begun in defense of national interest, but as the hostilities had expanded and drawn in most of the continent, and the Third Reich had shown its true colors, it had become increasingly clear that the British and their Allies also fought for a higher principle. As reports of unspeakable atrocities seeped out from occupied Europe, Hitler emerged as an enemy unlike any other the British people had faced.

Shortly before Christmas, Eden read a statement in Parliament, criticizing the "barbarous Hitlerite tyranny" for its slaughter of Jews and had, to the cheers of the legislators, vowed that "those responsible for these crimes shall not escape retribution." Jimmy de Rothschild, a Jewish MP, pointed out, in a voice shaking with emotion, that many British Jews had only been in the country for a generation or so, arguing that "but for the grace of God they themselves might have been among the victims of Nazi tyranny at the present time." The entire parliament then stood up in silence in protest against the mass murder.[18] David Lloyd George, who had been prime minister during the latter part of World War I, was impressed by the unprecedented show of unity, defiance and resolve. "I cannot recall a scene like that in all my years in Parliament," he told Eden.[19]

Victor Gollancz, who was writing his pamphlet *Let My People Go* just as Eden delivered the statement, was unconvinced that it was sufficient to make a difference. The execution after the war of German criminals or their East European helpers would not save any lives now, he argued. "Will the death of these," he wrote, "reduce by one jot or tittle the agony of a Jewish child who perhaps at this very moment at which I write on Christmas day, three hours after the sweet childish carol, 'O come, all ye faithful,' was broadcast before the seven o'clock news, is going to her death in a sealed coach, her lungs poisoned with the unslaked lime with which the floor is strewn, and with the dead standing upright about her, because there is no room for them to fall?"[20]

Churchill shortly afterwards called for "two or three" heavy air raids to be carried out against Berlin, adding that "during the course of the raids, leaflets should be dropped warning the Germans that our attacks were reprisals for the persecution of the Poles and the Jews."[21] This suggested a victorious mood, but the sad fact was that given the depletion of its resources, having faced the Germans alone for so long after the fall of France, Britain could only do so much on its own without the backing of the Americans.

Churchill had pushed for a conference with President Franklin D. Roosevelt, and before Christmas he was still waiting for word from Roosevelt about where the two were to meet. The lack of certainty annoyed the British prime minister, as it made it difficult to make any plans. "I don't know whether I should stand on my head or sit on my tail," Churchill complained to his staff.[22] Soon after, the Americans lightened his mood by agreeing to a meeting in the city of Casablanca in northwest Africa in January, and that was not their only Christmas present.

The US Army had a special treat for Churchill. It had prepared a specially made 750-pound globe as a Christmas present for the prime minister. Captain B. W. Davenport, an aide to George C. Marshall, personally accompanied the globe, with a diameter of 50 inches, to Britain by plane. He used a private airplane, which was to travel via Greenland, but it was diverted by bad weather in Maine, and instead had to go via South America, St. Helena, Ghana and Gibraltar. On the last leg of the journey, approaching England, a German plane pursued and shot at the aircraft. Finally, on December 23, Davenport arrived in London, being given access straight to the prime minister's office at 10 Downing Street. An impatient Churchill was waiting. "Where the hell have you been, Davenport?" he asked.[23]

Churchill was not really vexed—the British–American brotherhood praised by the king in his speech was in evidence after all. It was a happier Churchill who spent Christmas at Chequers, a 16th-century mansion located 40 miles northwest of London. He took it easy and got up late on Christmas Day, his personal secretary reported home in a letter: "That morning he was in a grand temper and left us in peace most of the time and just sat up in bed reading a book and looking like a benevolent old cherub."[24]

* * *

When the war had lasted for little more than a year, back in December 1940, the British people had experienced a Christmas harassed by German bombs and had dubbed it "Blitzmas." Two years on, the German bombing offensive had been reduced significantly, and the total amount of bombs dropped over the nation during all of 1942, estimated at 6,500 tons, was no more than what had been expended by the *Luftwaffe* in the course of a single month during the winter of 1940 and 1941. Furthermore, half of the German fighter-bombers deployed in northern France for operations against the British Isles had been moved south to Provence in response to the Allied invasion in North Africa.[25]

The sign of growing enemy weakness in the air was duly noted by the Royal Air Force. Air Marshal Trafford Leigh-Mallory, the commander-in-chief of Fighter Command, sounded a victorious note: "On this fourth Christmas of the war Fighter Command, with its record of some 5,000 enemy aircraft destroyed, looks forward in confidence and strength to a new year of great import," he said in a special order of the day, issued to the men and women he led. "To each one of you I send Christmas greetings and wish you all the best of luck in 1943 and damnation to the Luftwaffe."[26]

Still, while it was no longer the overwhelming threat it had been during the Battle of Britain, the *Luftwaffe* remained a presence in the daily lives of the British population in December of 1942, and it retained its capacity for spreading terror on the ground. Vere Hodgson, a 41-year-old woman working for a charity in London, received a letter from her aunt, Margaret Hodgson, in the southeast of England, talking about terrifying raids. "A Nazi got in and machine-gunned a woman pegging out the clothes—and a baby in a pram may be killed," she wrote in her diary on December 20. "Bomb fell on a shop full of people on the South Coast the other afternoon. Horrible."[27]

Six Focke-Wulf Fw 190 fighter aircraft were observed over the southeastern coast of England on December 20, the British Air Ministry reported, claiming that half of them had been shot down.[28] Earlier in the month, German aircraft, acting alone or in pairs, had shot up an empty train in the southwest of England, killing the train driver, while also swooping down on a street full of shoppers in a town in the same part of the country, succeeding only in injuring one person, as the crowd quickly scattered and dived in the gutters for protection.[29]

Many could not bring themselves to believe that the horrors of the blitz were truly over, fearing that the German foe might be hiding something up his sleeve. "There are some who discuss the present lull in air raiding and say that the *Luftwaffe* will never attack again. They are bold men," an editorial writer opined in *The South Wales Gazette and Newport News*. "Let us hope they are right—but let us also be prepared for them to be proved wrong."[30]

Meanwhile, the Royal Air Force was bringing the war to German cities. "They sowed the wind, and now they are going to reap the whirlwind," Air Marshal Arthur Harris, the commander-in-chief of Bomber Command, had said. Commonly known as "Bomber Harris," he repeated that sentiment in his Christmas message to his men, at the same time revealing his driven nature. "Greetings at Christmas 1942. Another milestone of the sweep of the road to victory. There is further but not so far to travel. The gradient eases. From that we gain advantage not respite," he said. "With stout hearts and unswerving purpose go forward, assuming that the roused echoes of your unfaltering treads have struck chill to the very marrow of the King's enemies. Upon you depends in large measure—and you will not fail—whether the end of 1943 will bring but another milestone on the road or a real Christmas of peace and goodwill."[31]

Still, even for people as unrelenting as "Bomber Harris," Christmas was different. American airmen, newly arrived in Britain to take part in the strategic bombing offensive mean to bring Hitler's Reich to its knees, were surprised to find that something like a Christmas truce prevailed with the Germans. Two pilots of the US Army Air Forces landed at an airport near London on Christmas Eve, surprised to find it nearly deserted. "Don't you people know that even the Nazis celebrate Christmas?" said the only Royal Air Force officer present, himself getting ready to celebrate. "We have an armistice on Christmas. We don't bomb them and they don't bomb us."[32]

* * *

As the threat from the air receded, the Britons turned their attention to more prosaic concerns. Chief among these was food. For Vere Hodgson, the 41-year-old Londoner, the problem of stocking up for the upcoming holiday was significant enough that it merited detailed treatment in her diary entry for December 13: "Thought I was going to be clever and get some Chinese figs for Xmas. Waiting in shop for ten minutes only to be told: A sweet ration and a half! Ruefully left the shop. Don't know what they will manage to get at home. As long as we have Bread Sauce with an onion, I don't mind."[33]

Despite the challenge of sourcing scarce food items under the existing rationing regime, some managed to eat well during Christmas, especially in the countryside. Betty Armitage, a retired theatrical dresser and seamstress who lived in rural Norfolk and supplemented her income by cooking in the local pub, was keen to spoil the servicemen who were stationed in the area and had become frequent visitors. In her diary for Christmas 1942, she listed with pride the dishes laid out for "the boys" on two tables placed together: "We are having turkey and pheasant, sprouts, roast potatoes, artichokes, peas, carrots, bread sauce of course, followed by Christmas pudding and my Christmas pie."[34]

Britain had worked hard to reach a level where its population was not starving. A key part of its efforts went into resisting German attempts to bar overseas supplies from arriving at its ports. Shipments of food from the United States—condensed milk, dried egg, frozen meat and Spam—largely managed to make their way through the blockade instituted by the German U-boats. Indeed, even at the height of the U-boat campaign in 1942, only nine percent of the American cargoes were lost.[35] In addition, Britain had stepped up efforts to expand its own agricultural sector. While the country had imported almost all its wheat prior to the war, it had managed to turn pasture into farmland and was now producing half its own bread grain.[36]

More exotic items often associated with Christmas were scarcer. "Reminders of the grim background of war were the absence of bowls of oranges, nuts and grapes, or boxes of dates, almonds and other goodies," the *People* newspaper noted.[37] The *Western Times*, published in Devon, suggested the proper way to describe the holiday was "Austerity Christmas," where "we must cut the coat of enjoyment according to the strictly rationed cloth." It was, however, not all gloom, the paper argued: "The festival need not be less happy for that. True happiness, indeed, does not depend upon an overloaded stomach and an overflow of wine. Rather we shall find it in grateful hearts... At last we have not only reached, but passed, the bend in the lane of adversity."[38]

Official Britain was doing its best to keep morale high. "It will take more than Hitler to stop the British housewife from setting a festive table at Christmas time," the Ministry of Food said in an infomercial. "Yes, the food will be the same—rations, vegetables, grain foods—no Christmas specials; because ship-saving matters more than ever now we have gone over to the offensive. But by dressing up the old favourites, by using little tricks of flavouring, garnishing and serving we can still put up a festive show."[39]

The ministry provided recipes for "mock goose," which was all vegetarian, and "mock turkey," which was made from mutton. It also taught citizens how to make cinnamon toast, which, it said, could act as a substitute for cake, and was made in a simple procedure: "Take 1 tablespoonful margarine, 1 dessertspoonful of sugar, 1 teaspoonful of cinnamon. Cream all the ingredients together, spread on hot toast and grill for two minutes."[40]

A bigger concern for many families was the fates of relatives serving overseas, especially if they had been taken prisoner and were locked up in camps with few chances of communication. British soldier George Sweetman of the Royal Wiltshire Yeomanry had been taken prisoner in North Africa a few weeks prior to Christmas and now languished in a camp in Italy. The camp inmates had been given a limited number of Christmas cards that they could send home to their relatives. There were not enough to go around, and a lottery decided who was given the privilege. Sweetman got lucky and won the right to send a card home.

Apart from that, it was a bleak Christmas. The food was the same unexciting fare as usual, apart from an orange for each prisoner handed out by the Italian captors. The prisoners had hoped for a special Christmas parcel from the Red Cross, but it did not turn up. "A great disappointment," Sweetman wrote in his diary. "And so to bed hungry & that was how we spent Christmas Day 1942 in our P.O.W. camp. I thought of home, all the good food. That's all we think about hear [sic] is food."[41]

* * *

More languages were spoken more widely in Britain in December 1942 than at any other time in its previous history. It was the staging area for the great multinational effort to free Europe of Nazi tyranny. Poles, French, Czechs, Dutch, Belgians and others whose countries had come under the Nazi heel were preparing to take back their continent. Inevitably, there were tensions. At North Weald airbase northeast of London, a huge brawl developed internally among Norwegian air force personnel. Members of the Royal Norwegian Air Force Joint Command clashed with pilots and mechanics of two squadrons over a petty dispute, and 24 had to be hospitalized. No disciplinary action was taken afterwards.[42]

However, by far the biggest foreign presence on the British Isles in late 1942 was the Americans. One of them was Colonel Curtis LeMay, who spent Christmas with 305th Bomb Group on Chelveston Airfield in England. Unlike the American ground units in England, which were still training for the planned invasion of Europe, he and his men were already in the middle of things. The war was becoming more real and was hitting closer to home. He had lost two bombers during a raid on Saint-Nazaire in France a few weeks earlier, and he was hoping that the men had managed to bail out and were now in prison camp.

"It doesn't seem much like Christmas over here with no lights or decorations," he wrote to his wife Helen. "However, we did have a holiday today. [Hot food] and sleeping until noon was the best Christmas we have received. I opened the pipes today and smoked both, and they are both going to be good." The US crews at Chelveston threw a party for 200 British war orphans aged between four and 15, he told her. "We had some entertainment perform for them. They certainly had a tough time. They can sing 'Deep in the Heart of Texas' as good as any [Texan] when they learned the words."[43]

Leonard Larsen, an Army officer stationed in England, wrote to his wife just before Christmas 1942, "I'm feeling a little lonely right now. I can't help but think of you without feeling so. We haven't been getting much mail and there's no place to go. So it's pretty lonesome here. When you have no diversion, there's nothing else to do, and naturally your thoughts turn to home. Of course I'm always thinking of you hons, but more so at a time such as this."[44]

The local population often did its best to mitigate the homesickness of the young soldiers. At the pub in rural England where Betty Armitage worked, a large Christmas tree had been placed in the corner. "When the fire is lit in the grate it all looks very homely," she wrote in her diary. "What we all need at Christmas and especially those who are away from their loved ones."[45] In 1942, over 500,000 free cards were distributed throughout the United Kingdom. Each had a photograph of American soldiers listening to the London Choir School in front of St. Mark's Church and was inscribed with the message "Christmas Greetings from Somewhere in Britain." If they were mailed from a military camp to somewhere in the United States, postage was not necessary.[46]

The Anglo-American Relations Committee noted that for Christmas 1942 the offers of hospitality by the British had been four or five times greater than the number of Americans to be entertained.[47] According to British censor reports for Christmas 1942, many letters expressed "utmost gratitude to the British, both organizations and private people for the way they have tried to recompense U.S. soldiers on being away from home, especially at Christmas time."[48]

The Americans were encouraged to fill "the chairs left empty by British fighting men," and entertained the locals with their own seasonal traditions while learning about the British ones. "They taught us about Advent calendars and Advent candles and hanging gingerbread biscuits on the Christmas tree—but we showed them Christmas crackers, which they'd never seen before," a former American airman recollected later.[49] A group of children, who were about the age where they had stopped believing in Santa Claus, were invited to an American base and met a Father Christmas with an American accent. "We were more confused than ever," one of them said later.[50]

CHAPTER 10

Weihnachtsberg

North Africa and the Atlantic

Most American and British soldiers had expected North Africa to be hot and dry, but during Christmas 1942, it was cold and humid. The rain was pouring down over the infantrymen shivering in their foxholes on Longstop Hill, on the road to Tunis. In front of them, across no-man's-land, were members of Germany's famed and feared Afrika Korps, who had waged a highly successful desert campaign for nearly two years and now, with their backs to the Mediterranean, were clearly determined to make the Allies pay dearly for every inch of African soil.

Artillery Major Edward A. Raymond of the US Army had been in Africa for six weeks since landing on the continent's northwestern edge in early November as part of Operation *Torch*, the first American invasion of Axis-controlled territory. Progress since then had been anything but smooth, and the mood was predictably bad. "Christmas was still another rainy day. Almost everything had bogged down, and the Catholic chaplain greeted members of the battalion staff with 'Muddy Christmas'," he wrote. "The staff ate genuine turkey dinner, sitting in an open shed in a barnyard with a full set of accompanying sounds and odors, reveling in their luxury."[1]

Longstop Hill was actually a series of ridges, two miles in length and rising to a height of 800 feet,[2] most of it covered in knee-high rosemary and coarse heather.[3] From the top of the hills, the Medjez plain could be viewed all the way to Tunis. It was a strategic point on the road to victory in North Africa.[4] The British Army's Coldstream Guards were in bivouac in the area after seizing most of the hill from German troops who had fought with only small arms but made up for their lack of heavy weaponry with death-defying fanaticism and in the end had held on to their positions equipped with only bayonets.[5]

Many of the Coldstream Guards had not seen action since Dunkirk in 1940, and Lance Sergeant Derrick Jackson knew they could use encouragement. Despite the rain, he moved around his section wishing the soldiers a happy Christmas and received mostly sarcastic replies: "My thoughts went back to home where my family would be welcoming Christmas Day. Here I was on a hillside seven hundred feet up in the Tunisian mountains with one tin of sardines and a bottle of rainwater. However, I still had my life, which was more than the rain-washed bodies had which lay out in front of us."[6] It was not an uplifting thought, but Jackson believed there might be a Christmas truce like in 1914. "It turned out the opposite," he noted tersely.[7]

The Coldstream Guards had pulled back from Longstop Hill, handing over their positions to 1st Battalion, 18th US Infantry. The Germans counterattacked on December 23, determined to regain Longstop Hill, and succeeded in pushing back the American units from most of the hill area. "The fighting was sullen and bitter," according to a post-war account by a US officer. "Pouring rain added to the misery of trying to dig in on rocky ground under heavy mortar and machine gun fire."[8] Most of the mortar rounds came from a ridge that formed part of the Longstop Hill area but had not been recognized due to flawed Allied reconnaissance, and therefore had never slipped out of German hands.[9] "Our people learned fast, though in almost every case they learned the hard way by getting hurt first," the American military officer commented.[10]

The US forces on Longstop Hill warned that unless they received reinforcements, Longstop Hill might be lost altogether. No other units were available than the Coldstream Guards who had just pulled out of the area and were now ordered back up onto the ridges they had fought bitterly to take only hours before. The seesaw battle culminated on Christmas Eve, when British and German troops wrestled desperately over the ridgeline that had been missed by Allied scouts. In the meantime, field hospitals just behind the frontline were filling up. "We were so busy with the flood of wounded that we did not realize it was Christmas," a medical officer wrote later.[11]

At dawn on Christmas Day the Germans launched their final, decisive strike against the remaining British troops on Longstop Hill. The Coldstream Guards saw themselves nearly surrounded and decided to pull back. The victorious Germans promptly named the hill *Weihnachtsberg*, "Christmas Mountain." Meanwhile, the mauled Allies counted their casualties. The Americans had lost 356 killed, injured and missing. The British reported 178.[12] After the battle for Longstop Hill, platoons voted on whether to keep Christmas presents sent to those killed in the battle or return them unopened.[13]

The British and American troops were to have taken Longstop Hill quickly as a preliminary to a much larger offensive aimed at Tunis. Now the whole enterprise was in jeopardy, not just because of the Germans but also due to the atrocious weather. General Dwight D. Eisenhower, commander of Allied forces in Northwest Africa, toured the frontline during Christmas and witnessed an incident that drove home to him the obstacles posed by the incessant downpour. A little off the main road, four men were struggling to extricate a motorcycle from the mud. The harder they tried, the more the motorcycle was bogged down into the sticky clay. Perhaps more than anything else, this convinced him that the ongoing offensive was hopeless. "We went back to headquarters and I directed that the attack be indefinitely postponed," he wrote in his memoirs. "It was a bitter decision."[14]

* * *

Eisenhower would later publish his recollections about the war against Germany under the title *Crusade in Europe*, and there was indeed an almost religious undertone to the American campaign in North Africa. *The New York Times* described how the area had been a battleground for competing faiths throughout history, arguing that the ongoing struggle was also a clash of incompatible worldviews. "For the real threat North Africa has had to wait until Hitler's Africa Corps arrived in Libya to establish the new religion of Valhalla slaughters and racial hates."[15]

Many Americans exhibited a zealous attitude to the conduct of war that allowed for no relaxation during Christmas. "How can there be a Christmas party?" a ranking American officer asked. "We might be fighting on Christmas."[16] Others allowed a more laid-back demeanor. American fliers at a desert outpost in the Libyan province of Tripolitania had fashioned a bar from the wing of a downed Messerschmitt 109 fighter plane. It was decorated with holly and real flowers, and an artistic member of the unit had created life-sized crayon drawings of shapely American girls.[17]

Men of the Reconnaissance Company, 13th Armored Regiment, on the frontline near the ancient town of Teboursouk, were delighted to receive Christmas presents from home, brought to them personally by the regimental commander Brigadier General Paul McDonald Robinett, even if many of the gifts proved of limited use. A red bathrobe and a pair of house slippers triggered roars of laughter. But here as elsewhere around the world, Christmas was mostly about food. "Some of the outfits managed to collect pigs or chickens to add to the C-ration which had become our steady diet," Robinett wrote. "But there was not turkey, duck, goose, cranberry sauce, or mince pie for anyone." Corporal Donald E. Steele of the US Army's 27th Armored Field Artillery Battalion wrote a sarcastic verse:

'Twas the night before Christmas in Africa's plain,
The men were drenched in deep drizzling rain.
Tomorrow our folks will eat turkey and duck,
We'll probably have C-ration down by the truck
...
So bring on the turkey, bring on the duck,
We'll sit here and cuss, confound the luck![18]

As elsewhere, the Americans befriended the local children. The military newspaper *Stars and Stripes* reported that men of the 12th Air Force held a party in the city of Algiers for a group of orphans, featuring a Santa Claus and a 16-foot Christmas tree as well as magicians, acrobats, and a choir of 20 soldiers. They "dished out 150,000 francs, plus candy, soap and gum rations to 200 orphans of four faiths—Protestant, Catholic, Jewish and Moslem," according to the paper.[19]

Others befriended the local girls. Hollis Stabler, an Omaha Indian serving in a US Army Ranger battalion, got caught in a German air raid while waiting on the railway station in the Allied-held city of Casablanca on December 24. He sought refuge in a tunnel with a buddy of his, and while waiting for the bombing to be over, they talked to two Arab girls. They followed them and were taken to a restaurant. "Those girls danced for us. We spent the night there and then went back to the railroad station," he said.[20]

At the other end of the American Army hierarchy, General George S. Patton, who had led the Western Task Force during the landing in Northwest Africa the month before and was prone to periods of depression, was particularly gloomy during Christmas. Earlier that month, his chief rival, Mark Clark, had been promoted over his head to command the entire Fifth Army, whereas he himself remained in command of a corps.[21] "I had expected this but it was a shock," Patton wrote in his diary then. "I felt so awful that I could not sleep for a while but I shall pass them yet."[22]

His diary at the end of December reflected his somber mood: "Woke up with terrible sore throat. Went shooting saw nothing came home & went to bed," he wrote one day, followed the next by an even briefer entry: "Stayed in bed all day."[23] His diary suggested Christmas came and went without any special celebration, except perhaps for one act of kindness after church on

Christmas Day, once again betraying the American kindness to children: "Gave candy to a little half French girl and boy."[24]

* * *

General Mark Clark, Patton's nemesis, was getting ready to leave his office early in Algiers, hoping to attend a Christmas Eve dinner, when Robert D. Murphy, President Roosevelt's top diplomatic envoy in the region, came rushing in. "They've shot the Little Fellow," he said. Clark knew immediately who he was referring to. The "Little Fellow" was French Admiral Francois Darlan, a major thorn in the Allied side during the North African campaign.[25] Darlan had been the chief representative of the collaborationist government of France in North Africa, and the western Allies had considered it necessary to reach an understanding with him when they invaded, as he alone could order the French forces in the region to cease resistance to the disembarking armies.

Still, it was not a very palatable choice. Churchill had been forced to defend it vigorously in front of a hostile parliament. "In war, it is not always possible to have everything go exactly as one likes," he had told a secret session in early December.[26] Now the problem had been solved, by an assassin's bullets fired at pointblank range into Darlan's face and torso at the entrance of the admiral's office at Palais d'Été, also in Algiers. "He's on the way to hospital," Murphy said. "Let's go," Clark replied, heading out for a car. When they arrived at the hospital, Darlan had already been pronounced dead. Clark noticed he looked calm and quiet, wondering if death might be a relief to the French admiral, who had been in a devilishly difficult situation since the Allied invasion one and a half months earlier.[27]

The idea to coopt Darlan was very much a product of American diplomacy, and upon learning about the shots fired at Darlan, General George C. Marshall, the US Army chief of staff, wrote a quick message, believing the admiral was still alive: "I am grieved and shocked by the news of the assault on you. You are rendering a service of vast importance to our armed forces and I pray that your injuries are not serious and that you will soon be able to resume your vital share in the great task of destroying the power of the Axis in Africa in the first great step to free France."[28] By the time the message reached North Africa, Darlan had already been long dead. Churchill was probably more honest in his post-war assessment: "Darlan's death, however criminal, relieved the Allies of their embarrassment of working with him."[29]

Darlan's death had cleared up a muddled political situation, and even though they had suffered a military setback at Longstop Hill, the Allies knew they were on the road to victory in Africa, and that the Axis stronghold of Tunis would fall soon. A clear sign that the Allies were coming were their regular air raids against the city. On Christmas Eve, the Allied planes flew in again, and the civilians sought shelter where they could. Among them were a French family of four, two middle-aged parents and their teenage children, huddling in their own basement. That night they were joined by 14 others, and it was Christmas. They had to celebrate.

The mother of the family had saved food items over the preceding weeks despite strict rations, and she had enough for a traditional French Christmas dinner. The Christmas tree was a broomstick with branches from an orange tree tied to it. In between the sound of exploding bombs, the family sang Christmas carols. Suddenly the father of the family got up and walked to the furthest end of the basement. When he returned, he held two bottles of St. Emilion red wine in his hands. He had kept them out of sight, hiding them from the German occupation force, which might have punished him severely for not handing them over. "To him it was worth it," his daughter said. "The Germans had already taken his country, they were also not going to take his St. Emilion!"[30]

An injured Allied soldier being treated at a German hospital in Tunis told General Hans-Jürgen von Arnim, the newly appointed commander of the Fifth Panzer Army, not to bother to send him to a prisoner camp in Italy, since the American and British forces would take the city by Christmas. "I do not think that your people will arrive that quickly," the German officer replied.[31] German Propaganda Minister Joseph Goebbels was following events from afar, with great interest and with a similar level of confidence. Shortly before Christmas, an orderly from the headquarters of Field Marshal Erwin Rommel, the commander of the Afrika Korps, visited him. "I pack his entire plane with Christmas presents for the Marshal and his immediate collaborators," Goebbels wrote in his diary.[32] He was gloating at the fact that the British forces seemed to have stalled: "The English soldiers must celebrate Christmas in the desert. It must be tough and embarrassing for them, since they had been promised that they would be in [the Libyan port city of] Tripoli by Christmas."[33]

The Mareth Line in southern Tunisia was key in securing a continued foothold for the Afrika Korps on the continent. The German defenders had been involved in heavy fighting with British and French troops in the days before Christmas, but on Christmas Eve, the fighting stopped completely. No shot was heard, and no explosion. It was if the warring parties had agreed tacitly to keep the peace. Could it be repetition of the famous truce of 1914 that most had heard about but so far not seen copied in the new war?

Just before midnight, the old carol *"Stille Nacht"* could be heard from scattered places all along the German line, and within minutes the singing was joined all along the front. Shortly afterwards, the song *"Minuit, chrétiens, c'est l'heure solennelle"* was heard from the French lines, and finally from the British trenches, hundreds of voices sang "Silent Night." Nico Ossemann, a young soldier in the Afrika Korps, was unable to fall asleep that night, even though the frontline was more peaceful than at any time in recent days. He was too overcome with emotion. "So many of these men were unable to hold back their tears," he wrote long after the war, stating it was as if "fate joined the soldiers of enemy nations."[34]

A different kind of communication with the German enemy revealed itself to Don Whitehead, a reporter for the Associated Press, as he toured a recently conquered town during Christmas and was exposed to a defiant foe, arrogant even in defeat. On the walls of pock-marked walls, he saw caricatures of Churchill, Stalin and Roosevelt, and graffiti saying, "We'll see you again at Alamein," "We'll be back," and "He laughs best who laughs last, Englishman!"[35]

* * *

Shortly before Christmas, General Bernard Law Montgomery, the commander of the legendary Eighth Army, received a letter from an anonymous English woman. "Dear Sir," it read, "to wish you and our lads of the Eighth Army a very happy Christmas. Good health. Good luck. And by the Grace of God Victory in 1943. Keep 'em on the run, Monty. Best wishes from a Yorkshire lass with a lad in the Eighth Army." Upon reading the letter, "Monty" was so delighted that he shared it with all the men under his command.[36]

The Eighth Army had advanced 1,200 miles since its victory over the Afrika Korps not even two months earlier, and Montgomery had decided to give his tired soldiers a Christmas break before the final push against Tripoli and the expulsion of the Germans and Italians from North Africa. "No offensive operations would take place until after Christmas, and we would all spend that day in the happiest way that conditions in the desert allowed," Montgomery wrote in his memoirs. "It was very cold. Turkeys, plum puddings, beer, were all ordered up from Egypt and the staff concentrated on ensuring that it all arrived in time: and it did."[37]

There was immense pride in the Eighth Army at the achievements during the last months of 1942, but also a slightly concerning feeling among the rank and file that once Tripoli had been reached, the job had been done. That was not the case, and while toasts were being drunk at a sergeant's mess, an old sergeant-major stood up and calmly explained that the end of hostilities in Africa would only conclude one chapter. "A long struggle lies ahead," he said, "when we have cleared the Axis Powers from Africa we shall have to carry the war into Europe, and finally into Germany. Only when we have defeated Germany in Europe, will we be able to return to our families honourable men."[38]

* * *

A long struggle was ahead for millions of men around the globe, including 20-year-old Norwegian sailor Ole Johan Næss, who found himself in Scotland in December 1942. Shortly before Christmas he was ordered to join the 41-member crew of the 3,978-ton steam merchant *Ingerfem*, which was due to leave Loch Ewe in Scotland for the east Canadian port city of Halifax. Næss had just completed a short training course at the Norwegian Navy's gunnery school at Dumbarton, and he had hoped for something a little more glamorous. "I wasn't particularly happy about that order. I knew it was an old ship built before World War I, and I didn't exactly expect any luxury on board," he said.[39]

Næss had been only 17 years old when Germany had invaded Norway in April 1940. He had been a cabin boy on board a Norwegian ship en route to Bermuda and had avoided coming under the Nazi yoke. Similar to thousands of other Norwegian sailors, he had opted to continue sailing in the service of Free Norway. With a fleet of about 1,000 vessels and 30,000 sailors, their contribution over the next two years had been vital to the Allied war effort.[40] "Norwegian tankers," the parliamentary secretary to the minister of transport Philip Noel-Baker had said in April 1942, "are to the battle of the Atlantic what the Spitfires were to the Battle of Britain."[41]

The *Ingerfem* departed on Christmas Eve, joining convoy ON 156. The ageing vessel soon encountered engine trouble, and eventually it was forced to drop out of the convoy. Three days into the journey, it was spotted by two British aircraft in the middle of the North Atlantic. They signaled that they would return with instructions as to whether the *Ingerfem* should continue on its route towards Canada or return to Scotland to have its engine repaired. This was the last contact the ship had with any friendly forces.[42]

While waiting for instructions, it was detected shortly before midnight by the German U-Boat *U-631* commanded by Oberleutnant Jürgen Krüger, who ordered a torpedo to be sent against its hull. Næss was below deck at the time of the impact. "I was sleeping and hadn't felt anything unusual when suddenly one of the gunners rushed into the cabin, shouting that we had been torpedoed," he said.[43] Næss jumped out of his hammock and rushed up the stairs, emerging onto the chaos on deck. Two lifeboats were lowered into the water, and he hastily climbed into one of them. The captain and two crew members attempted to launch a third lifeboat from the bridge, but within seconds the hull broke into two and sank, taking the men with them into the frothing ocean. The men on Næss' lifeboat shone lights into the ocean, hoping to find survivors, but quickly had to turn them off again as crew of the surfaced U-boat directed small-arms fire at them.

The sea was choppy, and the two remaining lifeboats soon lost sight of each other. "It was bitterly cold, and we were wet and shivering from the cold. I had a lighter and a few cigarettes, and we shared them among us," Næss said. The next days turned out to be a struggle against the elements, as high waves threatened to sweep them overboard and caused the lifeboat to capsize twice. A brief glimmer of hope flashed through their dulled brains one day when an aircraft, possibly friendly, appeared over the horizon. Even though they were weakened from thirst and hunger, they jumped to their feet, waving a yellow flag like mad. They felt it like a death sentence when the plane turned away and disappeared in the distance.

One by one, the men succumbed to thirst and exposure. In the end, only Næss was left, and he was on the point of losing his mind. Driven desperate by the abject feeling of loneliness, he tried to drown himself by plunging his face into a pool of seawater in the bottom of the boat and drifted in and out of hallucination-filled sleep. Finally, after 12 days at sea, he was observed by an American fruit carrier 500 nautical miles west of Scotland. At that time, his fingers were frozen so stiff he was almost unable to grab the rope ladder that was rolled down to him. There was no sign of the other lifeboat. He was the sole survivor.

* * *

On Christmas Eve, the cold killed yet another crew member of the cargo ship SS *Chulmleigh*. The 58 men had run aground in early November on South Cape, part of the Svalbard archipelago. They had managed to get to safety on land and found shelter amid the vast, featureless expanse in a hut left empty by hunters. They had tried to stay alive with their meager provisions, but one after another had succumbed to the elements. The ship's captain Daniel M. Williams knew that waiting for rescue would likely be deadly. "I therefore decided to make a final attempt to get help, or die in the effort," he said later.[44]

Williams set out with two other men to seek help in a settlement known to be in the area. However, the strong, chilly wind forced the three to turn around and walk back to the hut. Now all hope seemed gone. Out of the *Chulmleigh's* original complement of 58, only nine remained alive. All that was left was to lie down and wait to die. Then the miracle happened. Two hunters passed the hut and quickly arranged an evacuation of the shipwrecked crew. Sleighs arrived from the settlement, and the survivors were brought to safety. "Our clothes were soaked with pus from gangrenous limbs and gave off a horrible stench," Williams recalled later.[45]

The ocean was a watery desert, and the few islands scattered across the North Atlantic were oases where those lucky enough to chance upon them could get a lease of life. It was an inhospitable part of the world, but it was a place where men of both warring sides needed to be. There was no getting around it. It was the scene of the feared but vital Murmansk run, allowing British and American planners to ship supplies to the Soviet ally. During the last months of 1942, it became even more fraught with risk. Due partly to the need for warships for the effort in North Africa, convoys had been abandoned in October, and instead individual ships were dispatched on dangerous voyages to the north, taking advantage of the long polar nights. It was a procedure with the potential for massive loss of life, as *Chulmleigh's* story showed.[46]

Now, however, the convoys had resumed. On Christmas Eve, at the exact time when Williams decided to go looking for help, convoy JW 51A, consisting of 15 ships and a fleet oiler, and protected by an escort of seven destroyers and five smaller ships, arrived in waters near Murmansk. It had covered the entire route without being detected by the German enemy, who operated from bases along the rugged Norwegian coastline, but had to literally grope in the dark as the sun barely appeared above the horizon.[47]

The next convoy was already on the way. On Christmas Day, the 14-ship JW 51B met off Iceland with its escort of six destroyers and five smaller ships and embarked on its perilous route northeast. This time, the German Navy was lying in wait. A force of two heavy cruisers and six destroyers sought an encounter with the convoy, but in the perennial twilight that reigned when the two sides met on the last day of the year, only confused fighting ensued. All 14 transport ships made it to Russia.[48]

Admiral Erich Raeder, the commander-in-chief of the German Navy, described how the news was received at home: "Hitler thereupon flew in an uncontrolled rage, unjustifiably claiming that information had deliberately been withheld from him," Raeder wrote in his memoirs.[49] The *Führer* recorded in the war diary that heavy ships were "utterly useless," and ordered them laid up immediately. Raeder protested the rash reaction, inevitably triggering a clash with Hitler. The end result, several weeks later, was that Raeder had to resign.[50]

* * *

Admiral Karl Dönitz, the commander of the German U-boats and soon-to-be successor of Raeder, was not the sentimental type who made a big fuss out of Christmas, but he was in a good mood this December. Things were going his way, he thought. Yet, the Battle of the Atlantic, one of the most crucial theaters of the entire war, was still hanging in the balance. There was no clear winner, not yet. Germany was far from beaten. Nine new U-boats entered into service in December 1942, with the result that by the end of the month, 164 were operative in the Atlantic Ocean alone.[51]

On the other hand, the German losses were not negligible, and they were growing. In the period from July to December 1942, nearly nine percent of all U-boats had been lost at sea, up from less than four percent in the first six months of the year. Furthermore, each time a U-boat went to the bottom of the ocean, there was a high likelihood that it took all of its highly trained crew with it. Still the numbers were better than they had been in both 1940 and 1941, Dönitz argued. "In the second half of 1942, the battle for the convoys were waged with shifting luck, but still with reasonable success overall," he wrote after the war.[52]

Given what was at stake, intensive espionage efforts were carried out to win an edge in the Atlantic. During Christmas, German U-Boat *U-505* was in the French port of Lorient for repairs. Late at night, one of the crew members, Hans Goebeler, was guarding the vessel armed with a submachine gun, when a man dressed in an officer's uniform sought to embark. Goebeler stopped him, and even though the officer tried to pull rank, superiors were called to the scene. It turned out to be an enemy agent. "The spy was led away to what, I presume, was a very unpleasant fate," Goebeler wrote later, with a remarkable lack of pity.[53]

The biggest gains, however, were linked to efforts in the field of signal intelligence. Unbeknownst to Dönitz, a development was taking place in Britain in December which ultimately had a decisive impact on the course of the war. In early 1942, the German Navy had suddenly thrown British military intelligence into the dark by adding another level of complexity to the Enigma encoding machines it used to encrypt its communications, and for months German U-boats could operate in relative secrecy.

British codebreakers had worked frantically to solve the problem, and by December they were once again able to read the German messages. Partly, they were able to achieve a breakthrough due to the dense, centralized radio communication reflecting Dönitz's firm belief that Enigma was secure. This Allied advantage would last until the end of the war. Thus, with the involuntary assistance of Dönitz himself, communication between him and his U-boats had become an open book to the Allies.[54]

Command of the ocean was essential not just to carry vital supplies to the British Isles, but also in order to send the troops who were eventually to launch the invasion of Europe. Key in this endeavor were the ocean liners *Queen Mary* and *Queen Elizabeth*, and despite the constant threat from German surface vessels and especially U-boats, it was an endeavor that was paying off. In the course of the second half of 1942, a total of 194,850 American troops were carried across the North Atlantic to Britain.[55]

Joseph Schott, the 19-year-old sailor on board the troop transport SS *Westernland*, who had heard "White Christmas" for the first time while preparing to cross the Atlantic, had left New York shortly before Christmas. "After that, we were on our way to open ocean to join a huge convoy for the trans-Atlantic voyage to Scotland."[56] It was Convoy HX 219 bound for Liverpool. "Christmas Day we still had four more days to go to get to Scotland, and they had a mass outdoors on the deck. It was snowing."[57]

* * *

The Atlantic was enormous, and while Schott was passing Christmas in a chilly snowstorm, down near the Equator, Danish sailor Niels Ole Kiil was spending the holiday between two missions in Freetown, a British-controlled colonial city in West Africa, where the sandy beaches were a bright white in the stark sunshine, and the local markets were crammed with colorful fishes and tropical fruits he had never heard about before. "There was no 'White Christmas.' Christmas Eve passed in the local tradition with loud revelry in the streets," he wrote in his memoirs. "Christmas Day was celebrated in a more appropriate manner. We were served Christmas dinner and sang Christmas carols, accompanied by cute nurses from the military hospital."[58]

The waters off Africa were now seeing only scattered activity. Towards the end of 1942, Dönitz increasingly focused his efforts on the northern Atlantic. Allied convoys that passed through the southern part of the ocean on their way to Africa or the Mediterranean were left alone, as fuel shortages made it uneconomical to send German U-boats so far away. The day before Christmas the German Navy decided to end all operations against convoys headed for Northwest Africa.[59]

U-Boat *U-181*, which had been on a long combat patrol in the Indian Ocean and passed around the Cape of Good Hope in mid-December, celebrated Christmas between Ascension and St. Helena. The crew prepared a Christmas tree made from wire and toilet paper dyed green. "Merry Christmas to everyone at home from the South Atlantic," the *U-181*'s commander Wolfgang Lüth radioed to Dönitz's headquarters. "We are celebrating in tropical heat with accordion and tree at a depth of thirty meters."[60]

The crew of Italian submarine *Enrico Tazzoli* marked Christmas off Brazil. It had been on a patrol since mid-November and had sunk three Allied freighters, most recently the British-owned *Queen City*, which had been sent to the bottom of the ocean on December 21. The Italian crew, too, fashioned a makeshift tree from wire, decorated with figures cut out of wood and cardboard. The illusion was not perfect, and a crew member hung a sign on it, saying "I am the Christmas tree."[61]

Three of the participants in the Christmas party were not Italian. One, a boy named Jim, was a survivor from the *Queen City*; also present were the captain and first engineer of the Dutch vessel SS *Ombilin* sunk in the middle of the month. The Dutch captain asked for permission to speak. Speaking in English, he thanked them for letting them attend, praising the ceremony's simplicity and solemnity, in sharp contrast to "the fiery atmosphere of the senseless hatred that is shaking all the peoples of the world." He concluded by saying a prayer to the Almighty, asking for the "damn war" to end soon. Then he stepped back, blushing, hiding behind the massive bulk of his engineer, who was noisily blowing his nose.[62]

CHAPTER II

A Happier Christmas

Americas

Shortly before Christmas 1942, Thomas and Aletta Sullivan of Waterloo, Ohio, received letters from their five sons. The brothers were serving together in the US Navy, aboard the same ship, the light cruiser USS *Juneau*. The letters were dated November 8 and had been mailed just before their ship had departed with its crew of 673 officers and men from New Caledonia for the ongoing campaign in waters near Guadalcanal. The letters were the last that the Sullivans would ever receive from their sons. They did not know it yet, but by the time they opened the thin envelopes, all five had already been dead for more than a month.[1]

The first inkling that everything was not right came a few days after Christmas. A neighbor received a letter from her son, who was also in the Navy: "Isn't it too bad about the Sullivan boys? I heard that their ship was sunk," he wrote. The neighbor alerted Aletta Sullivan, who was numb with worry. "When I went to bed that night I could hardly sleep. When I did fall asleep, I had terrible dreams in which my boys were in danger. I wanted to help them and couldn't. In my nightmare I could even hear their voices calling 'Mother'," she wrote some months later.[2] It would be yet more days before the Sullivans received the terrible news that they had lost all five sons.

The five sons had died in mid-November. On November 13, the *Juneau* was hit by a torpedo fired from Japanese submarine *I-26*. The ship's magazine ignited, causing a huge explosion, and it had disappeared below the surface of the water within 20 seconds.[3] Four of the brothers, Francis, Joseph, Madison and Abel, died immediately in the blast.[4] The last brother alive, George, made it a few days on a lifeboat, but he was injured and starting to fall apart mentally. One day he took off all his clothes and said he wanted to go for a swim. Before anyone could stop him, he jumped in. "A shark came and grabbed him and that was the end of him. I never saw him again," said one of the only 10 crew members who survived, out of an original complement of nearly 700.[5]

The Sullivan family's loss was uniquely tragic. The Navy had been aware of the risk associated with having close family serving together, and in this case it had only been made possible because the brothers had petitioned the government not to be divided among different ships. Still, it highlighted a fear that millions of Americans had in common. The dreaded visit by a grim-faced military officer with information that a son, father or brother had given his life for the nation was the ultimate nightmare, and the concern was heightened during Christmas, when families normally got together.

It was a source of particular anxiety that no news was not always good news. Information from the theaters of war could be painfully slow, due to censorship concerns and bureaucratic red tape, and it could be weeks before relatives received the message that a family member had been harmed. Two long months passed before the Sullivans received final confirmation that all five sons were dead. Until then, it was not even widely known that the *Juneau* had been sunk, owing to a deliberate attempt by US military authorities to keep the Japanese in the dark.

Strictly speaking, December 1942 was America's second Christmas at war, but during the previous holiday, held amid the shock and uncertainty brought about by the recent attack of Pearl Harbor, the war that was carried out beyond the borders had still felt unreal and distant. Now almost every American family was enmeshed in the global conflict. It was hard to find someone who did not have relatives serving overseas or training in camps throughout the continental United States, awaiting deployment abroad.

Women, too, were serving in growing numbers. The Women's Army Auxiliary Corps had trained 12,000 members by late 1942, with ambitious plans to boost that number to more than a million. In her Christmas message to her staff, the corps' director Oveta Culp Hobby anticipated much work in the coming months and years. "May God bless you and give you strength for the task ahead," she said.[6] It would require toil and also sacrifice, and in a reminder of the risks involved, the corps lost its first member at Christmas 1942. Eleanor Campbell Nate was killed while on leave, when her husband, who was a major in the Army, crashed their plane over the Gulf of Mexico.[7]

It was a telltale sign of longing for family members away in uniform that the overseas mail service exploded towards the end of 1942. In the October and November Christmas mailing period, Americans sent 50 million letters and greeting cards, as well as 2.5 million packages.[8] Often they dwelled on everyday subjects, as if to pretend that these were still ordinary times where little things mattered. In a letter that Saidee R. Leach of Edgewood, Rhode Island wrote to her son, Navy Ensign Douglas Leach, in December 1942, when he was serving in the Central Pacific, she focused on the small inconveniences of life on the home front. "Dad could not start the car this morning [...] so after two busses had passed us because of being loaded to capacity, we managed to get to work. My shop is so cold that I have put on a furlined overcoat," she wrote, and then concluded with what might have been her most important message and what the entire letter was really about: "We all hope that you have a very pleasant and unusual Christmas and you know that you will be in our thoughts many, many times during the day."[9]

Likewise, Helen Larsen of upstate New York told her husband Leonard Larsen, stationed in England, about preparations for Christmas at home, including the Christmas tree: "It really looks beautiful with all the decorations around it and all." Then she went on to explain how much she missed her husband: "I'm very lonesome for you. I guess its cause it's getting so near to the holidays." She continued: "Gee I wish you could have helped me sweets. I sure miss you. This is the first year in forever that we won't be together... I don't feel much like Christmas honey. I wish it would come and go in a hurry."[10]

* * *

President Franklin D. Roosevelt spent the last days before Christmas at his estate in Hyde Park, New York. He slept late, and often signed documents in bed, partly due to his secret disability, brought about by a midlife attack of polio, which caused him to use a wheelchair. Unlike the previous Christmas, the international situation left him in an excellent mood, and he was particularly satisfied to see the German Army bled dry in the Russian snow. "Stalin is pursuing a policy of attrition," he told his staff, "the same as I am doing in the Southwest Pacific. He is destroying German tanks and matériel faster than they can be replaced."[11]

The last two evenings at Hyde Park were devoted to parties for the soldiers who guarded the president, as well as staff on his estate, Springwood. "A grand party it turned out to be," the president's secretary William D. Hassett wrote in his diary. "The President [...] received all comers. There was a gaily decorated Christmas tree, around which the crowd gathered for the singing of carols which started the party."[12] The following night, Roosevelt again invited off-duty soldiers, who sat in a circle around him while he told stories about his time as assistant secretary of the Navy in the previous war. "It was a successful party," Hassett commented.[13]

While at Hyde Park, Roosevelt received a letter from General Marshall informing him that he would get the same Christmas present as Churchill.

"The battles now in progress make a most important introduction to the New Year because I am confident that they foreshadow great victories," the general wrote. "That you may be better able to follow the course of these battles we wish to install a special globe in your office, the duplicate of which is being delivered to 10 Downing Street."[14] Roosevelt arrived in the White House to find the 750-pound globe and was delighted. "I am made very happy [...] by the special Globe which I have set up in my office directly behind my chair," he wrote in a letter to Marshall. "I can swing around and figure distances to my great satisfaction. The newspaper men were much interested in it at the conference yesterday."[15]

Well in advance of the holiday, Roosevelt had prepared his Christmas message to be broadcast to the American people in the evening of December 24. It struck a more upbeat note than a year earlier, but the president could not afford to encourage complacency at a time when final victory was still far in the future. "I cannot say 'Merry Christmas'—for I think constantly of those thousands of soldiers and sailors who are in actual combat throughout the world," he said, "but I can express to you my thought that this is a happier Christmas than last year in the sense that the forces of darkness stand against us with less confidence in the success of their evil ways." As one of the leaders of a global coalition he also understood the need to reach out to other nations: "In sending Christmas Greetings to the Armed Forces and merchant sailors of the United Nations we include therein our pride in their bravery on the fighting fronts and on all the seas."

America's First Lady Eleanor Roosevelt struck a similar note in her syndicated column "My Day," which appeared in newspapers across the nation. "How completely the character of Christmas has changed this year. I could no more say to you: 'A Merry Christmas' without feeling a catch in my throat than I could fly to the moon!" She knew what she was talking about after having spent part of the holiday at the Walter Reed Hospital in Washington, D.C. visiting soldiers who had been so gravely injured in Africa that their treatment required evacuation back across the Atlantic.

She continued, "We all know that for too many people this will be anything but a Merry Christmas. It can, however, be a Christmas Season of deep meaning to us all." She said the example of Jesus Christ and his willingness to pay the supreme sacrifice had added significance in the extraordinary times America was going through. "Many of the young people today are doing their jobs in the present world crisis with exactly the same hope in their hearts, and it is this spirit of divine sacrifice and love for your fellow human beings which gives to the Christmas Season its real spiritual significance."[16]

The ongoing slaughter of Jews and other people considered racially inferior by the Nazis did not merit a mention in most public declarations by American politicians and other opinion makers, but the subject did not escape public attention altogether. Dorothy Thompson, a prominent journalist who had been expelled from Germany as early as 1934 due to her critical reporting, took the initiative to release a "Christmas Declaration by men and women of German ancestry." The signatories denounced "the Hitler policy of cold-blooded extermination of the Jews of Europe," raising their voices against "the barbarities committed by the Nazis against all other innocent peoples under their sway."[17]

The declaration, which carried the names of 50 well-known German-Americans, including baseball legend Babe Ruth, warned the citizens of Germany that they were being made complicit in the crimes of the Nazis, resulting in a sinister bond between people and regime amid universal hatred of the Third Reich: "Hitler is creating a deep loathing of all things German in the heart of mankind." It stated that the hour had struck for the German people to rise against its rulers. "We call on them to overthrow a regime which is the infamy of German history," the declaration said.[18]

* * *

In Fitchburg, a Massachusetts city of about 40,000 inhabitants, this was a war Christmas like no other it had experienced. "Christmas will come to a new Fitchburg this year, a city geared smoothly and almost totally to the great war effort of the nation," said the *Fitchburg Sentinel*. "A city short of fuel, short of many essential foods, plagued by transportation problems and concerned for the welfare of 2,500 of her sons and daughters on the many fronts around the world, but a city cheerful, a city dedicated without reserve to the winning of the war."[19]

Residents working in the city's war industries could look forward to three days off from work, their first vacation in a year, but supplies were scarce, and the means to celebrate a proper Christmas were lacking. Beef and butter were hard to get, and many families would have to forgo the traditional turkey. "Others will find that coffee must be eliminated from the holiday menu and lack of sugar may bring unusual desserts to the Christmas board," the reporter wrote.[20] The challenge of celebrating Christmas with a minimum of sugar was universal. In Council Grove, a town of 2,800 in Kansas, the readers of the *Council Grove Republican* were urged to serve cheese and fresh fruit or use syrup and honey as substitute sweeteners.[21]

Paradoxically, given shortages and rationing of certain product categories necessitated by the war, consumption was in general more free-wheeling across the United States in December 1942 than it had been at any time during the recession-ravaged decade of the 1930s. "Santa Claus Is No War Casualty," the *Los Angeles Times* proclaimed in an editorial and explained how the total industrial payroll of all of California had reached 1.35 billion dollars annually, twice the amount of a year earlier, as up to a quarter million more Californians had found jobs.[22] War was good for the economy. People had more money to spend, but just as importantly, consumption was a patriotic statement. The *Charleston Daily Mail* asked rhetorically if Christmas should be celebrated in wartime, and answered the question itself: "The answer, we think, is yes—as never before. It is the symbol of what we are fighting for."[23]

Of all products on sale for the American public, children's toys were among the categories most affected by the war. "From now on because so many of the things that go into toy-making are needed for war, the glamour of today is going to be replaced by the simplicity of yesterday in little Johnnie's toy," argued Robert H. McCready, publisher of *Playthings*, the toy manufacturers' magazine. "There will be plenty of toys for Christmas 1942, but there will be far fewer of the items made with steel—such as mechanical toys, tool chests, boats—and rubber products like balls… There will be more games made of wood and cardboard, wooden wagons, and even perhaps wooden velocipedes, such as grandpa used to navigate the country lanes."[24]

Some mothers were concerned that the ongoing war had an unhealthy impact on their children's play. In an article titled "Shall I Let My Child Play with War Toys?" the magazine *Women's Home Companion* pointed out that "children naturally carry out through play the activities they see and hear about," arguing that "in this war play children are probably working off vague and undefined worries."[25] A similar concern was triggered by the frequent appearance in advertisement of Santa Claus in a military outfit. An opinion piece in the periodical *Printer's Ink* warned in jest that it would not be long "before the aroused and indignant parents of the nation, seeing that the business won't clean up its own abuses, will call for government control of Santa Claus."[26]

It was inevitable that the war would become a major theme in Christmas celebrations that year, and one of the primary ways in which it became part of the holiday was in drives to urge citizens to buy war bonds as gifts. A single page in mid-December 1942 in the *Cushing Daily Citizen*, published in Cushing, Oklahoma, reflected the support this campaign received from corporate America. Local businesses such as Hall's Transfer & Storage, Abercrombie's Farm Supplies, Neva's Sandwich Shop, Cushing Refining & Gasoline, and Hinds Shore Store all urged their customers to buy war bonds, many of them adding that their own staff would spend 10 percent of their payroll on the purpose. "I help save the very lives of American boys, fighting in distant lands. For I am the means of translating America's desperate need for war materials into actual guns, planes, and tanks," First National Bank's branch in Cushing said in its advert. "I am the gift that will mean safety, and security, and freedom to celebrate all our future Christmases."[27]

* * *

Other residents of the United States had completely different concerns that Christmas. Matsushita Hanaye, a 44-year-old Japanese-born Christian woman now living in Seattle, spent Christmas in tears. She had been inseparable from her six-year-older husband Iwao since they had both immigrated to the United States from Japan in 1919, but after the attack on Pearl Harbor he had been interned as part of the general drive to round up Japanese along the US west coast, and one year on, he languished at Fort Missoula, a camp deep in Montana's countryside.

When Hanaye saw happy families gathering for the holiday in Seattle, she felt a lump in her throat. "I imagine you spent a lonely Christmas too," she wrote to her husband. "This year's was more sad and lonely than last year's or any I've had."[28] Iwao tried to comfort his wife in his letters, describing how his camp was covered in a deep layer of snow, making it look "as pretty as a Christmas card."[29] He, too, however could not hide his sadness: "I'm awfully sorry that you already had to spend two lonely Christmases," he wrote in a letter, adding: "I know that the Lord will answer our prayers one day and the sun will also shine."[30]

Iwao sent her a package for Christmas. It contained a heart-shaped stone which Iwao had picked up from Missoula River and had polished with great effort, carving an H before sending it to his wife. "If you could let it rest on your Bible as I did, it'll surely make the stone happy. Our hearts are like this stone... without blame," he wrote. "Let us pray that the war will end soon and 'Peace on earth and blessings to mankind' will again prevail..."[31]

At Minidoka War Relocation Center in Idaho, thousands of Japanese-American internees passed Christmas, quietly meditating on how different this Christmas was from the ones they had experienced in the past. In the camp newspaper, *The Minidoka Irrigator*, one of the internees, Sally Nakamoto, wrote a wistful poem:

> Christmas, 1941, meant tables groaning with good things
> And tummy aches were nothing new
> That's Christmas, '41.

> But Christmas, 1942, tho' lacking in so many ways
> Will still be quite a pleasant day
> Of that I am assured.[32]

At the same time, the internees made a visible effort to signal that the Japanese empire was the common enemy of all, Americans and others alike. Fukuyama Tsutomu, a minister for the young, lamented in the same paper a Christmas marked by the "hollow mockery of diabolical warfare," describing the misery of "the evacuees from Burma in India, Chinese refugees of a memorable trek to West China," and expressing sadness over "loved ones who have been killed by brother men in jungles of Bataan."[33] Others were eager to emphasize their patriotism: "Here behind barbed wires on top of sage brush cleared soil, we are about to celebrate our Christmas in an atmosphere none too familiar to us; but in an atmosphere where the Yuletide spirit will not go unprecedented. Christmas in an American relocation center... the American way," a writer commented in the same paper.[34]

It was not all harmonious. At the Manzanar Camp at the foot of the Sierra Nevada mountains in California, violence had broken out only a few weeks earlier. On December 7, the first anniversary of the attack on Pearl Harbor, a riot had erupted due to internal tensions among the inmates, and an explosive situation had developed when military police called to the scene confronted the protesting Japanese-Americans. "Some fellows were thumbing their noses at the soldiers," an eyewitness said. "I saw several of them go right up to the M.P., then turn around, point at their own rear ends in derisive fashion and dare the M.P. to shoot." In the end, the military police had fired into the crowd, killing one and injuring 10, one of whom died later of his wounds.[35]

Many camp internees, however, experienced a reconciliatory attitude from their neighbors. Ichihashi Yamato wrote to an acquaintance from Tule Lake Relocation Center in eastern California: "We are fast approaching the Christmas and New Year. One of our neighbors brought us a small xmas tree, and I fixed it with a few ornaments which I made myself, as I could not buy any here this year. Still another neighbor gave us Point-cetters [poinsettias] in a pot, artificial ones, of course, I put them in an appropriate corner. Therefore even our one-room tenement appears rather cheery and bright now. Yesterday morning another woman gave us an English holly and some other evergreens... I am sure we will have a turkey dinner for Christmas and special rice cakes [a traditional Japanese New Year food] for New Year's Day."[36]

'Twas the Season

Christmas 1942 in memory and imagination

In a letter sent to her son just before Christmas 1942, the Rhode Islander Saidee Leach joked about "Bing Crosby boop-a-dooping for a 'White Christmas'," and then hastily added, realizing that the musical sensation might not yet have reached the Central Pacific, where he was serving: "Have you heard that latest song of his from *Holiday Inn*?"[1] By Christmas 1943, American letter writers no longer would have to ask this kind of question. Even though a new seasonally themed Crosby tune had hit the airwaves in the form of "I'll Be Home for Christmas," his sentimental ballad from the year before had already achieved the status of a classic. "White Christmas" had become part of a common frame of reference, and it could be safely assumed that everyone knew about it.

Irving Berlin, the song's creator, did not intend it to be associated with war. "What is a war song?" he asked *Variety* just after Christmas 1942. "Some songs are popular during war and others aren't. Goodness knows 'White Christmas' isn't a war song by the farthest stretch of the imagination, but boys in the Solomons and boys in Africa are singing it. So—it's a war song."[2] More specifically, "White Christmas" became the quintessential song about Christmas at war. Bing Crosby, whose mellow voice played an essential part in its popularity, made that link explicit when starring in the 1954 eponymous movie, playing a GI performing in front of a crowd of weary and dirty soldiers in a wintry and bombed-out landscape somewhere in Europe on Christmas Eve 1944.

Perhaps the song owed at least part of its popularity to the specific time when it started crawling up the charts. It was a time when, after a year marked mostly by defeats, things finally started looking up for the Americans and their Allies. US forces were winning their first campaign on Guadalcanal, and together with British and French comrades-in-arms, they were in the process of pushing Axis forces out of the African continent. In Russia, an entire German Army was facing annihilation. Along came "White Christmas" with its gentle promise of what was waiting ahead, after victory.

William M. Reddig, an editor with the *Kansas City Times*, looked into the future with uncanny prescience, when on the first day of 1943 he imagined a television show as it would be beamed into American living rooms on a random night in 1953. Bing Crosby would be in it, and he would be picking some of his past hits to entertain his audience. One was sure to be among them: "White Christmas," even though his fans might have forgotten "what 'A White Christmas' meant to American boys in Guadalcanal and North Africa and to their folks back home in 1942… Many of them may not realize how much it was associated with the great events of World War II in the fall and winter of 1942, when the Americans took the offensive."[3]

Still, "White Christmas" was not a victory hymn. Its basic mood was melancholy. It was a reminder of what had been lost, and a meditation on what might have been if there had been no war. Fundamentally, it was, without ever even hinting at it in its lyrics, an elegy on the terrible loss brought about by human conflict.

Singing the song on the war loan radio program *Let's Talk Turkey to Japan* in November 1944, Bing Crosby explained what it meant to him and his millions of fans: "On a holiday like this, is when our men overseas have to swallow the biggest lumps, thinking of the cozy, quiet warmth of home on a holiday. They asked to hear 'White Christmas.' I hesitated, it made them sad. Heaven knows making them sad wasn't my job, but every time I tried to slack it they'd holler for it. Sometimes we all got a little dewy-eyed."[4]

His nephew Howard Crosby confirmed the sadness that was also part of the story of "White Christmas" during World War II. "I once asked Uncle Bing about the most difficult thing he ever had to do during his entertainment career," he told a reporter. "He didn't have to think about it. He said in December, 1944, he was in a… show with Bob Hope and the Andrews Sisters. They did an outdoor show in northern France… At the end of the show, he had to stand there and sing 'White Christmas' with 100,000 GIs in tears without breaking down himself. Of course, a lot of those boys were killed in the Battle of the Bulge a few days later."[5]

* * *

There is a special poignancy to Howard Crosby's story. None of the thousands of soldiers who watched his uncle's performance could know that this would be their last Christmas, but surely many of them must have asked themselves if this was the case. That was the uniquely heart-breaking thing about Christmases at war. Like birthdays, they were occasions to both look back and look ahead, considering the change that the past year had brought, and contemplating the change that might lie in the future. But given the special circumstances, this implied contemplating if one would even be alive one year on.

Thoughts of this nature must have occupied the soldiers marking Christmas in 1942. The Germans observing the holiday in the freezing trenches in Stalingrad knew full well that they were in a terrible position, but not many of them would have guessed that only weeks into the future, the entire Sixth Army would capitulate, and its soldiers would march into years of captivity. Even fewer would have believed it if they had been told that among them, only a tiny handful would survive. Out of 91,000 taken prisoner, a mere 5,000 would return home.

The British and American troops fighting the Axis around the globe faced better odds, although they could of course not know it. The battle of Buna was over in late January 1943, and the last Japanese troops were evacuated from Guadalcanal in early February. In North Africa, the Allies were in for more hardship at the hands of the skillful German enemy, but in late spring Tunisia was in their hands, and the Axis presence south of the Mediterranean was history.

None of them could have known this in December 1942. The fundamental uncertainty about the future made the emotional burden that Christmas almost unbearable, especially when it was compounded with longing for loved ones. Being separated from one's wife, one's parents or one's children, was an experience shared by soldiers everywhere. Many of the soldiers were just out of adolescence and had grown up in an innocent age where it was not unusual to reach the late teens without having been in a relationship. As British military historian John Keegan has pointed out in his history of the Normandy campaign, fond memories of favorite sisters occurred with surprising frequency in the thoughts of the soldiers.[6] It may have been longing for siblings that was at work when young men during Christmas 1942 paid special attention to children and adolescents who emerged, seemingly out of nowhere: the girl singing in Hawaii, the child's voice in Burma, the "angel" in Poland.

The psychological stress brought about by danger and separation was often countered with alcohol. Drunkenness, to the extent that it was at all possible, appears to have been a big part of Christmas for men at or near the front, although it was only incompletely recorded in the sources. The American

Marines celebrating Christmas on the northeastern shores of New Zealand and the Danish SS volunteers marking the holiday in their trenches south of Leningrad had little in common, fighting on opposing sides in the vast conflict, but they both did what young men often do when they get together. They drank, to lift the mood and to forget.

With the help of drinking or without it, humans have a both profound and disturbing ability to get used to new things, soon accepting that unusual conditions are now the new normal. War is the most extreme example of this. Only rarely do participants in conflict stop and wonder what they are actually doing. Christmas is one of those rare occasions. This is so partly because it confronts them with the essential message of peace and brotherly love, which is of course mostly a concern to the religious individuals, but also because it reminds them of home and of the life they left behind.

People were prepared to go to great lengths to recreate life as they had known it prior to the war. There was even a willingness to take considerable risks, as the middle-aged French civilian in Tunis showed, hiding two bottles of St. Emilion despite the threat of German reprisals. Special attention was paid to the children, except in the Nazi concentration and extermination camps. Makeshift Christmas trees were prepared, and striking inventiveness was mobilized in order to give children presents, even in prison camps.

For many who lived through December 1942, it was the most terrifying Christmas of their lives, but it was also the one that stuck in memory when all the other Christmases had been long forgotten. Lithuanian-American Eleonora Carneckis spent Christmas Eve in a Siberian camp above the Arctic circle "in terror, hunger, cold, polar night, with dying [...] on all sides," yet remembered this Christmas as "the most unforgettable, memorable and meaningful of all."

It was a unique Christmas, because the conditions were uniquely awful, but it encompassed something else which was not entirely terrible but had some kind of value not found in peacetime. Often it was a specific aspect of Christmas 1942 that made people remember. Julian J. Gates, held at a camp near Osaka, got a simple Christmas meal spiced up with a few extra ingredients carefully saved for the occasion, and was sure that even if he lived to be 100, he would never forget that dinner.

It is testimony to a general insight expressed by many who have been in wars: war is pain, suffering and loss, but war is also something else. As a World War II veteran said of his experience seven decades after the conflict, "I wouldn't have traded that for anything in the world although I wouldn't do it again for anything, either."[7] It is a sentiment voiced by many veterans, not just of World War II but of any war. Participating in war, possibly the most intense experience available to humankind, provides a new perspective on life and death, but at a price paid in blood.

* * *

Christmas Eve 1942 was completely dark and quiet in waters off Iceland. Hardly a ripple could be seen. The convoy was scattered across the surface of the ocean, as the shadows of the crews walked around on deck speaking to each other in muffled voices. The danger of German U-boats was imminent and ever-present, and the slightest noise was to be avoided. Suddenly familiar notes were ringing through the chilly air with crystal clarity: "Silent night, holy night." The skipper of a Norwegian freighter had hooked a gramophone to the ship's loudspeaker. Ships nearby signaled frantically for the music to stop, but the signal was ignored.

In the middle of this chaos, signal lights flared briefly over the horizon. A cluster of German U-boats, which had been observing the convoy from a distance, proposed a 12-hour Christmas truce. The Allied ships agreed, and the U-boats approached, as their crews emerged from below. For the next hours, young men from opposing nations—Canadians, Britons, Norwegians and Germans—put the war on hold to mark Christmas. A Canadian sailor later described the unreal feeling of seeing the Germans standing on the decks of their U-boats, singing carols in their native language. "I swear you could see the whites of their eyes," he said. Early on Christmas Day, 12 hours after the truce had been agreed on, the German U-boats disappeared into the darkness again. Shortly afterwards, one of them sent a torpedo against an Allied ship. The men who had been celebrating Christmas together were now back at it, killing each other. The war had started again.[8]

The 1942 Christmas truce in the northern Atlantic is a remarkable story, and according to naval historians, it never happened.[9] It is based on the testimony of one sailor made 60 years later, and there is otherwise no record of it taking place. Besides, quite apart from the fact that a truce would have breached all standing orders on both sides, it is hard to see how it could possibly have taken place, given the ferocity with which the war was being waged in the Atlantic, often marked by German U-boat crews machinegunning survivors from shipwrecks while they were floating helpless in the water.

A similar story from Christmas 1942 is from the opposite end of the earth, in the steaming jungles of New Guinea. A group of starving Japanese infantrymen were sitting in their pillbox, smelling the food that the Americans were preparing only a few yards away. One of the Japanese, who spoke passable

English, rose and said, "I've had it." He undressed until he was wearing only his loincloth, in order to show that he was unarmed, and then moved towards the American lines.

A long time passed. The Japanese who had stayed behind in the pillbox only heard muffled talk and occasional burst of laughter from the American positions and they started being seriously concerned about what had happened. Finally, their comrade returned, carrying a large load of food. "We were having a good time eating and drinking, whether we were enemies or not," he told the other soldiers, who were staring in disbelief. "I got something for you guys, too, so share this around," he said.[10]

In a battlefield where cannibalism was in evidence, and prisoners of the Japanese were rumored to be used as live targets in bayonet practice, while American infantrymen rarely gave any quarter when rooting out pockets of resistance, the story also does not ring true. The question is how these accounts emerged and were told by veterans who seemed to believe their own words. The most likely explanation in both cases is that the veterans had heard tall stories from their comrades, and in the course of decades, as memories became more blurred, they started inserting themselves into the accounts.

It is also likely that the stories were influenced by what happened both before and after in history. The Japanese veteran's tale may have been molded by knowledge of how the American–Japanese friendship evolved after 1945 to the extent that a few years after the war, the idea of young men from the two nations sharing a Christmas dinner together was no longer fanciful.

While the Japanese veteran looked ahead in time, the Canadian sailor more likely was looking back, to the famed Christmas truce of 1914, to find inspiration for his narrative. Nothing like the Christmas truce happened in 1942, at least not to the same extent as in 1914. World War II was in many ways more relentless than World War I. Even though cameras were much less widespread from 1914 to 1918, photos of soldiers comforting and treating captured and often injured enemies seem more numerous from that conflict. During the global conflagration of the early 1940s national differences were exacerbated by ideological and racial hatreds, and it is much more common to see snapshots of soldiers treating captured men from the other side with contempt and disgust, if not cruelty.

The editorial writer in the camp newspaper of Changi prison, Singapore, expressed the notion eloquently: "Never in the history of the last 2,000 years has the spirit of Christmas been so lacking among the nations of the earth. In olden days the soldiers of opposing armies could forget their enmity at Christmastide and join in merry-making to celebrate the birth of the Prince of Peace. Only a quarter of a century ago, British and Germans, true to the traditions of Christendom and their common heritage, laid aside their weapons for a few hours on this day to fraternise in No-man's-land. To-day, we may be sure, no considerations of this sort will prevent the bomber from taking off with its deadly load. There can be no truce, even for a moment, when there is no trust; in losing their faith in God the nations have lost faith in one another. And yet never before have so many people in the world longed for peace."[11]

In this new war, Christmas ended up, in some cases at least, having almost the opposite meaning to what it had had in 1914. It was used by the Germans as proof of being uniquely civilized. Importantly, it was in their view a mark of *German* civilization, not Western civilization in a broader sense. The idea of Christmas as being common to all people was anathema to the Nazis, who mobilized the holiday and its traditions for an effort to underline the peculiarity of German culture and, of course, its inherent superiority. This was apparent in the stern opposition to German nuns teaching their students to sing "Silent Night" in English, and in the insistence of the SS on referring to the holiday as *Jul*, the word used in Old Norse and living on in modern Scandinavian languages, in reference to its pre-Christian roots.

* * *

The German view was a reflection of the unforgiving nature of the war, but it was extreme, after all. The Nazi insistence on the national specifics of Christmas traditions collided with the more widely held belief that Christmas stood for something entirely different. It was a holiday that brought people together across political and cultural boundaries, even in a time of war. In this, Germany was "on the wrong side of history," to use a modern expression. The very fact that Christmas was celebrated in similar fashion throughout much of the world in 1942 suggested a post-war era in which mankind would in some ways be more unified than ever before.

People at the time were busy achieving victory, and to the extent that they were even thinking about what the world would look like after peace had been restored, they could necessarily only have hazy notions. However, there were tantalizing hints already in 1942 about the world to come. GIs brought their version of Christmas to children as far apart as India and England, and they were worshipped for it by the young generations. It was a first signal of the powerful pull of American culture, which, along with the military and economic clout of the United States, would contribute to making Pax Americana the dominant theme of the second half of the 20th century.

When one looks at photos of American soldiers from the war years, it is hard to convince oneself that they are actually 80 years old. They look so modern, with their baseball caps and aviator sunglasses and broad white smiles. This could be because the Americans won the war, of course in conjunction with their allies, and more importantly won the peace, and as a result a big part of the world subsequently became Americanized in its cultural tastes and habits. By the same token, Christmas was to a significant extent to be celebrated the American way, from Manchester to Manila, from Cologne to Kyoto. Many foreigners, especially in old Europe, bemoaned this state of affairs, but the fact is that the American way of life would not have been so successful if it was not so attractive to a large number of people. The world became American because it wanted to, and when we look at look at those 80-year-old photos, we are in a way actually looking at ourselves. That is why the GIs of three generations ago seem so modern.

The end of the war coincided with an era of globalization that to a great extent happened on American terms. The example of Hawaii, the place where World War II began for the Americans, is instructive as it demonstrates how this trend came about and what facilitated it. About a million soldiers, sailors and war workers spent time in Hawaii during World War II, and many who could afford it returned as tourists after 1945.[12] Tourism was helped by improved infrastructure and enhanced means of transport, much of it the derived effects of the technological breakthroughs prompted by global conflict. Prior to the war, it took a Boeing 314 up to 20 hours to carry no more than 25 passengers from San Francisco to Honolulu. By 1959, a Boeing 707 could transport 150 passengers across the same distance in four and a half hours.[13]

The frequent travel to Hawaii in the years after 1945, making Waikiki Beach and Diamond Head as familiar to many Americans as Mount Rushmore and the Golden Gate Bridge, is a striking example of how the world had shrunk. To be sure, the tourism boom is just one aspect of globalization, along with for example trade and communication, but it is a significant indicator of how a globalized outlook became normal for ordinary people. It is one thing to consume an imported food product or read a translated book. It is quite another thing to travel abroad yourself and immerse yourself in a foreign culture. A mental barrier has to be broken. It was broken by the millions of young men and women who were forced overseas during the war. Both then and after the war, they were cultural ambassadors, bringing their own habits and practices, including their ways of celebrating Christmas, to other peoples. This fostered growing cross-border understanding and made globalization possible.

Now, however, globalization as we know it may be coming to an end. Or at least the globalization that began with World War II may have run its course. The future may see a more compartmentalized form of globalization, divided into at least two parts: an American-dominated one in the west, and another with China setting the tone in the east. True globalization, encompassing the whole world, may be a thing of the past. At the very least, the US-led global world order that underpinned globalization for nearly eight decades after 1945 is unlikely to be sustained for long as new centers of political and economic power arise, the mighty Chinese dragon the most prominent of them. Perhaps Chinese New Year will be the new Christmas, and then again, maybe not.

* * *

All that was still unknowable future back in December 1942. Realizing that the future would be radically different, but not being privy to much else and thus unable to prepare, would seem to be a recipe for despair. Still, it was counterbalanced by a sense of hope which permeated much of what was said and written that Christmas.

Eleanor Roosevelt expressed this hope when she wrote her column "My Day" on December 28, 1942, describing a family wedding in Fairfax, Virginia. "When you see young people today trusting to the future enough to start a new life together, it not only fills you with admiration for their courage, but you cannot escape a certain emotional tension which is apparent in the general feeling which runs through the guests at almost any wedding today."[14]

Those who lived through that Christmas seemed often to sense that they were standing at the dawn of a new age. On December 24, the young Nebraskan newspaper editor Ray McConnell Jr. wrote an essay to his 13-day-old son, trying to fathom what kind of world he would live to see as a grown man. "The birth of the Messiah will not likely mean the same thing in 1970 as we understand it to mean today; anymore than today it conveys to us what it did to the shepherds in the time of Augustus Caesar."[15] He was speaking in religious terms that may seem alien to some modern readers, and familiar to others, but the essence of his message was clear. History was in the process of turning a decisive corner. Life would never be the same. It was terrifying, but it was also exciting.

It was understood that this new age would be built on the sacrifice of those who continued to give their lives in the ongoing conflict. One of them was 29-year-old Major Patrick Hore-Ruthven, who died on Christmas Eve 1942 in an Italian field hospital in the Libyan city of Misurata. Four days before, the major, who was the only son of Australian Governor-General Alexander Hore-Ruthven, had taken part in a paratroop commando raid that had resulted in a fierce firefight, and severely injured he had ordered his men to abandon him in the field, allowing himself to fall into enemy hands.[16]

Hore-Ruthven, a Cambridge graduate, was also an aspiring poet who in one of his last poems, "The Young Men," had described the strange attraction of war—that unique and sometimes intoxicating experience of bursting bombs, streaming blood, and screaming bullets which no outsider would ever completely understand—while also acknowledging the terrible cost that it exacted:

> For this we were ordained. Love's beauties lie
> Along strange ways that we at last shall roam
> True to our laughing gods, we young men die.[17]

Post-1942 fates of individuals appearing in the text

Abels, Jacques. Survived the war.

Adam, Wilhelm. Captured with Sixth Army in early 1943. Died in 1978.

Alcaraz, Ramon A. Died in 2009.

Aldebert, Bernard. Died in 1974.

Alexander, Irvin. Survived the war.

Armitage, Betty. Survived the war.

Arnim, Hans-Jürgen von. Died in 1962.

Aumeier, Hans. Executed in Poland in 1948.

Baarova, Lida. Died in 2000.

Badley, Charles. Survived the war.

Bailey, Stanley William. Survived the war.

Barr, Ruth. Interned with her family in a Japanese-run camp at Shanghai in spring 1943 and liberated at the end of the war.

Beach, Edward. Survived the war.

Beebe, Lewis. Remained a prisoner of the Japanese in camps in Taiwan, Japan and Manchuria until he was liberated in August 1945. Died in 1951.

Belov, Nikolai. Killed in action in Germany in May 1945.

Berlin, Irving. Died in 1989.

Bilek, Tony. Survived the war.

Blamey, Thomas. Died in 1951.

Blancaflor, Louise Fillmore. Survived the war.

Bohnhoeffer, Dietrich. Arrested in April 1943 and hanged in April 1945.

Bolszakow, Wasyl. Executed in January 1943.

Bormann, Martin. Killed in Berlin in May 1945.

Bose, Subhas Chandra. Killed in plane crash in August 1945.

Bosenberg, Carl. Survived the war.

Böttcher, Herbert. Executed in Poland in 1950.

Bratteli, Trygve. Died in 1984.

Braun, Felicja. Survived the war.

Bronson, Joseph C. Survived the war.

Brooke, Alan. Died in 1963.

Brydon, Donald. Survived the war.

Brynski, Antoni. Survived the war.

Carneckis, Eleonora. Survived the war.

Carter, Emmett N. Left Russell Island in January 1943 after the end of his team's mission. He survived the war.

Chaudhuri, Nirad. Died in 1999.

Chennault, Claire. Died in 1958.

Chiang Kai-shek. Died in 1975.

Chunn, Calvin Ellsworth. Survived the war.

Churchill, Winston S. Died in 1965.

Ciano, Galeazzo. Executed by Fascist government in January 1944.

Clark, Mark. Died in 1984.

Clarke, Burnett. Died in 1974.

Clements, Olen W. Survived the war.

Cohen, Elie. Survived the war.

Coldiron, Johnny. Survived the war.

Cordingly, Eric. Died in 1976.

Crosby, Bing. Died in 1977.

Cukierman, Hersz. Escaped from Sobibor during the uprising in October 1943 and survived the war.

Curtin, John. Died in July 1945.

Dai Li. Died in 1946.

Davenport, B. W. Survived the war.

Daye, Pierre. Survived the war and fled to Argentina. Died in 1960.

Deschamps, Henri. Died in 1968.

Dedman, J. J. Died in 1973.

Dönitz, Karl. Died in 1981.

Dorn, Frank. Died in 1981.

Durlacher, Gerhard. Died in 1996.

Eden, Anthony. Died in 1977.

Edmundson, James V. Survived the war.

Eichelberger, Robert L. Died in 1961.

Eisenhower, Dwight D. Died in 1969.

Elizabeth, Queen Mother. Died in 2002.

Elrod, Roy H. Survived the war.

Emmons, Delos. Died in 1965.

Epstein, Karl. Survived the war.

Feigl, Peter. Survived the war.

Feinberg, Kai. Died in 1995.

Fergusson, Charles. Died in 2004.

Fiebig, Martin. Executed in Yugoslavia in October 1947.

Finnegan, Joseph. Died in 1980.

Frank, Hans. Executed in 1946.

Fraser, Peter. Died in 1950.

Fukuyama Tsutomu. Died in 1988.

Fünten, Ferdinand Hugo aus der. Released from Dutch prison in 1989, shortly before his death.

Gates, Julian J. Died in 2001.

Gehring, Frederic. Survived the war.

Gemmeker, Albert Konrad. Released from Dutch prison in 1951. Died in West Germany in 1982.

George VI. Died in 1952.

Glatstein, Cyna. Survived the war hiding among gentiles and later emigrated to the United States.

Glowa, Stanislaw. Survived the war.

Goebeler, Hans. Survived the war.

Goebbels, Hedwig. Killed by her parents in Berlin on May 1, 1945.

Goebbels, Heidrun. Killed by her parents in Berlin on May 1, 1945.

Goebbels, Helga. Killed by her parents in Berlin on May 1, 1945.

Goebbels, Helmut. Killed by his parents in Berlin on May 1, 1945.

Goebbels, Hildegard. Killed by her parents in Berlin on May 1, 1945.

Goebbels, Holdine. Killed by her parents in Berlin on May 1, 1945.

Goebbels, Joseph. Committed suicide in Berlin on May 1, 1945.

Goebbels, Magda. Killed by her husband in Berlin on May 1, 1945.

Gollancz, Victor. Died in 1967.

Goodman, E. W. Survived the war.

Gorbachevsky, Boris. Survived the war.

Göring, Hermann. Committed suicide in October 1946.

Grieben, Hans. Killed in an accidental explosion in February 1945.

Griffin, David. Survived the war.

Grigg, James. Died in 1964.

Griss, Jack. Survived the war.

Grüneberg, Alex David. Survived the war.

Grupe, Friedrich. Survived the war.

Grzywa, Kazimiera. Survived the war.

Halsey, Bill. Died in 1959.

Happe, Hans. Reported missing in Stalingrad in January 1943. He was either killed in action or died in captivity.

Harris, Arthur. Died in 1984.

Harrison, Frank. Survived the war.

Hartley, Frank. Died in 1971.

Hassett, William D. Died in 1965.

Haubach, Theodor. Executed in January 1945.

Heagy, Daniel. Survived the war.

Hennig, Liemar. Died in 1954.

Henk, Emil. Died in 1969.

Herring, Edmund. Died in 1982.

Herzberg, Abel. Survived the war.

Herzog, Franek. Survived the war.

Hibbs, Ralph Emerson. Survived the war.

Hillen, Ernest. Survived the war.

Himmler, Heinrich. Committed suicide in May 1945.

Himmler, Marga. Died in 1967.

Hodgson, Vere. Survived the war

Hobby, Oveta Culp. Died in 1995.

Hodson, Harry. Died in 1999.

Holloway, Eric. Survived the war.

Holmes, Wilfred Jay. Died in 1986.

Hore-Ruthven, Alexander. Died in 1955.

Hori Tomokazu. Died in 1944.

Höss, Rudolf. Executed in Poland in 1947.

Hoth, Hermann. Died in 1971.

Huq, A. K. Fazlul. Died in 1962.

Ichihashi Yamato. Died in 1963.

Jackson, Derrick. Survived the war.

Jacobs, Eugene C. Survived the war.

Jones, Frederick. Died in 1966.

Joseph, Inge. After a failed attempt to escape from France, she finally managed to flee into neutral Switzerland. She survived the war.

Jung, Richard. Survived the war.

Kenney, George. Died in 1977.

Kiil, Niels Ole. Survived the war.

Kirkpatrick, Charles C. Died in 1988.

Klehr, Josef. Survived the war. Imprisoned from 1965 until shortly before his death in 1988.

Klemperer, Victor. Died in 1960.
Knappe, Siegfried. Survived the war.
Koch, Ferdinand. Unknown.
König, Wolfhilde von. Died in 1993.
Krotova, Natalya Grigorevna. Unknown.
Krüger, Jürgen. Sunk along with his crew on board *U-631* southeast of Greenland in October 1943.
Küsel, Otto. Died in 1984.
Larsen, Helen. Unknown.
Larsen, Leonard. Unknown.
Leach, Douglas. Survived the war.
Leach, Saidee. Unknown.
Leigh-Mallory, Trafford. Killed in a plane crash in 1944.
Leckie, Robert. Died in 2001.
LeMay, Curtis. Died in 1990.
Lévy, Jean-Pierre. Died in 1996.
Lindgren, Astrid. Died in 2002.
Linlithgow, Victor Alexander John Hope, 2nd Marquess of. Died in 1952.
Lloyd George, David. Died in March 1945.
Logue, Lionel George. Died in 1953.
Loustaunau-Lacau, Georges. Died in 1955.
Lüth, Wolfgang. Accidentally killed by German sentry days after end of war in May 1945.
Lutjens, Paul R. Died in 1977.
MacAdoo, Geraldine. Survived the war.
MacArthur, Douglas. Died in 1964.
Margaret, Princess. Died in 2002.
Marks, Ken. Survived the war.
Marshall, George C. Died in 1959.
Martinez, Anthony. Survived the war.
Martinsen, Knud Børge. Executed in Denmark in 1949.
Mary of Teck, Queen. Died in 1953.
Masters, John "Bud". Died in 1987.
Matsushita Hanaye. Died in 1965.
Matsushita Iwao. Died in 1979.
Matthews, Herbert L. Died in 1977.
McConnell, Ray Jr. Died in 1979.
McCready, Robert H. Died in 1952.
McGillivray, Jack S. Survived the war.
Michailovic, Dragoljub. Executed in Yugoslavia in 1946.

Mielert, Harry. Killed in action, December 1943.

Mierendorff, Carlo. Killed in Allied air raid in December 1943.

Mikosz, Stanislaw. Survived the war.

Miles, Milton E. Died in 1961.

Miller, Glenn. Disappeared while flying between Britain and France in December 1944.

Millican, Moke. Missing and presumed killed when his submarine *Escolar* disappeared in the Sea of Japan in October 1944.

Minier, Lee. Survived the war.

Molesworth, George. Died in 1968.

Monro, John. Survived the war.

Montgomery, Bernard Law. Died in 1976.

Morriss, Mack. Survived the war.

Moses, Ken. Survived the war.

Murphy, Robert D. Died in 1978.

Myers, Harry W. Repatriated in 1942 and died in the United States in August 1945.

Naf, Rösli. Survived the war.

Nakamoto, Sally. Unknown.

Nansen, Odd. Died in 1973.

Natasha. Unknown.

Nimitz, Chester W. Died in 1966.

Noel-Baker, Philip. Died in 1982.

Næss, Ole Johan. Died in 1984.

Osborne, Francis d'Arcy. Died in 1962.

Ossemann, Nico. Survived the war.

O'Toole, James. Survived the war.

Palitzsch, Gerhard. Demoted and expelled from the SS. Assigned to a penal unit, and was reported killed in action on December 7, 1944, possibly in Hungary.

Patton, George S. Killed in a traffic accident in December 1945.

Paulus, Friedrich. Captured with the Sixth Army in early 1943. Died in 1957.

Pietzcker, Hans. Killed in February 1943 in Russia.

Pius XII. Died in 1958.

Pohl, Oswald. Executed in Germany in 1951.

Poindexter, Joseph. Died in 1951.

Quästl, Roland. Unknown.

Quintero, Joseph. Died in 2000.

Raeder, Erich. Died in 1960.

Randhawa, Katyun. Survived the war.

Raymond, Edward A. Survived the war.

Reddig, William M. Died in 1968.

Redlich, Gonda. Deported to Auschwitz in October 1944 and presumably killed shortly afterwards.

Redwine, Fred. Survived the war.

Reineck, Hermann. Survived the war.

Reuber, Kurt. Died in January 1944 in a Russian camp.

Ribbentrop, Joachim von. Executed in October 1946.

Ritter, J. R. Survived the war.

Robertson, J. McKee. Survived the war.

Robinett, Paul McDonald. Died in 1975.

Rommel, Erwin. Forced to commit suicide in October 1944.

Roosevelt, Eleanor. Died in 1962.

Roosevelt, Franklin D. Died in April 1945.

Ross, Barney. Survived the war.

Ruth, Babe. Died in 1948.

Sajer, Guy. Died in 2022.

Sandburg, Carl. Died in 1967.

Sarno, Phil. Survived the war.

Savary, Gladys. Died in 1985.

Scazighino, Feliks. Survived the war.

Schenkl, Emilie. Died in 1996.

Schlagintweit, Willi. Survived the war.

Schott, Joseph. Survived the war.

Shavin, Sidney. Survived the war.

Sheedy, Irvin. Survived the war. Died in 2004.

Sierakowiak, David. Died in the Lodz ghetto in August 1943.

Simmet, Helmut. Survived the war.

Skrjabina, Elena. Survived the war.

Smith, Steward Worth. Unknown.

Song Meiling. Died in 2003.

Soong, T. V. Died in 1971.

Spencer, Murlin. Survived the war.

Speyer, Donald G. Survived the war.

Stabler, Hollis. Survived the war.

Stangl, Franz. Escaped after the war but was later incarcerated. Died from a heart attack in 1971.

Stangl, Theresa. Survived the war.

Steele, Donald E. Unknown.
Stefanile, Francesco. Survived the war.
Stephens, Ian. Died in 1984.
Stevens, Frederic H. Survived the war.
Stilwell, Joseph. Died in 1946.
Streit, Kurt. Survived the war.
Stresau, Hermann. Died in 1964.
Sullivan, Aletta. Died in 1972.
Sullivan, Thomas. Died in 1965.
Sweetman, George. Survived the war.
Sørensen, Per. Missing presumed killed during battle of Berlin, April 1945.
Tardini, Domenico. Died in 1961.
Terwiel, Rosemarie. Guillotined in August 1943.
Thompson, Dorothy. Died in 1961.
Tittmann, Harold. Died in 1980.
Tojo Hideki. Executed in December 1948.
Turner, Kelly. Died in 1961.
Turkiewicz, Leszek. Survived the war.
Twiss, Frank. Died in 1994.
Ugaki Matome. Committed suicide by flying on a kamikaze mission after
    Japan's surrender in 1945.
Vargas, Jorge B. Died in 1980.
Vašek, Anton. Tried and executed in 1946.
Veltjens, Josef. Died in a plane crash in October 1943.
Villarosa, Duchess of. Died in 1982.
Volckmann, Russell W. Died in 1982.
Vrba, Rudolf. Died in 2006.
Wachholz, Paul F. Survived the war.
Wainwright, Jonathan M. Died in 1953.
Wassner, Fernando. Survived the war.
Wijze, Louis de. Survived the war.
Williams, Daniel M. Unknown.
Wilson, James E. Survived the war.
Wituska, Krystyna. Executed by guillotine in June 1944.
Wood, Dick. Survived the war.
Young, Eunice. Died in 1995.
Zuckerman, Yitzhak. Died in 1981.

Endnotes

Preface

1   Carlos P. Romulo, *I Saw the Fall of the Philippines* (Garden City, NY: Doubleday, Doran & Co., 1942), 263.

Introduction

1   Joseph Schott, "White Christmas," private manuscript.
2   Joshua Eli Plaut, *A Kosher Christmas: 'Tis the Season to Be Jewish* (New Brunswick, NJ: Rutgers University Press, 2012), 89.
3   "National and Regional Sheet Music Best Sellers," *The Billboard*, October 24, 1942: 24.
4   "National and Regional Best Selling Retail Records," *The Billboard*, October 31, 1942: 24.
5   "Songs with Most Radio Plugs," *The Billboard*, November 14, 1942: 24.
6   Joseph R. Carlton, "Selling Records and Sheet Music," *The Billboard*, November 14, 1942: 25.
7   James C. Rill, *A Narrative History of the 1st Battalion, 11th Marines During the Early History and Deployment of the 1st Marine Division, 1940–43* (Bennington, VT: Merriam Press, 2006), 64.
8   Bill Fitsell, "Christmas 1942 is remembered," *The Kingston-Whig Standard*, December 23, 1980: 16.
9   Paul Fussell, *Wartime: Understanding and Behavior in the Second World War* (Oxford: Oxford University Press, 1989), 186.
10 Fussell, *Wartime*, 186.
11 Quoted in James Kaplan, *Irving Berlin: New York Genius* (New Haven, CT and London: Yale University Press, 2019), 202.
12 Bruce David Forbes, *Christmas: A Candid History* (Berkeley, CA: University of California Press, 2007), 133.
13 Oral history interview with Donald J. Brydon, Aleutian World War II National Historic Area Oral History Project, https://www.nps.gov/aleu/learn/photosmultimedia/upload/Donald-Brydon-final-508.pdf, 6.
14 "Letters," *The Culver Citizen*, November 25, 1942: 4.
15 Oral history interview with Carl O. E. Bosenberg, Rutgers Oral History Archives of World War II, https://oralhistory.rutgers.edu/images/PDFs/bosenberg_carl_part1.pdf, 17.
16 Raymond L. Daye, "Area vets recall battle at Guadalcanal," *The Town Talk*, August 9, 1992: 11.
17 Sugata Bose, *His Majesty's Opponent: Subhas Chandra Bose and India's Struggle against Empire* (Cambridge, MA and London: The Belknap Press of Harvard University Press, 2011), 229–30.
18 "Wherever you may be… Merry Christmas!" *The Daily Oklahoman*, December 25, 1942: 5.
19 *Völkischer Beobachter*, December 24, 1942: 6.

20 *Völkischer Beobachter*, December 25, 1942: 11.
21 Catherine Merridale, *Ivan's War: The Red Army at War 1939–45* (London: Faber & Faber, 2005), 251.
22 "Facing the Future with Confidence: The King's Broadcast to the Empire," The *Guardian*, December 28, 1942: 3.
23 "Forward to Victory: P.M.'s Stirring Message," *The Age*, December 26, 1942: 3.
24 Ken Marks, Interview, National Museum of the Pacific War, https://digitalarchive.pacificwarmuseum.org/digital/collection/p16769coll1/id/5510/rec/1, 4.
25 "Christmas, 1942," *The Cincinnati Enquirer*, December 25, 1942: 4.
26 Penne Lee Restad, *Christmas in America: A History* (Oxford: Oxford University Press, 1997), 29ff.
27 Isaac Mickle, *A Gentleman of Much Promise: The Diary of Isaac Mickle, 1837–1845*, vol. 2 (Philadelphia, PA: University of Pennsylvania Press, 1977), 344.
28 Restad, *Christmas in America*, 50.
29 *The Random House Book of Poetry for Children* (New York, NY: Random House, 1983), 51.
30 John Chalmers Vinson, *Thomas Nast: Political Cartoonist* (Athens, GA: University of Georgia Press, 2014), 1.
31 Vinson, *Thomas Nast*, fig. 10.
32 Wendy Wick Reaves, "Thomas Nast and the President," *The American Art Journal*, vol. 19, no. 1 (Winter, 1987): 61.
33 J. Chal Vinson, "Thomas Nast and the American Political Scene," *American Quarterly*, vol. 9, no. 3 (Autumn, 1957): 339.
34 Joe Perry, *Christmas in Germany: A Cultural History* (Chapel Hill, NC: University of North Carolina Press, 2010), 98.
35 Ingeborg Weber-Kellermann, *Das Weihnachtsfest: Eine Kultur- und Sozialgeschichte der Weihnachtszeit [The Christmas Celebration: A Cultural and Social History of Christmas]* (Luzern and Frankfurt am Main: Verlag C. J. Bucher, 1978), 118–19.
36 Perry, *Christmas in Germany*, 110.
37 "Voices of the First World War: The Christmas Truce." Imperial War Museums, https://www.iwm.org.uk/history/voices-of-the-first-world-war-the-christmas-truce.
38 Fridolin Mayer's War Diary, December 24 and 28, 1916, https://tagebuch.hypotheses.org/page/2.
39 Betty Armitage, *Betty's Wartime Diary, 1939–1945*, ed. Nicholas Webley (London: Thorogood, 2002), 180.
40 Odd Nansen, *Fra dag til dag [From Day to Day]* (Oslo: Dreyers Forlag, 1946), 182.

Chapter 1

1 E. B. Potter, *Nimitz* (Annapolis, MD: Naval Institute Press, 1976), 16.
2 John R. O'Brien, "Blackout and Scarce Merchandise Put Damper On Hawaii Christmas," *The Baltimore Sun*, December 23, 1942: 1, 11.
3 Ibid.
4 Gwenfread Elaine Allen, *Hawaii's War Years, 1941–1945* (Honolulu, HI: University of Hawaii Press, 1952), 113.
5 Beth Bailey and David Farber, *The First Strange Place: Race and Sex in World War II Hawaii* (Baltimore, MD: The Johns Hopkins University Press, 1992), 209.
6 W. J. Holmes, *Double Edged Secrets: U.S. Naval Intelligence Operations in the Pacific* (Annapolis, MD: Naval Institute Press, 1979), 120.

7   Ibid., 119–20.
8   Allen, *Hawaii's War Years*, 139.
9   "Gen. Emmons Greets Officers, Enlisted Men," *The Honolulu Advertiser*, December 25, 1942: 1.
10 "Hawaii Military Rule Assailed," *The Honolulu Advertiser*, December 25, 1942: 1.
11 Potter, *Nimitz*, 16.
12 "Nimitz Sends Christmas Message to Servicemen," *The Sun*, December 26, 1942: 9.
13 James C. Olson, "The Gilberts and Marshalls," in Wesley Frank Craven and James Lea Cate (eds.), *The Pacific: Guadalcanal to Saipan, August 1942 to July 1944 [The Army Air Forces in World War II]* (Chicago, IL: University of Chicago Press, 1951), 283–4.
14 Olen W. Clements, "All Planes Come Back Safely," *San Francisco Examiner*, January 2, 1943: 1, 3.
15 Ibid.
16 Olson, "The Gilberts and Marshalls."
17 Robert Trumbull, "Heaviest Air Blow in Pacific Hit Foe at Wake by Surprise," *The New York Times*, January 2, 1943: 1, 3.
18 Donald M. Goldstein and Katherine V. Dillon (eds.), *Fading Victory: The Diary of Admiral Matome Ugaki 1941–1945* (Annapolis, MD: Naval Institute Press, 1991), 312.
19 Goldstein and Dillon (eds.), *Fading Victory*, 83.
20 Clay Blair Jr., *Silent Victory: The US Submarine War against Japan* (Philadelphia, PA and New York, NY: J. P. Lippincott, 1975), 334; Naval History and Heritage Command, *Triton III* (SS-201) https://www.history.navy.mil/content/history/nhhc/research/histories/ship-histories/danfs/t/triton-iii.html.
21 Blair Jr., *Silent Victory*, 351; Naval History and Heritage Command, *Thresher I* (SS-200) https://www.history.navy.mil/research/histories/ship-histories/danfs/t/thresher-i.html.
22 Denise Goolsby, "Cup of coffee leads to submarine duty," *The Desert Sun*, May 15, 2010: B3.
23 Blair Jr., *Silent Victory*, 336.
24 Edna May Tubbs, "Boys in North Pacific Don't Dream of White Christmas, Aleutian Veteran Says," *Corpus Christi Caller-Times*, November 14, 1943: 6.
25 J. R. Ritter, *From Texas to Tinian and Tokyo Bay: The Memoirs of Captain J. R. Ritter, Seabee Commander during the Pacific War, 1942–1945* (Denton, TX: University of North Texas Press, 2019), 48.
26 Ibid., 48.
27 James E. Wilson, Interview, National Museum of the Pacific War, https://digitalarchive.pacificwarmuseum.org/digital/collection/p16769coll1/id/3362/rec/11, 15–16.
28 Clay Gowran, "Yanks in Hawaii Take Time Out for Yule Turkey," *Chicago Daily Tribune*, December 25, 1942: 3.
29 Forrest C. Pogue, *George C. Marshall, vol. 3 Organizer of victory, 1943–1945* (New York, NY: Viking Press, 1973), 80.
30 "Remembrances of Christmases gone by," *Imperial Beach Star-News*, December 25, 1983: 1.
31 Command Summary ("Graybook"), December 24, 1942, Papers of Fleet Admiral Chester W. Nimitz, Archives Branch, Naval History and Heritage Command.
32 William F. Halsey and J. Bryan III, *Admiral Halsey's Story* (New York, NY and London: McGraw-Hill Publishing Co., 1947), 141.
33 "Vet Details World War II Christmas Memories," *Portage Daily Register*, December 24, 1994: 13.
34 Mack Morris, *South Pacific Diary, 1942–1943*, ed. Ronnie Day (Lexington, KY: University Press of Kentucky, 1996), 51.
35 Ibid., 48.

36   Ibid., 51.
37   Ibid., 53.
38   Ibid., 53.
39   Eileen Pech, "Dirty Business: Ciceronian Recalls Guadalcanal," *The Life*, November 11, 1990: 1.
40   Stanley Coleman Jersey, *Hell's Islands: The Untold Story of Guadalcanal* (College Station, TX: Texas A&M University Press, 2008), 355.
41   Roy H. Elrod, *We Were Going to Win, or Die There: With the Marines at Guadalcanal, Tarawa, and Saipan* (Denton, TX: University of North Texas Press, 2017), 120.
42   Rill, *A Narrative History of the 1st Battalion, 11th Marines*, 78–9.
43   Jersey, *Hell's Islands*, 355–6.
44   "Christmas 'Over There'", *The Town Talk*, December 24, 1990: 29.
45   Robert Leckie, *Helmet for My Pillow: From Parris Island to the Pacific* (London: Ebury Press, 2010), 136–7.
46   James Edmundson, *Letters to Lee: From Pearl Harbor to the War's Final Mission* (New York, NY: Fordham University Press, 2009), 121.
47   Ibid., 119.
48   Douglas Century, *Barney Ross: The Life of a Jewish Fighter* (New York, NY: Shocken Books, 2006), 125.
49   Ibid., 126.
50   Ross in interview with columnist Jimmy Breslin, quoted in Ron Grossman, "Looking for a Christmas lesson in tolerance? Here's one from the foxholes of WWII in 1942," *Chicago Tribune*, December 24, 2019.
51   Jersey, *Hell's Islands*, 337–40.

Chapter 2

1   "American Visitors: Send-Off This Morning," *The Gisborne Herald*, December 29, 1942: 2.
2   Norman T. Hatch, Oral History, United States Marine Corps, 72–3.
3   "Historic Event: Marines in Gisborne," *The Gisborne Herald*, December 24, 1942: 2.
4   Hatch, Oral History, United States Marine Corps, 74.
5   "American Forces Returning To-morrow: Beaten at Own Game," *The Gisborne Herald*, December 28, 1942: 2.
6   "Faith in Future," *New Zealand Herald*, December 31, 1941: 6.
7   "New Zealand Troops: Premier's Message," *Manawatu Standard*, December 24, 1942: 2.
8   "Festive Season: Christmas Spirit," *New Zealand Herald*, December 26, 1942: 4.
9   "Motions. United States Forces. 70th Anniversary of Arrival in New Zealand During World War II." Transcript. New Zealand Parliament, June 14, 2012.
10   Nancy M. Taylor, *The Home Front Volume I [The Official History of New Zealand in the Second World War 1939–1945]* (Wellington: Historical Publications Branch, 1986), 633.
11   Ibid., 625.
12   "Middle East Division: Minister Defends Dispatch," *Nelson Evening Mail*, January 29, 1943: 3.
13   Joseph H. Alexander, *Edson's Raiders: The 1st Marine Raider Battalion in World War II* (Annapolis, MD: Naval Institute Press, 2001), 231.
14   Ibid., 230–1.
15   Harry Bioletti, *The Yanks are Coming: The American Invasion of New Zealand, 1942–1944* (Auckland: Century Hutchinson, 1989), 5–7.
16   "Christmas Eve: Brisk Sales in Shops," *New Zealand Herald*, December 26, 1942: 4.

17 Bioletti, *The Yanks are Coming*, 112.
18 "Young Bootblacks: Practice Discouraged," *Evening Post*, February 25, 1942: 4.
19 "Forward to Victory: P.M.'s Stirring Message," *The Age*, December 26, 1942: 3.
20 "Crowds Throng the Churches," *The Age*, December 26, 1942: 3.
21 Eli Daniel Potts and Annette Potts, *Yanks Down Under, 1941–45: The American Impact on Australia* (Melbourne: Oxford University Press, 1985), 211.
22 Kate Darian-Smith, "The Home Front and the American Presence in 1942," in *Australia 1942: In the Shadow of War*, ed. Peter Dean (Port Melbourne: Cambridge University Press, 2013), 79.
23 Kate Darian-Smith, "Remembrance, Romance, and Nation: Memories of Wartime Australia" in *Gender & Memory*, ed. Selma Leydesdorff, Luisa Passerini, and Paul Thompson, (New York, NY: Routledge, 2017), 161.
24 Michael Duffy and Nick Hordern, *World War Noir: Sydney's unpatriotic war* (Sydney: University of New South Wales Press, 2019), 88–114.
25 Ibid., 88–114.
26 Kate Darian-Smith, *On the Home Front: Melbourne in Wartime, 1939–1945* (Melbourne: Oxford University Press, 1990), 45.
27 Ibid., 42–3.
28 *Australian Women's Weekly*, December 19, 1942.
29 "Christmas Hampers for Forces," *The Age*, December 15, 1942: 2.
30 "Aircraft Drop 'Presents'," *The Sydney Morning Herald*, December 26, 1942: 6.
31 Murlin Spencer, "Traditional Yule for GI Again Is Announced – Again It's Not So," *Fort Worth Star-Telegram*, December 21, 1945: 10.
32 Samuel Milner, *Victory in Papua [United States Army in World War II]* (Washington, D.C.: US Government Printing Office, 1957), 114.
33 Ibid., 115.
34 George C. Kenney, *General Kenney Reports: A Personal History of the Pacific War* (New York, NY: Duell, Sloan and Pearce, 1949), 150.
35 James Jay Carafano, *Brutal War: Jungle Fighting in Papua New Guinea 1942* (Boulder, CO: Lynne Rienner Publishers, 2021), 193.
36 Milner, *Victory in Papua*, 263.
37 Kenney, *General Kenney Reports*, 164.
38 Geoffrey Tebbutt, "West Front Touch," *The Courier-Mail*, December 28, 1942: 3.
39 "Chaplain Killed in New Guinea," *Sydney Morning Herald*, January 2, 1943: 11.
40 F. J. Hartley, *A Christmas in New Guinea* (Melbourne: The Book Depot, 1944), 20–30.
41 F. J. Hartley, *Sanananda Interlude* (Melbourne: The Book Depot, 1949), 36.
42 Dudley McCarthy, *South-West Pacific Area – First Year: Kokoda to Wau [Australia in the War of 1939–1945. Series 1 (Army), vol. 5]* (Canberra: Australian War Memorial, 1959), 507.
43 Hartley, *A Christmas in New Guinea*, 30.
44 Phil Sarno, "Heavy bombers brought hope for the holidays," *Standard-Speaker*, February 21, 1984: 19.
45 D. Clayton James, *The Years of MacArthur*, vol. 2 (Boston, MA: Houghton Mifflin, 1975), 247.
46 Phil Sarno, "Heavy bombers," 19.
47 "Comforts for the Troops," *The Age*, December 24, 1942: 3.
48 Geoffrey Hutton, "It's An Austere Christmas in the Front Line," *Newcastle Morning Herald and Miners' Advocate*, December 24, 1942: 2.
49 Kenney, *General Kenney Reports*, 170–1.
50 William Manchester, *American Caesar* (New York, NY: Little, Brown and Company, 1978), 326; Robert L. Eichelberger, *Our Jungle Road to Tokyo* (New York, NY: The Viking Press, 1950), 47.

51   Eichelberger, *Our Jungle Road*, 47.
52   Ibid., 47.
53   "Buna Veteran Does Death Act for Japs," *The Missoulian*, March 15, 1944: 1; "Has 57 Wounds," *The South Bend Tribune*, March 16, 1944: 9.
54   Paul Handel, *The Vital Factor* (Sydney: Australian Military History Publications, 2004), 164.
55   Ibid., 167–8.
56   Ibid., 64.
57   D. Clayton James, *The Years of MacArthur*, vol. 2 (Boston, MA: Houghton Mifflin, 1975), 269–70.
58   Eichelberger, *Our Jungle Road*, 43.
59   Ibid., 47.
60   *Papuan Campaign: The Buna-Sanananda Operation 16 November 1942–23 January 1943* (Washington, D.C.: Center of Military History, 1990), 51.
61   Eichelberger, *Our Jungle Road*, 46.
62   "Christmas Fare at Buna," *The New York Times*, December 25, 1942: 3.
63   Eichelberger, *Our Jungle Road*, 46.
64   Robert L. Eichelberger, *Dear Miss Em: General Eichelberger's War in the Pacific 1942–1945* (Westport, CT: Greenwood Press, 1972), 48.
65   Eichelberger, *Dear Miss Em*, 48.
66   Eichelberger, *Our Jungle Road*, 47.
67   Eichelberger, *Dear Miss Em*, 49.

Chapter 3

1   Heyo Hamer, "Die letzten Japan-Missionare der Ostasien-Mission (OAM). Ein Beitrag zur Geschichte der Auflösung der OAM 1947" ["The Last Japan Missionaries of the East Asia Mission (OAM): A Contribution to the History of the Dissolution of the OAM in 1947"] in *Wege und Welte der Religionen [Roads and Worlds of the Religions]*, ed. Jürgen Court and Michael Klöcker (Frankfurt am Main: Verlag Otto Lembeck, 2009), 181–2.
2   Ibid.
3   "Rev. Dr. Harry W. Myers," *The New York Times*, August 7, 1945: 23.
4   "Kansai Notes," *Japan Times Advertiser*, December 23, 1942: 2. "90 Years of Kobe Union Church," *Mainichi Daily News*, May 29, 1961, reprinted in https://www.evkobe.org/deutsch/150th-anniversary-of-kobe-union-church/90-years-of-kuc-iii-trials-of-growth-and-war-1904-1942/; on Hennig, see Hamer, "Die Letzten Japan-Missionare," 182 n12.
5   "Japanese People Giving Up Their New Year's Day; Adopt Christmas," *Honolulu Star-Bulletin*, November 19, 1930: 17.
6   "Christmas in Japan," *The Pomona Progress Bulletin*, January 16, 1930: 8.
7   Paul Rusch, "Christmas in Japan," *The Courier-Journal*, January 6, 1931: 4.
8   "Jap Regime Curbs Christmas Gaiety," *The Tampa Daily Times*, December 24, 1938: 1.
9   "Anti-Communist Flags Replace Beloved Santa in Japan's Christmas," *Evening Herald*, December 20, 1938: 4.
10   "Kansai Notes," *Japan Times Advertiser*, December 23, 1942: 2.
11   Jane M. J. Robbins, "Tokyo Calling: Japanese Overseas Radio Broadcasting, 1937–1945" (PhD diss., University of Sheffield, 1997), 127.
12   Ibid., 96, 127.
13   "Hori Raps Leaders of U.S. and Britain," *Japan Times Advertiser*, December 25, 1942: 1, 3.

14 "Peace on Earth," *Japan Times Advertiser*, December 25, 1942: 6.

15 Ezequiel L. Ortiz and James A. McClure, *Don Jose: An American Soldier's Courage and Faith in Japanese Captivity*, (Santa Fe, NM: Sunstone Press, 2012), 57.

16 Gene O'Connell and Tony Bilek, *No Uncle Sam: The Forgotten of Bataan* (Kent, OH: Kent State University Press, 2003), 112.

17 Ralph Emerson Hibbs, *Tell MacArthur to Wait* (New York, NY: Carlton Press, 1988), 169.

18 Van Waterford, *Prisoners of the Japanese in World War II* (Jefferson, VA: McFarland and Company, 1994), 42.

19 Irvin Alexander, *Surviving Bataan and Beyond: Colonel Irvin Alexander's Odyssey as a Japanese Prisoner of War*, ed. Dominic J. Caraccilo (Mechanicsburg, PA: Stackpole Books, 2005), 157.

20 Calvin Ellsworth Chunn, *Of Rice and Men: The Story of Americans Under the Rising Sun* (Los Angeles, CA: Veterans' Publishing Company, 1947), 28.

21 Eugene C. Jacobs, *Blood Brothers: A Medic's Sketch Book* (New York, NY: Carlton Press, 1985), 58.

22 Oritz and McClure, *Don Jose*, 59.

23 Gladys Savary, *Outside the Walls* (New York, NY: Vantage Press, 1954), 81–2.

24 Morgan Byrn, "Christmas in a World War II POW Camp," Tennessee State Museum, https://tnmuseum.org/Stories/posts/christmas-in-a-world-war-ii-pow-camp.

25 Ibid.

26 James Wharton, "Christmas in Captivity," Forces.net, December 24, 2020, https://www.forces.net/heritage/wwii/christmas-captivity.

27 See for example, Thomas Dooley, Jerry C. Cooper, John A. Adams Jr., and Henry C. Dethloff, *To Bataan and Back: The World War II Diary of Major Thomas Dooley* (College Station, TX: Texas A&M University Press, 2006), 123.

28 Jonathan M. Wainwright and Robert Considine, *General Wainwright's Story: The Account of Four Years of Humiliating Defeat, Surrender, and Captivity* (Garden City, NY: Doubleday, 1946), 200.

29 Brigadier E. W. Goodman, Diary, December 25, 1942, https://www.britain-at-war.org.uk/WW2/Brigadier_EW_Goodman/html/taiwan.htm.

30 Lewis Beebe and John M. Beebe, *Prisoner of the Rising Sun: The Lost Diary of Brig. Gen. Lewis Beebe* (College Station, TX: Texas A&M University Press, 2006), 123.

31 Wainwright and Considine, *General Wainwright's Story*, 199.

32 Dooley *et al.*, *To Bataan and Back*, 124.

33 Wainwright and Considine, *General Wainwright's Story*, 199.

34 Andy Reed, "The Curious Case of the Changi Christmas Dinner," Faculty of Medicine, University of Queensland, https://medicine.uq.edu.au/blog/2018/12/curious-case-changi-christmas-dinner.

35 "Obituaries: Admiral Sir Frank Twiss," *The Daily Telegraph*, January 28, 1994: 19.

36 Frank Twiss, *Social Change in the Royal Navy, 1924–1970: The Life and Times of Admiral Sir Frank Twiss, KCB, KCVO, DSC*, comp. and ed. Chris Howard Bailey (Stroud: Sutton Publishing, 1996), 88–9.

37 Eric Cordingly, *Down to Bedrock: The Diary and Secret Notes of a Far East Prisoner of War Chaplain 1942–45*, ed. Louise Cordingly (Norwich: Art Angels, 2013), 91–2.

38 Wainwright and Considine, *General Wainwright's Story*, 198.

39 Beebe and Beebe, *Prisoner of the Rising Sun*, 125–6.

40 Ibid., 123.

41 Ibid., 125–6.

42 Doole *et al.*, *To Bataan and Back*, 124.

43 Beebe and Beebe, 126–7.

44 Wainwright and Considine, *General Wainwright's Story*, 199.
45 Olga Moss, "Bantjeuj," *Fidelity* no. 61 (2006), https://metanthonymemorial.org/VernostNo61.htm.
46 Ruth Barr, *Ruth's Record: The Diary of an American in Japanese-occupied Shanghai 1941–45* (Hong Kong: Earnshaw, 2017).
47 Gladys Savary, *Outside the Walls* (New York, NY: Vantage Press, 1954), 76.
48 Geoffrey Charles Emerson, *Hong Kong Internment, 1942–1945: Life in the Japanese Civilian Camp at Stanley* (Hong Kong: Hong Kong University Press, 2008), 84.
49 Evelyn M. Monahan and Rosemary Neidel-Greenlee, *All This Hell: U.S. Nurses Imprisoned by the Japanese* (Lexington, KY: University Press of Kentucky, 2003), 109.
50 Staff Sergeant James O'Toole, transcript of diary, December 25, 1942, https://www.far-eastern-heroes.org.uk/James_OToole/html/dairy_1942.htm.
51 Frederic H. Stevens, *Santo Tomas Internment Camp* (New York, NY: Stratford House, 1946), 356.
52 Ibid., 353–9.
53 Celia Lucas, *Prisoners of Santo Tomas* (London: Leo Cooper, 1975), 63–4.
54 Stevens, *Santo Tomas*, 39.
55 Gavin Souter, "The determined alderman," *The Sydney Morning Herald*, July 19, 1972: 7; Keith James, "A happy end to the horror of war camp," *The Sydney Morning Herald*, August 29, 1991: 4; "Obituaries: Sir David Griffin," *The Daily Telegraph*, April 10, 2004: 23.
56 Ernest Hillen, *The Way of a Boy: A Memoir of Java* (London: Penguin, 1993), 63.
57 Diary of Louise Fillmore Blancaflor, December 20, 1942, The Philippine Diary Project, https://philippinediaryproject.com/1942/12/20/december-20-1942/.
58 Ibid.
59 Ibid.
60 Ibid.
61 "Army's Generosity Responsible for Celebration of X'mas Today," *The Tribune*, December 25, 1942: 3.
62 Mike Guardia, *American Guerrilla: The Forgotten Heroics of Russell W. Volckmann* (Philadelphia, PA: Casemate Publishers, 2010), 88.
63 Diary of Ramon A. Alcaraz, December 25, 1942, The Philippine Diary Project, https://philippinediaryproject.com/1942/12/25/december-25-1942/.
64 Ibid.

Chapter 4

1 Milton E. Miles, *A Different Kind of War* (Garden City, NY: Doubleday & Company, 1967), 111.
2 Charles E. Romanus and Riley Sunderland, *Stilwell's Mission to China [United States Army in World War II: China-Burma-India Theater]* (Washington, D.C.: United States Army Center of Military History, 1953), 256.
3 Hannah Davies, *Among Hills and Valleys in Western China* (London: S. W. Partridge & Co., 1901), 37–8.
4 Sarah Pike Conger, *Letters from China* (Chicago, IL: A. C. McClurg & Co., 1909), 37.
5 "Asiatics Like Christmas," *The New York Times*, December 25, 1899, 7.
6 Bae Kyounghan, "Chiang Kai-shek and Christianity: Religious life reflected from his diary," *Journal of Modern Chinese History*, vol. 3, no. 1 (June 2009): 4–5.
7 Miles, *A Different Kind of War*, 110.

8 Bae, "Chiang Kai-shek and Christianity," 6.

9 Ibid., 6.

10 Mary Monro, *Stranger in my Heart* (London: Unbound, 2018), 146–7.

11 Bae, "Chiang Kai-shek and Christianity," 7.

12 "Christmas in China," *The New York Times*, December 24, 1942, 14.

13 Chiang Kai-Shek, Albert French Lutley *et al.*, *Resistance and Reconstruction: Messages during China's Six Years of War, 1937–1943* (New York, NY: Harper and Brothers, 1943), 319.

14 "Christmas Cheer to U.S. Troops," *The Times of India*, December 25, 1942: 7.

15 John D. Plating, *The Hump: America's Strategy for Keeping China in World War II* (College Station, TX: Texas A&M University Press, 2011), 68

16 Herbert L. Matthews, "Unsung Heroes Fly Supplies to China," *The New York Times*, December 2, 1942: 10.

17 "An incredible untold story of WWII," *New Zealand Herald*, January 23, 2016.

18 "Battle Diary of an Oakland War Eagle," *Oakland Tribune*, April 4, 1943: 51.

19 Julian Thompson, *Forgotten Voices of Burma: The Second World War's Forgotten Conflict* (London: Ebury Press, 2009), 47.

20 Frank Harrison, interview, Imperial War Museums, https://www.iwm.org.uk/collections/item/object/80016194.

21 "A Silent Night in 1942," *Surrey Leader*, December 23, 1987: 14.

22 Quoted in Janam Mukherjee, *Hungry Bengal: War, Famine and the End of Empire* (Oxford: Oxford University Press, 2015), 81–2.

23 Herbert L. Matthews, "Americans Swarm in Misty Calcutta," *The New York Times*, December 22, 1942: 5.

24 "Year-Old Cake: Journey to Calcutta Takes Long Time," *The Leader-Post*, January 4, 1943: 3.

25 Ian Stephens, *Monsoon Morning* (London: Ernest Benn, 1966), 81–2.

26 "How Japanese Raid on Calcutta Failed," *The Times of India*, December 28, 1942: 7.

27 Stephens, *Monsoon Morning*, 82.

28 "Calcutta Raid Casualties Total 25 Killed & 100 Injured," *Amrita Bazar Patrika*, December 27, 1942: 3.

29 Ishan Mukherjee, "The Elusive Chase: 'War Rumour' in Calcutta During the Second World War," in *Calcutta The Stormy Decades*, eds. Tanika Sarkar and Sekhar Bandyopadhyay (London: Routledge, 2017), 66; "Enemy Air Raid on Calcutta," *The Times of India*, December 22, 1942: 1.

30 "Chief Minister's Message," *Amrita Bazar Patrika*, December 24, 1942: 1.

31 "Fifth Japanese Air Raid on Calcutta Area," *Amrita Bazar Patrika*, December 31, 1942: 6.

32 Philip P. Crosland, "Arden Couple Who Lived in India, Follows News," *The News Journal* (Wilmington, Delaware), December 3, 1948: 6.

33 "What Calcutta Wants," *Amrita Bazar Patrika*, December 31, 1942: 2.

34 "Calcutta Takes It," *Amrita Bazar Patrika*, December 24, 1942: 2.

35 Stephens, *Monsoon Morning*, 83.

36 Ibid., 82.

37 Ken Moses, "My RAF Service with 194 Squadron," Burma Star Memorial Fund, https://burmastarmemorial.org/archive/stories/1405932-my-raf-service-with-194-squadron-ken-moses?q=.

38 "What Calcutta Wants," *Amrita Bazar Patrika*, December 31, 1942: 2.

39 Philip P. Crosland, "Arden Couple Who Lived in India, Follows News," *The News Journal* (Wilmington, Delaware), December 3, 1948: 6.

40 Stephens, *Monsoon Morning*, 83.

41 Eric Holloway, *The Stars Are My Friends* (Darlington: Serendipity, 2005), 36.

42 G. N. Molesworth, *Curfew on Olympus* (Bombay: Asia Publishing House, 1965), 247.
43 Ibid., 246.
44 Nirad C. Chaudhuri, *Thy Hand, Great Anarch! India 1921–1952* (London: Chatto & Windos, 1987), 722.
45 Molesworth, *Curfew on Olympus*, 246.
46 William McGaffin, "Yanks Have Bright Yule in New Delhi," *The Knoxville Journal*, December 27, 1942: 8.
47 "Parties Through-out China-India Spread Goodwill," *CBI Roundup*, December 31, 1942.
48 "Parties Through-out China-India Spread Goodwill," *CBI Roundup*, December 31, 1942.
49 "6,000 Orphans Get Havens," *The New York Times*, October 17, 1942: 12.
50 Sunaina Kumar, "During WWII, Polish Refugees Found a Home in India," *Atlas Obscura*, November 28, 2018.
51 Testimony of Kazimiera Grzywa. Chronicles of Terror, Pilecki Institute, https://www.zapisy-terroru.pl/publication/2346.
52 Preston Grover, "Paderwski Fame Brings Haven to Polish Orphans," *The Greeneville Sun*, June 10, 1944: 1.
53 Anuradha Bhattacharjee, *The Second Homeland: Polish refugees in India* (Los Angeles, CA: SAGE, 2012).
54 Eleonora Carneckis, "Woman remembers, treasures Siberian Christmas," *The Marshall News Messenger*, December 9, 1990: 21.
55 "Christmas in Russia," *The Bee* (Danville, Florida), January 7, 1943: 8.
56 David M. Nichol, "One Christmas Tree Moscow's Only Touch of Holiday Spirit," *The Province* (Vancouver, British Columbia), December 24, 1942: 23.

Chapter 5

1 Richard Jung, "90 Minuten Aufenthalt (Begegnung mit einem Engel)," ["90 Minute Stop (Meeting an Angel]" in *Weihnachtsgeschichten aus schwerer Zeit erzählt von Freunden und Förderern des Volksbundes Deutsche Kriegsgräberfürsorge [Christmas Stories from Difficult Times Told by Friends and Supporters of the German People's League for the Care of War Cemeteries]*, ed. Martin Dodenhoeft (Kassel: Volksbund Deutsche Kriegsgräberfürsorge, 2017), 47.
2 Siegfried Knappe with Ted Brusaw, *Soldat: Reflections of a German Soldier, 1936–1949* (New York, NY: Dell Book, 1992), 214 and 222.
3 Walter Bähr and Hans W. Bähr, *Kriegsbriefe gefallener Studenten [War Letters from Fallen Students]* (Tübingen and Stuttgart: Rainer Wunderlich Verlag, 1952), 155–6.
4 V. M. Bogdanov, "A Daring Raid," *Soviet Military Review*, no. 11 (November 1982): 39.
5 Bogdanov, "A Daring Raid," 39; Joel S. A. Hayward, *Stopped at Stalingrad: The Luftwaffe and Hitler's Defeat in the East, 1942–1943* (Lawrence, KS: University Press of Kansas, 1998), 271–2.
6 Hayward, *Stopped at Stalingrad*, 272.
7 Wilhelm Adam, *Der schwere Entschluss [The Difficult Decision]* (Berlin: Verlag der Nation, 1965), 230.
8 Erik Haaest, *Frostknuder [Frostbites]* (Copenhagen: Bogan, 2005), 69.
9 Claus Bundgård Christensen, Niels Bo Poulsen, and Peter Scharff Smith, *Under hagekors og Dannebrog: Danskere i Waffen SS 1940–45 [Under Swastika and Dannebrog: Danes in the Waffen-SS 1940–45]* (Copenhagen: Aschehoug, 1998), 182–3.
10 Ibid., 184.

11 Hans Heintel, "Weihnachten bei Matka" ["Christmas with Matka"], *Unter den Sternen: Weihnachtsgeschichten aus schwerer Zeit erzählt von Freunden und Förderern des Volksbundes Deutsche Kriegsgräberfürsorge [Under the Stars: Christmas Stories from Difficult Times Told by Friends and Supporters of the German People's League for the Care of War Cemeteries]*, ed. Martin Dodenhoeft and Henning Unverhau (Kassel: Volksbund Deutsche Kriegsgräberfürsorge, 2007), 20.

12 Harry Mielert, *Russische Erde: Kriegsbriefe aus Russland [Russian Soil: War Letters from Russia]* (Stuttgart: Reclam-Verlag, 1950), 43.

13 Fernando Wassner, "Feldpostbrief" ["Letter from the Front"], *Unter den Sternen: Weihnachtsgeschichten aus schwerer Zeit erzählt von Freunden und Förderern des Volksbundes Deutsche Kriegsgräberfürsorge [Under the Stars: Christmas Stories from Difficult Times Told by Friends and Supporters of the German People's League for the Care of War Cemeteries]*, ed. Martin Dodenhoeft and Henning Unverhau (Kassel: Volksbund Deutsche Kriegsgräberfürsorge, 2007), 29–30.

14 Boris Gorbachevsky, *Through the Maelstrom: A Red Army Soldier's War on the Eastern Front, 1942–1945* (Lawrence, KS: University Press of Kansas, 2008), 200.

15 Ibid., 200–1.

16 Guy Sajer, *The Forgotten Soldier* (Washington, D.C.: Potomac Books, 1990), 26.

17 Joe Perry, *Christmas in Germany: A Cultural History* (Chapel Hill, NC: University of North Carolina Press, 2010), 100.

18 Ibid., 101.

19 Ibid., 110.

20 Mielert, *Russische Erde*, 43–4.

21 Hayward, *Stopped at Stalingrad*, 279.

22 Jung, "90 Minuten Aufenthalt" 45.

23 *Kriegsweihnachten 1942: Eine Scheswig-Holsteinische Infanteriedivision im Osten [War Christmas 1942: A Schleswig-Holstein Infantry Division in the East]* (Riga: Deutsche Verlags- und Druckerei-Gesellschaft im Ostland, 1942), 15–16.

24 Perry, *Christmas in Germany*, 109.

25 Friedrich Grupe, *Jahrgang 1916: Die Fahne war mehr als der Tod [Born in 1916: The Flag Meant More than Death]* (Munich: Universitas, 1989), 274.

26 *Kriegsweihnachten 1942*, 15.

27 Joseph B. Perry, "The Madonna of Stalingrad: Mastering the (Christmas) Past and West German National Identity after World War II," *Radical History Review*, no. 83 (Spring 2002): 14.

28 Wassner, "Feldpostbrief".

29 Heintel, "Weihnachten bei Matka."

30 Bähr and Bähr, *Kriegsbriefe*, 194.

31 Laurie R. Cohen, *Smolensk under the Nazis: Everyday Life in Occupied Russia* (Woodbridge: Boydell & Brewer, 2013), 199.

32 Bähr and Bähr, *Kriegsbriefe*, 182–3.

33 Cohen, *Smolensk under the Nazis*, 115.

34 Ibid., 118.

35 Elena Skrjabina with Norman Luxenburg, *After Leningrad: From the Caucasus to the Rhine, August 9, 1942 – March 25, 1945: A Diary of Survival during World War II* (Carbondale, IL: Southern Illinois University Press, 1978), 53–5.

36 Anatoly Golovchansky, Valentin Osipov, Anatoly Prokopenko, Ute Daniel and Jürgen Reulecke (eds.), *"Ich will raus aus diesem Wahnsinn." Deutsche Briefe von der Ostfront 1941–1945 aus sowjetischen Archiven ["I Want to Escape from this Madness." German Letters from the Eastern Front in Soviet Archives]* (Wuppertal: Peter Hammer Verlag, 1991), 163.

37 Torsten Diedrich, *Paulus: Das Trauma von Stalingrad [Paulus: The Trauma of Stalingrad]* (Paderborn: Ferdinand Schöningh, 2009), 262–9.

38 Adam, *Der schwere Entschluss*, 222.

39 Ibid.

40 Ibid.

41 Ibid., 223.

42 Joseph Goebbels, *Die Tagebücher von Joseph Goebbels [Joseph Goebbels' Diaries]*, Part 2, vol. 6 (October–December 1942), ed. Hartmut Mehringer (Munich: K. G. Sauer, 1996), 513.

43 Hope Hamilton, *Sacrifie on the Steppe: The Italian Alpine Corps in the Stalingrad Campaign, 1942–1943* (Havertown, PA and Oxford: Casemate Publishers, 2011), 68.

44 Francesco Stefanile, "La vigilia del Natale '42," https://www.idiariraccontano.org/estratti/la-vigilia-del-natale-42/.

45 Jürgen Brautmeier, "Frontbewährung in Stalingrad. Feldpostbriefe des Gefreiten Hans Happe aus Delbrück/Westfalen" ["Proving One's Worth at the Front in Stalingrad: Letters from Sergeant Hans Happe from Delbrueck/Westphalia"], in *Geschichte im Westen. Halbjahres-Zeitschrift für Landes- und Zeitgeschichte*, volume 2 (1993), 185–6.

46 Golovchansky, *Ich will raus*, 162.

47 Ibid., 159–60.

48 Brautmeier, "Frontbewährung in Stalingrad," 185–6.

49 Diedrich, *Paulus*, 269.

50 Perry, "The Madonna of Stalingrad," 12.

51 Ibid., 25 n17.

52 Bähr and Bähr, *Kriegsbriefe*, 199.

53 Jochen Kummer, "Weihnachten in Stalingrad," *Welt am Sonntag*, November 22, 1992, 29; quoted in Perry, "The Madonna of Stalingrad," 25 n14.

Chapter 6

1 Yitzhak Zuckerman, *A Surplus of Memory: Chronicle of the Warsaw Ghetto Uprising*, transl. and ed. Barbara Harshav (Berkeley, CA: University of California Press, 1993), 235–9.

2 Gusta Davidson Draenger, *Justyna's Narrative*, ed. Eli Pfefferkorn and David H. Hirsch (Amherst, MA: University of Massachusetts Press, 1996), 27.

3 Bähr and Bähr, *Kriegsbriefe*, 216.

4 *Trials of the Major War Criminals before the International Military Tribunal, vol. XL Documents and Other Material in Evidence Bormann-11 to Raeder-7* (Nuremberg: International Military Tribunal, 1949), 147. Some secondary works erroneously state that the quote was published in the *Völkischer Beobachter*.

5 Testimony of Dina Winder, December 31, 1947. Chronicles of Terror, Pilecki Institute, https://www.zapisyterroru.pl/dlibra/publication/2848; Testimony of Józef Manela, June 1947. Chronicles of Terror, Pilecki Institute. https://www.zapisyterroru.pl/dlibra/publication/2845.

6 Testimony of Antoni Brynski, October 20, 1947. Chronicles of Terror, Pilecki Institute. https://www.zapisyterroru.pl/dlibra/publication/5571

7 Testimony of Wladyslaw Sowinski, October 1, 1945. Chronicles of Terror, Pilecki Institute, https://www.zapisyterroru.pl/dlibra/publication/2068.

8 Testimony of Antoni Sobania and Adam Szczepaniak, November 16, 1948. Chronicles of Terror, Pilecki Institute, https://www.zapisyterroru.pl/dlibra/publication/4547.

9   Roy MacLaren, *Canadians Behind Enemy Lines, 1939–1945* (Vancouver: UBC Press, 2004), 137.

10   Walter R. Roberts, *Tito, Michailovic and the Allies, 1941–1945* (New Brunswick, NJ: Rutgers University Press, 1973), 70–1.

11   *Trials of War Criminals before the Nuernberg Military Tribunals under Control Council Law No. 10, vol. 11* (Washington, D.C.: United States Government Printing Office, 1950), 813–14.

12   Joseph R. White, *The United States Holocaust Memorial Museum Encyclopedia of Camps and Ghettos, 1933–1945, vol. 3* (Bloomington, IN: Indiana University Press, 2012), 856.

13   Béla Weichherz and Daniel H. Magilow, *In Her Father's Eyes: A Childhood Extinguished by the Holocaust* (New Brunswick, NJ: Rutgers University Press, 2008), 164.

14   Gonda Redlich, *The Terezin Diary of Gonda Redlich* (Lexington, KY: University Press of Kentucky, 1992), 89.

15   Wolfgang Benz, *Theresienstadt: Eine Geschichte von Täuschung und Vernichtung [Theresienstadt: A History of Deception and Annihilation]* (Munich: C.H. Beck, 2013), 155.

16   Redlich, *The Terezin Diary of Gonda Redlich*, 92.

17   *Trials of War Criminals before the Nuernberg Military Tribunals under Control Council Law No. 10, vol. 4* (Washington, D.C.: United States Government Printing Office, 1950), 972–973.

18   Ibid., 972.

19   *Trials of War Criminals before the Nuernberg Military Tribunals under Control Council Law No. 10, vol. 5* (Washington, D.C.: United States Government Printing Office, 1950), 903.

20   Ibid., 1157.

21   *Trials of War Criminals before the Nuernberg Military Tribunals under Control Council Law No. 10, vol. 4* (Washington, D.C.: United States Government Printing Office, 1950), 503.

22   Richard Rashke, *Escape from Sobibor* (Urbana and Chicago, IL: University of Illinois Press, 1995), 103.

23   White, *Encyclopedia of Camps and Ghettos*, 915.

24   Gitta Sereny, *Into That Darkness* (London: Andre Deutsch, 1974), 200.

25   Martin Gilbert, *The Holocaust: The Human Tragedy* (New York, NY: Rosetta Books, 2014), 375.

26   Gitta Sereny, *Into That Darkness* (London: Andre Deutsch, 1974), 209–210.

27   Hermann Langbein, *People in Auschwitz* (Chapel Hill, NC: University of North Carolina Press, 2004), 393; Rebecca Wittmann, *Beyond Justice: The Auschwitz Trial* (Cambridge, MA: Harvard University Press, 2012), 74.

28   Testimony of Stanislaw Glowa, September 30, 1946. Chronicles of Terror, Pilecki Institute, https://www.zapisyterroru.pl/dlibra/publication/4044.

29   Danuta Czech, *Kalendarium der Ereignisse im Konzentrationslager Auschwitz-Birkenau 1939–1945 [Chronology of Events in the Concentration Camp Auschwitz-Birkenau]* (Hamburg: Rowohlt, 1989), 16.

30   Testimony of Kai Fernberg, March 12, 1947. Chronicles of Terror, Pilecki Institute, https://www.zapisyterroru.pl/publication/3766.

31   Bernd G. Wagner, *IG Auschwitz* [vol. 3 in *Darstellungen und Quellen zur Geschichte von Auschwitz [Accounts and Sources of the History of Auschwitz]*] (Munich: K. G. Sauer 2000), 133.

32   Czech, *Kalendarium der Ereignisse im Konzentrationslager Auschwitz-Birkenau 1939–1945*, 365.

33   "Christmas Eve in Auschwitz as Recalled by Polish Prisoners," Memorial and Museum Auschwitz-Birkenau, December 23, 2005, http://auschwitz.org/en/museum/news/christmas-eve-in-auschwitz-as-recalled-by-polish-prisoners,47.html.

34   Langbein, *People in Auschwitz*, 427.

35 Rudolf Vrba, *I Escaped from Auschwitz* (Fort Lee, NJ: Barricade Books, 2002), 173.

36 Peter Kuon, "Weihnachten im Konzentrationslager" ["Christmas in the Concentration Camp"] in *Poetik des Überlebens: Kulturproduktion im Konzentrationslager [The Poetics of Survival: Cultural Production in the Concentration Camp]*, ed. Anne-Berenike Rothstein (Berlin: De Gruyter Oldenbourg, 2015), 36–7.

37 Ibid., 34.

38 He was writing about Christmas 1944. Kuon, 34–5.

39 Didier Durmarque, "Noël 1942 à Birkenau," http://didier.durmarque.com/2013/11/noel-1942-a-birkenau/.

40 Testimony of Leszek Turkiewicz, February 1, 1946. Chronicles of Terror, Pilecki Institute, https://www.zapisyterroru.pl/dlibra/publication/3864.

41 Hermann Reineck, "Ein grauenvoller Tag unterm Weihnachtsbaum" ["A Horrifying Day under the Christmas Tree"], *Lagergemeinschaft Auschwitz/Freundeskreis der Auschwitzer. Mitteilungsblatt [Newsletter of Auschwitz Camp Community/Circle of Friends of Former Auschwitz Prisoners]*, vol. 37 (December 2017): 4.

42 Czech, *Kalendarium der Ereignisse im Konzentrationslager Auschwitz-Birkenau 1939–1945*, 365.

43 Hermann Langbein, *Against All Hope: Resistance in the Nazi Concentration Camps, 1938–1945* (New York, NY: Paragon House, 1994), 268–9.

44 Langbein, *Against All Hope*, 268–9; Langbein, *People in Auschwitz*, 154.

45 Shmuel Krakowski and Orah Blaustein, *The War of the Doomed: Jewish Armed Resistance in Poland, 1942–1944* (New York, NY: Holmes and Meier, 1984), 245.

46 Marek Bem, *Sobibor Extermination Camp 1942–1943* (Amsterdam: Stichting Sobibor, 2015), 256.

47 Ibid., 256

48 Yitzhak Arad, *The Operation Reinhard Death Camps: Belzec, Sobibor, Treblinka* (Bloomington, IN: Indiana University Press, 2018), 314.

49 Testimony of Hersz Cukierman, Jewish Historical Institute in Warsaw, Holocaust Survivor Testimonies (coll. 301), Hersz Cukierman Testimony (301/14), https://early-testimony. ehri-project.eu/document/EHRI-ET-ZIH3010014, 8.

50 Dawid Sierakowiak, Alan Adelson, and Kamil Turowski, *The Diary of Dawid Sierakowiak: Five Notebooks from the Lodz Ghetto* (New York, NY: Oxford University Press, 1996), 241–2.

51 Shmuel Krakowski and Orah Blaustein, *The War of the Doomed: Jewish Armed Resistance in Poland, 1942–1944* (New York, NY: Holmes and Meier, 1984), 31.

52 Anita Brostoff and Sheila Chamovitz, *Flares of Memory: Stories of Childhood during the Holocaust* (New York, NY: Oxford University Press, 2001), 107–9.

53 "Portrait of Felicja Braun taken in the Warsaw ghetto," United States Holocaust Memorial Museum, https://collections.ushmm.org/search/catalog/pa1143497.

54 White, *Encyclopedia of Camps and Ghettos*, 727.

Chapter 7

1 The description of Karl Epstein is based on Karl Iosifowitsch Epstein, *Weihnachten 1942: Ein jüdischer Junge überlebt deutsche Massaker in der Ukraine und erlebt als ukrainischer "Ostarbeiter" eine deutsche Weihnacht in Berlin [Christmas 1942: A Jewish Boy Survives German Massacres in the Ukraine and Experiences a German Christmas in Berlin as a Ukrainian 'East Worker']* (Konstanz: Hartung-Gorre Verlag, 2017).

2 Joseph Goebbels, *Die Tagebücher von Joseph Goebbels*, Part 2, vol. 6 (October–December 1942), ed. Hartmut Mehringer (Munich: K. G. Sauer, 1996), 488.

3   Ibid., 469.
4   Ibid., 479–80.
5   Ibid., 474.
6   Ibid., 494.
7   Ibid., 494.
8   Ibid., 505.
9   Ibid., 472.
10 Ibid., 472.
11 Ibid., 479–80.
12 Ibid., 483–4.
13 Ibid., 505–6.
14 Ibid., 479.
15 Ibid., 506.
16 Ibid., 484.
17 Georg Bönisch, "Der Bock von Babelsberg" ["The Stud from Babelsberg"], *Der Spiegel*, November 22, 2010.
18 Peter Longerich, *Goebbels* (Berlin: Pantheon, 2012), 317.
19 Longerich, *Goebbels*, 389–93.
20 Ansgar Diller, "Die Weihnachtsringsendung 1942. Der Produktionsfahrplan der RRG" ["The Christmas Relay Broadcast 1942. The Production Plan of the Reich Broadcast Corporation"], *Rundfunk und Geschichte*, vol 29, no. 1–2 (2003): 47–51
21 Willi A. Boelcke (ed.), *Kriegspropaganda 1939–1941. Geheime Ministerkonferenzen im Propagandaministerium [War Propaganda 1939–1941. Secret Ministerial Conferences in the Propaganda Ministry]* (Stuttgart: Deutsche Verlags-Anstalt, 1966), 579.
22 *Kriegstagebuch der Seekriegsleitung 1939–1945 Teil A, Band 40: Dezember 1942 [War Diary of the Naval Command 1939–1945 Part A, vol. 40: December 1942]* (Herford and Bonn: Verlag E. S. Mittler & Sohn, 1993), 467.
23 Diller, "Die Weihnachtsringsendung 1942. Der Produktionsfahrplan der RRG," 48–51.
24 Ibid., 48. The authenticity of the *Ringsendung* has been thrown into doubt, and some scholars have suggested that all or part of the program was staged, with actors in a Berlin studio pretending to be soldiers and sailors far away from home. While this would certainly conform with the general Nazi history of lies and deceit, the sources do not support this thesis. Goebbels' copious diaries do not mention any deception such as this, and other participants are also not on the record as confirming that the broadcast was a work of fiction. The fact the German Navy allocated two submarines for participation in the broadcast on December 23 serves as evidence that the Berlin broadcaster was indeed in contact with frontline troops. *Kriegstagebuch der Seekriegsleitung 1939–1945 Teil A, Band 40*, 467. The program schedule, which came to light decades after the war, also shows no indication that it was all an act; see Diller, "Weihnachtsringsendung": 47–51. However, in his accompanying remarks, Diller states that it was "in no way a live production", ibid., 47. I am grateful for the help provided by Joe Perry, Georgia State University, in evaluating the sources.
25 Hilmar Hoffmann, John A. Broadwin *et al.*, *The Triumph of Propaganda: Film and National Socialism, 1933–1945* (Providence, RI: Berghahn Books, 1997), 93.
26 Goebbels, *Tagebücher*, 506.
27 Ibid.
28 Ibid., 505.
29 Sven Keller (ed.), *Kriegstagebuch einer jungen Nationalsozialistin: Die Aufzeichnungen Wolfhilde von Königs 1939–1946 [War Diary of a Young National Socialist: The Notes of Wolfhilde von Koenig 1939–1946]* (Berlin: Walter de Gruyter, 2015), 138.

30 Heinz Boberach (ed.), *Meldungen aus dem Reich: Die geheimen Lageberichte des Sicherheitsdienstes der SS 1938–1945 [Intelligence from the Reich: The Secret Situation Reports of the SS Security Service 1938–1945]*, vol. 12, (Herrsching: Pawlak Verlag, 1984), 4600.

31 Golovchansky, *Ich will raus*, 161–2.

32 Boberach, *Meldungen aus dem Reich*, 4634.

33 Marga Himmler, diary, November 29, 1942. Holocaust memorial.

34 Golovchansky, *Ich will raus*, 156–7.

35 Michael Fischer, "Der Vater steht im Feld und hält die Wacht: Die Schrift 'Deutsche Kriegsweihnacht' als Mittel der Propaganda im Zweiten Weltkrieg" ["Father is in the Field and Keeps Watch: The Publication 'German War Christmas' as a Means of Propaganda in World War Two"], *Lied und populäre Kultur/Song and Popular Culture* (2005/2006): 132.

36 The German title is *Feierbuch der deutschen Sippe*. Fischer, "Der Vater steht im Feld," 104.

37 Samuel Koehne, "Were the National Socialists a Völkisch Party? Paganism, Christianity, and the Nazi Christmas," *Central European History*, vol. 47 (2014): 777–8.

38 Perry, *Christmas in Germany*, 213.

39 Ibid., 210.

40 Ibid., 230; Boberach, *Meldungen aus dem Reich*, 3135–6.

41 Hemut Bauckner, "Der Tod kam am Heiligabend," ["Death Came During Christmas"], *Der Oberbadische*, December 23, 2021.

42 Bruno Blau, "The Jewish Population of Germany 1939–1945," *Jewish Social Studies*, vol. 12, no. 2 (April 1950): 161–72.

43 Viktor Klemperer, *Ich will Zeugnis ablegen bis zum letzten [I Will Bear Witness to the Last]*, vol. 2 (Berlin: Aufbau-Verlag, 1996), 295.

44 Hermann Stresau, *Als lebe man nur unter Vorbehalt: Tagebücher aus den Kriegsjahren 1939–1945 [As If You Lived Only Conditionally: Diaries from the War Years 1939–1945]*, ed. Peter Graf and Ulrich Faure (Stuttgart: Klett-Cotta, 2021), 300.

45 Otto Dov Kulka and Eberhard Jäckel, eds., *Die Juden in den geheimen NS-Stimmungsberichten 1933–1945 [The Jews in the Secret National Socialist Public Opinion Reports 1933–1945]* (Düsseldorf: Droste Verlag, 2004), 510.

46 *Das Deutsche Reich und der Zweite Weltkrieg, vol. 9/1: Die deutsche Kriegsgesellschaft 1939 bis 1945. Politisierung, Vernichtung, Überleben [The German Reich and the Second World War, vol. 9/1: German War Society from 1939 to 1945. Politicization, Annihilation, Survival]*, ed. Jörg Echternkamp (Munich: Deutsche Verlags-Anstalt, 2004), 245.

47 Martin Dieckhoff, *Die Stimmen meines Onkels: Ein Lesetagebuch gegen das Schweigen [The Voices of My Uncle: A Diary against Silence]* (n.p., 2015), 69–70.

48 J. L. Granatstein and Norman Hillmer, *Battle Lines: Eyewitness Accounts from Canada's Military History* (Toronto: Thomas Allen Publishers, 2004), 286.

49 Teresa Mikosz-Hintzke, *Six Years 'til Spring: A Polish Family's Odyssey* (San Jose, CA: Authors Choice Press, 2001), 233.

50 Krystyna Wituska and Irene Tomaszewski, *Letters of Krystyna Wituska, 1942–1944* (Detroit, MI: Wayne State University Press, 2006), 1.

51 Ibid., 3.

52 Testimony of Willi Schlagintweit, December 3, 1947. Chronicles of Terror, Pilecki Institute, https://www.zapisyterroru.pl/dlibra/publication/3736.

53 Peter Longerich, *Der ungeschriebene Befehl: Hitler und der Weg zur 'Endlösung' [The Unwritten Command: Hitler and the Road to the 'Final Solution']* (Munich: Piper Verlag, 2001), 169–170.

54 Boberach, *Meldungen aus dem Reich*, 701.

55 Max Braubach, *Der Weg zum 20. Juli 1944: Ein Forschungsbericht [The Road to July 20: State of the Research]* (Cologne and Opladen: Westdeutscher Verlag, 1953), 27.

56 Dietrich Bonhoeffer, *Widerstand und Ergebung: Briefe und Aufzeichnungen aus der Haft [Resistance and Devotion: Letters and Notes from Jail]* (Gütersloh: Gütersloher Verlagshaus, 1998), 36–7.

57 Helmut Simmet, "Bethlehem kann überall sein" ["Bethlehem can be everywhere"] in *Weihnachtsgeschichten aus schwerer Zeit erzählt von Freunden und Förderern des Volksbundes Deutsche Kriegsgräberfürsorge [Christmas Stories from Difficult Times Told by Friends and Supporters of the German People's League for the Care of War Cemeteries]*, ed. Martin Dodenhoeft, (Kassel: Volksbund Deutsche Kriegsgräberfürsorge, 2017), 187–90.

Chapter 8

1 Jean-Pierre Lévy, *Mémoires d'un franc-tireur: Itinéraire d'un resistant (1940–1944) [Memoirs of an Irregular: A Resistance Fighter's Journey (1940–1944)]* (Brussels: Éditions Complexe, 2000), 90–3.

2 Astrid Lindgren, *Krigsdagböcker [War Diaries]* (Lidingö: Salikon förlag, 2005), 150–1.

3 Ibid.

4 Odd Nansen, *Fra dag til dag [From Day to Day]* (Oslo: Dreyers Forlag, 1946), vol. 2, 161.

5 Ibid., 183.

6 Trygve Bratteli, *Fange i natt og tåke [Prisoner in Night and Fog]* (Oslo: Tiden Norsk Forlag, 1980), 37.

7 *Trial of the Major War Criminals before the International Military Tribunal*, vol. 39 (Nuremberg, 1949), 385–407.

8 Ibid., 391.

9 Ibid., 390–1.

10 Götz Aly, *Hitlers Volksstaat: Raub, Rassenkrieg und nationaler Socializmus [Hitler's People's State: Loot, Racial War and National Socialism]* (Frankfurt am Main: S. Fischer Verlag, 2005), 158.

11 *Trials of War Criminals before the Nuernberg Military Tribunals under Control Council Law No. 10, vol. 13* (Washington, D.C.: United States Government Printing Office, 1952), 835.

12 Ibid., 835.

13 Ibid.

14 *Trial of the Major War Criminals before the International Military Tribunal*, vol. 39 (Nuremberg, 1949), 385.

15 Mark Mazower, *Inside Hitler's Greece* (New Haven, CT and London: Yale University Press, 1993), 40.

16 Polymeris Voglis, "Surviving Hunger: Life in the Cities and the Countryside during the Occupation," in *Surviving Hitler and Mussolini: Daily Life in Occupied Europe*, eds. Robert Gildea, Olivier Wieviorka and Anette Warring (Oxford and New York, NY: Berg, 2006), 24.

17 "Noel to be Frugal in Drained France," *The New York Times*, December 24, 1942: 4.

18 Interview with Louis de Wijze, September 13 and 20, 1985, https://www.oorloginnijmegen.nl/images/PDF/579_117_Driever_30_Louis_de_Wijze_compleet.pdf.

19 Dick van Last Galen and Rolf Wolfswinkel, *Anne Frank and After: Dutch Holocaust Literature in a Historical Perspective* (Amsterdam: Amsterdam University Press, 1996), 75.

20 Ibid., 76, 81.

21 Ibid., 76, 81.

22 Elie A. Cohen, *The Abyss* (New York, NY: W. W. Norton, 1973), 71.

23 Jacob Presser, *The Destruction of the Dutch Jews* (New York, NY: E.P. Dutton, 1969), 460.

24 Etty Hillesum, *Etty: The Letters and Diary of Etty Hillesum 1941–1943* (Grand Rapids, MI: William B Eerdmans Publishing Company, 2001), 642–3.

25 Andere Tijden, "Kerstmis in Westerbork" ["Christmas in Westerbork"], https://anderetijden.nl/aflevering/406/Kerstmis-in-Westerbork-.

26 G. L. Durlacher, *Quarantaine [Quarantine]* (Amsterdam: Meulenhoff, 1993), 53.

27 Ibid., 54–5.

28 Tijden, "Kerstmis in Westerbork."

29 Peter Longerich, *Politik der Vernichtung: Eine Gesamtdarstellung der nationalsozialistichen Judenverfolgung [Politics of Annihilation: A Comprehensive Account of the National Socialist Persecution of the Jews]* (Munich: Piper, 1998), 500–1.

30 J. Presser, *Ashes in the Wind: The Destruction of Dutch Jewry* (London: Souvenir Press, 1968), 176–7.

31 David E. Gumpert, "Switzerland Begins To Confront Its Own Holocaust Past," *Forward*, November 5, 2014, https://forward.com/opinion/208252/switzerland-begins-to-confront-its-own-holocaust-p/.

32 David E. Gumpert and Inge Joseph Bleier, *Inge: A Girl's Journey through Nazi Europe* (Grand Rapids, MI: William B. Eerdmans, 2004), 177.

33 Alexandra Zapruder, *Salvaged Pages: Young Writers' Diaries of the Holocaust* (New Haven, CT: Yale University Press, 2014), 63–5.

34 Zapruder, *Salvaged Pages*, 76.

35 Zapruder, *Salvaged Pages*, 76.

36 "Text of Pope Pius XII's Christmas Message Broadcast from Vatican to the World," *The New York Times*, December 25, 1942: 10.

37 Galeazzo Ciano, *The Ciano Diaries*, ed. Hugh Gibson (Garden City, NY: Doubleday & Co., 1946), 558–9.

38 Goebbels, *Tagebücher*, 508.

39 Kulka and Jäckel, *Die Juden in den geheimen NS-Stimmungsberichten*, 512.

40 "Text of the Official Translation of the Pope's Christmas Eve Broadcast," *The New York Times*, December 25, 1941: 20.

41 "The Pope's Message," *The New York Times*, December 25, 1941: 24.

42 White, *Encyclopedia of Camps and Ghettos*, 406.

43 "Contact in time of war," *Sunday Telegraph*, July 4, 1993: 27.

44 Uki Goñi, *The Real Odessa: How Perón Brought the Nazi War Criminals to Argentina* (London: Granta Books, 2003).

45 Ciano, *The Ciano Diaries*, 249.

46 Saul Friedländer, *Pius XII and the Third Reich* (New York, NY: Knopf, 1966), 175–6.

47 Goñi, *The Real Odessa*.

48 Harold H. Tittmann Jr., *Inside the Vatican of Pius XII* (New York, NY: Image Books, 2004), 116.

49 Victor Gollancz, *Let My People Go* (London: Victor Gollancz Ltd., 1943), 31.

50 Owen Chadwick, *Britain and the Vatican during the Second World War* (Cambridge: Cambridge University Press, 1986), 199.

51 Michael Phayer, "'Helping the Jews is not an easy thing to do.' Vatican Holocaust Policy: Continuity or Change?" *Holocaust and Genocide Studies*, vol. 21, no. 3 (Winter 2007): 424.

52 Ibid., 424.

53 Ibid., 432.

54 Ibid., 432.
55 *Foreign Relations of the United States. Diplomatic Paper 1943, vol. 2: Europe* (Washington, D.C.: US Government Printing Office, 1964), 912.

Chapter 9

1 John W. Wheeler-Bennett, *King George VI: His Life and Reign* (London: Macmillan, 1958), 740–1.
2 Ibid., 741.
3 Ben Pimlott, *The Queen: Elizabeth II and the Monarchy* (London: HarperCollins Publishers, 2001), 64.
4 "The Royal Family's Christmas," *Birmingham Post*, December 28, 1942: 2.
5 Lisa Sheridan, *From Cabbages to Kings: The Autobiography of Lisa Sheridan* (London: Odhams Press, 1955), 115.
6 Eleanor Roosevelt, *This I Remember* (New York, NY: Harper & Brothers, 1949), 264.
7 Annette Tapert, *Lines of Battle: Letters from American Servicemen, 1941–1945* (New York, NY: Pocket Books, 1989), 53–5.
8 "King's 'Firm Confidence'," *Sunday Sun*, December 27, 1942: 8.
9 "Facing the Future with Confidence: The King's Broadcast to the Empire," *The Guardian*, December 28, 1942: 3.
10 Ibid.
11 "King's 'Firm Confidence'."
12 Mark Logue and Peter Conradi, *The King's War* (London: Quercus, 2018), 159.
13 "More People Went to Church, Fewer Went Traveling," *Sunday Dispatch*, December 27, 1942: 3.
14 Wheeler-Bennett, *King George VI*, 557.
15 Field Marshal Lord Alanbrooke, *War Diaries 1939–1945*, ed. Alex Danchev and Daniel Todman (Berkeley and Los Angeles, CA: University of California Press, 2001), 350–1.
16 Anthony Eden, *The Memoirs of Anthony Eden, Earl of Avon: The Reckoning* (Boston, MA: Houghton Mifflin Co., 1965), 417.
17 Ibid., 417.
18 "United Nations Declaration on Jewish Massacres: Mr. Eden's Statement," *The Guardian*, December 18, 1942: 6.
19 Eden, *Memoirs*, 415.
20 Gollancz, *Let My People Go*, 2.
21 Martin Gilbert, *Winston S. Churchill, Vol. VII: Road to Victory 1941–1945* (London: Heinemann, 1986), 287.
22 Eden, *Memoirs*, 416.
23 Arthur H. Robinson, "The President's Globe," *Imago Mundi*, vol. 49 (1997), 143–4.
24 Gilbert, *Winston S. Churchill*, 282.
25 Basil Collier, *The Defence of the United Kingdom [History of the Second World War: United Kingdom Military Series]* (London: Her Majesty's Stationery Office, 1957), 311.
26 "Road to Victory," *The Guardian*, December 24, 1942: 6.
27 Vere Hodgson, *Few Eggs and No Oranges* (London: Dennis Dobson, 1976), 277.
28 "Nazi Raiders Destroyed," *The Western Morning News*, December 21, 1942: 3.
29 "Day Raids on Coast Towns," *Liverpool Daily*, December 1, 1942: 1.
30 "Notes on News," *The South Wales Gazette and Newport News*, December 11, 1942: 2.

31 "Bomber Chief: 'The Gradient Eases'," *The Daily Telegraph*, December 24, 1942: 6.

32 Ralph H. Nutter, *With the Possum and the Eagle: The Memoir of a Navigator's War over Germany and Japan* (Denton, TX: University of North Texas Press, 2005), 83.

33 Hodgson, *Few Eggs*, 276.

34 Betty Armitage, *Betty's Wartime Diary, 1939–1945*, ed. Nicholas Webley (London: Thorogood, 2002), 180.

35 Lizzie Collingham, "The human fuel: Food as global commodity and local scarcity," in *The Cambridge History of the Second World War. Volume 3: Total War: Economy, Society and Culture*, eds. Michael Geyer and Adam Tooze (Cambridge: Cambridge University Press, 2015), 166.

36 Collingham, "Human fuel," 165.

37 "Christmas Cheer in 20 Words," *The People*, December 27, 1942: 5.

38 "Austerity Christmas," *The Western Times*, December 24, 1942: 6.

39 "Food Facts: Frugal but Festive," *Marylebone Mercury, Middlesex Independent and West London Star*, December 26, 1942: 2.

40 Ibid.

41 "Christmas Behind the Wire," Wiltshire & Swindon History Centre, https://wshc.org.uk/blog/item/christmas-behind-the-wire.html.

42 "Historien om Olav Bakke Stene," Bodø Lufthistoriske Forening, https://blhf.org/?id=142556726.

43 Benjamin Paul Hegi, *From Wright Field, Ohio, to Hokkaido, Japan: General Curtis E. LeMay's Letters to His Wife Helen, 1941–1945* (Denton, TX: University of North Texas Libraries, 2015), 106–7.

44 Samantha Desroches, "Tanks and Tinsel: The American Celebration of Christmas during World War II" (PhD diss., University of Western Ontario, 2018), 264.

45 Armitage, *Betty's Wartime Diary*, 180.

46 Desroches, "Tanks and Tinsel," 279.

47 Ibid., 286.

48 Ibid., 266.

49 Erik Dyreborg, *The Lucky Ones: Airmen of the Mighty Eighth* (San Jose, CA: Writers Cub Press, 2002), 30–1.

50 Caroline Taggart, *Christmas at War: True Stories of How Britain Came Together on the Home Front* (London: John Blake Publishing, 2019).

Chapter 10

1 Edward A. Raymond, "Long Toms in Action," *Field Artillery Journal*, vol. 33, no. 11 (November 1943): 803.

2 Rathvon M. Tomkins, "Reverse Slope Defense," *Marine Corps Gazette*, vol. 33, no. 7 (July 1949): 30.

3 E. R. Hill, "The Coldstream at Longstop Hill," *Military Review*, vol. 24, no. 3 (June 1944): 106.

4 Bruce Allen Watson, *Exit Rommel: The Tunisian Campaign, 1942–43* (Mechanicsburg, PA: Stackpole Books, 1999), 66.

5 George F. Howe, *Northwest Africa: Seizing the Initiative in the West [United States Army in World War II: The Mediterranean Theater of Operations]* (Washington, D.C.: Center of Military History, 1957), 341.

6 "War Memories of L/Sgt Derrick Jackson, 2nd Battalion, Coldstream Guards," *Britain at War*, https://www.britain-at-war.org.uk/ww2/Derrick_Jackson/html/body_long_stop_hill.htm.

7   Ibid.
8   Tomkins, "Reverse Slope Defense,"30.
9   Howe, *Northwest Africa*, 339; Tomkins, "Reverse Slope Defense," 30.
10 Tomkins, "Reverse Slope Defense,"31.
11 Allen N. Towne, *Doctor Danger Forward: A World War II Memoir of a Combat Medical Aidman, First Infantry Division* (Jefferson, NC and London: McFarland & Co., 2000), 29.
12 Howe, *Northwest Africa*, 343.
13 Rick Atkinson, *An Army at Dawn* (New York, NY: Henry Holt and Company, 2002), 255.
14 Dwight D. Eisenhower, *Crusade in Europe* (Baltimore, MD and London: The Johns Hopkins University Press, 1997), 124.
15 "Battle of the Creeds," *The New York Times*, December 24, 1942, 14.
16 "Christmas Spans Globe with AEF," *Leader-Telegram*, December 25, 1942: 1.
17 Ibid., 8.
18 Paul McDonald Robinett, *Armor Command* (Washington, D.C.: McGregor & Werner, 1958), 113.
19 Desroches, "Tanks and Tinsel," 297.
20 Hollis D. Stabler and Victoria Smith, *No One Ever Asked Me: The World War II Memoirs of an Omaha Indian Soldier* (Lincoln, NE: University of Nebraska Press, 2005), 44.
21 Carlo d'Este, *Patton: A Genius for War* (New York, NY: Harper Perennial, 1995), 444; Agostino Von Hassell and Ed Breslin, *Patton: The Pursuit of Destiny* (Nashville, TN: Thomas Nelson, 2010), 96.
22 George S. Patton Papers: Diaries, 1910–1945; Original; 1942, Sept. 24–1943, Mar. 5; Library of Congress: December 1, 1942.
23 Ibid., December 27 and 28, 1942.
24 Ibid., December 25, 1942.
25 Mark W. Clark, *Calculated Risk: His Personal Story of the War in North Africa and Italy* (London: George G. Harrap, 1951), 128–9.
26 Gilbert, *Winston S. Churchill*, 274–6.
27 Clark, *Calculated Risk*, 128–9.
28 George C. Marshall, *The Papers of George Catlett Marshall*, vol. 3, *"The Right Man for the Job," December 7, 1941 – May 31, 1943* (Baltimore, MA and London: The Johns Hopkins University Press, 1991), 492.
29 Winston S. Churchill, *The Second World War, vol. 4: The Hinge of Fate* (London: Cassell, 1951), 578.
30 Yolanda Maurer, "A Christmas Eve Never To Be Forgotten," *Fort Lauderdale News*, December 20, 1972: 13.
31 David Rolf, *The Bloody Road to Tunis: Destruction of the Axis Forces in North Africa, November 1942 – May 1943* (Redbridge: Greenhill Books, 2001), 69.
32 Goebbels, *Tagebücher*, 493.
33 Ibid., 503.
34 Nico Ossemann, "Chor der Chöre" ["Choir of Choirs"], in *Stille Nacht, Heilige Nacht. Weihnachtsgeschichten aus schwerer Zeit erzählt von Freunden und Förderern des Volksbundes Deutsche Kriegsgräberfürsorge [Silent Night, Holy Night: Christmas Stories from Difficult Times Told by Friends and Supporters of the German People's League for the Care of War Cemeteries]*, ed. Maurice Bonkat, (Kassel: Volksbund Deutsche Kriegsgräberfürsorge, 2008), 54.
35 John B. Romeiser, *Combat Reporter: Don Whitehead's World War II Diary and Memoirs* (New York, NY: Fordham University Press, 2006), 85.

36   Bernard Law Montgomery, *The Memoirs of Field-Marshal the Viscount Montgomery of Alamein* (London: Collins, 1958), 148–9.
37   Ibid., 148.
38   Ibid., 150.
39   Leif Vetlesen and Ingvald Wahl, *Syv fortellinger fra Norges krig på havet [Seven Tales from Norway's War at Sea]* (Oslo: Gyldendal Norsk Forlag, 1993).
40   Stig Tenold, *Norwegian Shipping in the 20th Century: Norway's Successful Navigation of the World's Most Global Industry* (London: Palgrave MacMillan, 2019), 139–40.
41   *News of Norway*, vol. 4, no. 1 (January 21, 1944): 88; "Land of Contrasts," *The Age*, March 19, 1949: 5.
42   Jon Rustung Hegland, *Nortraships flåte [Nortraship's Fleet]* (Oslo: Dreyers Forlag, 1976), 149, 151.
43   Vetlesen and Wahl, *Syv fortellinger*.
44   Michael G. Walling, *Forgotten Sacrifice: The Arctic Convoys of World War II* (Oxford: Osprey 2016), 234.
45   Ibid. 234.
46   S. W. Roskill, *War at Sea 1939–1945, vol. 2: The Period of Balance [History of the Second World War: United Kingdom Military Series]* (London: Her Majesty's Stationery Office, 1956), 287–9.
47   Ibid., 291.
48   Ibid., 291–9.
49   Erich Raeder, *My Life* (Annapolis, MD: United States Naval Institute, 1960), 370.
50   Raeder, *My Life*, 370–3; Karl Dönitz, *Zehn Jahre und zwanzig Tage [Ten Years and Twenty Days]* (Munich: Bernard & Graefe Verlag für Wehrwesen, 1977), 292.
51   Dönitz, *Zehn Jahre*, 308.
52   Karl Dönitz, *40 Fragen an Karl Dönitz [Forty Questions for Karl Dönitz]* (Munich: Bernard & Graefe Verlag für Wehrwesen, 1980), 105–6.
53   Hans Goebeler with John Vanzo, *Steel Boats, Iron Hearts: A U-Boat Crewman's Life Aboard U-505* (El Dorado Hills, CA: Savas Beattie, 2005), 123–5.
54   Robin Brodhurst, *Churchill's Anchor: The Biography of Admiral Sir Dudley Pound* (Barnsley: Pen and Sword, 2000), 272.
55   Roskill, *War at Sea*, 212.
56   Joseph Schott, "White Christmas," private manuscript.
57   Interview with Joseph Schott, https ://www.youtube.com/watch?v=epjPGxtzgvc&t=2s.
58   Niels Ole Kiil, "Sønderjyde på de store have," ["A South Jutland Sailor at Sea"], *M/S Museet for Søfarts årbog*, vol. 61 (2002): 32.
59   Karl Dönitz, *Zehn Jahre*, 278.
60   Jordan Vause, *U-boat Ace: The Story of Wolfgang Lüth* (Annapolis, MD: Naval Institute Press, 1990), 143–5.
61   Antonio Maronari, *Un sommergibile non è rientrato alla base [A submarine has not returned to base]* (Milan: Libreria Rizzoli, 1957), 323.
62   Ibid., 323.

Chapter 11

1   Bruce Kuklick, *The Fighting Sullivans: How Hollywood and the Military Make Heroes* (Lawrence, KS: University Press of Kansas, 2016), 68.
2   Aletta Sullivan, "I Lost Five Sons," *American Magazine* 137 (March 1944): 92–5. Quoted from Emily Yellin, *Our Mothers' War: American Women at Home and at the Front During World War II* (New York, NY: Free Press, 2004), 34–5.

3   *Juneau I* (CL-52). Naval History and Heritage Command, https://www.history.navy.mil/research/histories/ship-histories/danfs/j/juneau-i.html.
4   The Sullivan Brothers. Naval History and Heritage Command, https://www.history.navy.mil/browse-by-topic/disasters-and-phenomena/the-sullivan-brothers-and-the-assignment-of-family-members0.html.
5   Kuklick, *The Fighting Sullivans*, 66–7.
6   Mattie E. Treadwell, *The Women's Army Corps United States Army in World War II [United States Army in World War II: Special Studies]* (Washington, D.C.: Center of Military History, 1954), 110.
7   Doris Weatherford, *American Women during World War II: An Encyclopedia* (New York, NY: Routledge, 2010), 166.
8   "Overseas Yule Gifts Tripled Over Last War," *Washington Post*, December 20, 1942: L8, quoted from Desroches, "Tanks and Tinsel," 173–4.
9   Letter Written by Saidee R. Leach to her Son, Navy Ensign Douglas Leach, Dated December 21, 1942. Bryant Digital Repository. Bryant University, https://digitalcommons.bryant.edu/wwll_leach/22/.
10 Desroches, "Tanks and Tinsel," 160.
11 William D. Hassett, *Off the Record with F. D. R., 1942–1945* (New Brunswick, NJ: Rutgers University Press, 1958), 148–9.
12 Ibid., 147–8.
13 Ibid., 149.
14 Robinson, "President's Globe," 143.
15 Ibid., 143.
16 Eleanor Roosevelt, "My Day," December 25, 1942. Eleanor Roosevelt Papers Project, Columbian College of Arts & Sciences, The George Washington University, https://erpapers.columbian.gwu.edu/my-day.
17 "Christmas Declaration by men and women of German ancestry," *The Boston Globe*, December 28, 1942: 15.
18 Ibid.
19 "Christmas Has New Meaning for City," *Fitchburg Sentinel*, December 24, 1942: 1.
20 Ibid.
21 "To Save Sugar," *Council Grove Republican*, December 10, 1942: 3.
22 "Santa Claus Is No War Casualty," *Los Angeles Times*, December 23, 1942: 20.
23 "Christmas 1942," *Charleston Daily Mail*, December 25, 1942: 1, quoted from Desroches, "Tanks and Tinsel," 113–14.
24 Desroches, "Tanks and Tinsel," 29–30.
25 Adele McKinnie, "Shall I Let My Child Play with War Toys?" *Women's Home Companion*, November 1942: 52, quoted from Desroches, "Tanks and Tinsel," 265.
26 Desroches, "Tanks and Tinsel," 103.
27 *The Cushing Daily Citizen*, December 13, 1942: 8.
28 Louis Fiset, *Imprisoned Apart: The World War II Correspondence of an Issei Couple* (Seattle, WA: University of Washington Press, 1997), 219.
29 Ibid., 217.
30 Ibid., 216.
31 Ibid., 215–16.
32 Sally Nakamoto, "Christmas, 1942," *The Minidoka Irrigator*, 25 December 25, 1942: 6.
33 Fukuyama Tsutomu, "Bethlehem's Message," *The Minidoka Irrigator*, 25 December 25, 1942: 3.
34 Hiromura Yuji, "A Christmas Prayer," *The Minidoka Irrigator*, 25 December 25, 1942: 6.

35 Tanaka Togo, "A Report of the Manzanar Riot of Sunday, December 6, 1942." The Japanese American Evacuation and Resettlement: A Digital Archive, Bancroft Library, University of California, 105.

36 Yamato Ichihashi and Gordon H. Chang, *Morning Glory, Evening Shadow: Yamato Ichihashi and His Internment Writings, 1942–1945* (Stanford, CA: Stanford University Press, 1997), 164.

Postscript

1 Letter Written by Saidee R. Leach to her Son, Navy Ensign Douglas Leach, Dated December 21, 1942. Bryant Digital Repository. Bryant University, https://digitalcommons.bryant.edu/wwll_leach/22/.

2 "Music Biz Still Hunting That Boff War Song," *Variety*, January 6, 1943: 187. Quoted from Kathleen E. R. Smith, *God Bless America: Tin Pan Alley Goes to War* (Lexington, KY: University Press of Kentucky, 2003), 24.

3 W. M. Reddig, "Medley for 1942 Is Full of Hits in the Big Parade for Total Victory," *The Kansas City Times*, January 1, 1943: 18.

4 *Let's Talk Turkey to Japan*, NBC's Sixth War Loan Program, November 23, 1944, quoted in Smith, *God Bless America*, 25.

5 Nathan Weinbender, "Still Bright after 75 Years," *The Spokesman Review*, December 23, 2016: C3–C4.

6 John Keegan, *Six Armies in Normandy: From D-Day to the Liberation of Paris, June 6th – August 25th, 1944* (New York, NY: Viking Press, 1982), 82.

7 Bryan Hiatt, Interview with Sterling Mace. World War II Database, https://ww2db.com/doc.php?q=441.

8 Yvonne Zacharias, "A glorious Silent Night on wartime seas," *The Vancouver Sun*, December 24, 2002: 3.

9 I am indebted to Christopher Bell, Dalhousie University; Marcus Faulkner, King's College London; and David Kohnen, Naval War College for their help in evaluating this account.

10 Craig Collie and Hajime Marutan, *The Path of Infinite Sorrow: The Japanese on the Kokoda Track* (Crows Nest: Allen & Unwin, 2012), 253–4.

11 *The Changi Guardian, Xmas Number*, December 25, 1942, https://specialcollections-blog.lib.cam.ac.uk/wp-content/uploads/2015/12/christmas.jpg

12 David Farber and Beth Bailey, "The Fighting Man as Tourist: The Politics of Tourist Culture in Hawaii during World War II," *Pacific Historical Review*, vol. 65, no. 4 (November 1996), 641.

13 "Rising Tide of Tourism," Smithsonian National Air and Space Museum, https://airandspace.si.edu/exhibitions/hawaii-by-air/online/post-war-travel/rising-tide-of-tourism.cfm#

14 Eleanor Roosevelt, "My Day," December 28, 1942. Eleanor Roosevelt Papers Project, Columbian College of Arts & Sciences, The George Washington University, https://erpapers.columbian.gwu.edu/my-day.

15 Ray McConnell Jr., "Thirty Christmases to Come," *Lincoln Journal Star*, December 24, 1942: 1.

16 "Death of Lord Gowrie's Son," *Sydney Morning Herald*, February 16, 1943: 4.

17 "Happy Warrior and Poet," *The Age*, October 23, 1943: 6.

Bibliography

Articles

Bae Kyounghan. "Chiang Kai-shek and Christianity: Religious life reflected from his diary." *Journal of Modern Chinese History*, vol. 3, no. 1 (June 2009): 1–10.

Blau, Bruno. "The Jewish Population of Germany 1939–1945." *Jewish Social Studies*, vol. 12, no. 2 (April 1950): 161–72.

Brautmeier, Jürgen. "Frontbewährung in Stalingrad. Feldpostbriefe des Gefreiten Hans Happe aus Delbrück/Westfalen" ["Proving One's Worth at the Front in Stalingrad: Letters from Sergeant Hans Happe from Delbrueck/Westphalia"]. *Geschichte im Westen. Halbjahres-Zeitschrift für Landes- und Zeitgeschichte*, volume 2 (1993): 166–92.

Diller, Ansgar. "Die Weihnachtsringsendung 1942. Der Produktionsfahrplan der RRG" ["The Christmas Relay Broadcast 1942. The Production Plan of the Reich Broadcast Corporation"]. *Rundfunk und Geschichte*, vol. 29, no. 1–2 (2003): 47–51.

Farber, David and Beth Bailey. "The Fighting Man as Tourist: The Politics of Tourist Culture in Hawaii during World War II." *Pacific Historical Review*, vol. 65, no. 4 (November 1996): 641–60.

Fischer, Michael. "Der Vater steht im Feld und hält die Wacht: Die Schrift 'Deutsche Kriegsweihnacht' als Mittel der Propaganda im Zweiten Weltkrieg" ["Father is in the Field and Keeps Watch: The Publication 'German War Christmas' as a Means of Propaganda in World War II"]. *Lied und populäre Kultur/Song and Popular Culture* (2005/2006): 99–135.

Hill, E. R. "The Coldstream at Longstop Hill." *Military Review*, vol. 24, no. 3 (June 1944): 106–10.

Kiil, Niels Ole. "Sønderjyde på de store have" ["A South Jutland Sailor at Sea"]. *M/S Museet for Søfarts årbog*, vol. 61 (2002): 7–38.

Moss, Olga. "Bantjeuj." *Fidelity* no. 61 (2006). Available at: https://metanthonymemorial.org/VernostNo61.htm

Perry, Joseph B. "The Madonna of Stalingrad: Mastering the (Christmas) Past and West German National Identity after World War II." *Radical History Review*, no. 83 (Spring 2002): 7–27.

Phayer, Michael. "'Helping the Jews is not an easy thing to do.' Vatican Holocaust Policy: Continuity or Change?" *Holocaust and Genocide Studies*, vol. 21, no. 3 (Winter 2007): 421–53.

Raymond, Edward A. "Long Toms in Action." *Field Artillery Journal*, vol. 33, no. 11 (November 1943): 803–4.

Reaves, Wendy Wick. "Thomas Nast and the President." *The American Art Journal*, vol. 19, no. 1 (Winter, 1987): 60–71.

Reineck, Hermann. "Ein grauenvoller Tag unterm Weihnachtsbaum" ["A Horrifying Day under the Christmas Tree"]. *Lagergemeinschaft Auschwitz/Freundeskreis der Auschwitzer. Mitteilungsblatt [Newsletter of Auschwitz Camp Community/Circle of Friends of Former Auschwitz Prisoners]*, vol. 37 (December 2017): 4.

Robinson, Arthur H. "The President's Globe." *Imago Mundi*, vol. 49 (1997): 143–52.

Sullivan, Aletta. "I Lost Five Sons." *American Magazine*, no. 137 (March 1944): 92–5.

Tomkins, Rathvon M. "Reverse Slope Defense." *Marine Corps Gazette*, Vol. 33, No. 7 (July 1949): 30–3.

Vinson, J. Chal. "Thomas Nast and the American Political Scene." *American Quarterly*, vol. 9, no. 3 (Autumn, 1957): 337–44.

Books

Adam, Wilhelm. *Der schwere Entschluss [The Difficult Decision]*. Berlin: Verlag der Nation, 1965.

Alanbrooke, Field Marshal Lord. *War Diaries 1939–1945*, edited by Alex Danchev and Daniel Todman. Berkeley and Los Angeles, CA: University of California Press, 2001.

Alexander, Irvin. *Surviving Bataan and Beyond: Colonel Irvin Alexander's Odyssey as a Japanese Prisoner of War*, edited by Dominic J. Caraccilo. Mechanicsburg, PA: Stackpole Books, 2005.

Alexander, Joseph H. *Edson's Raiders: The 1st Marine Raider Battalion in World War II*. Annapolis, MD: Naval Institute Press, 2001.

Allen, Gwenfread Elaine. *Hawaii's War Years, 1941–1945*. Honolulu, HI: University of Hawaii Press, 1952.

Aly, Götz. *Hitlers Volksstaat: Raub, Rassenkrieg und nationaler Socializmus [Hitler's People's State: Loot, Racial War and National Socialism]*. Frankfurt am Main: S. Fischer Verlag, 2005.

Arad, Yitzhak. *The Operation Reinhard Death Camps: Belzec, Sobibor, Treblinka*. Bloomington, IN: Indiana University Press, 2018.

Armitage, Betty. *Betty's Wartime Diary, 1939–1945*, edited by Nicholas Webley. London: Thorogood, 2002.

Atkinson, Rick. *An Army at Dawn*. New York, NY: Henry Holt and Company, 2002.

Bähr, Walter and Hans W. Bähr. *Kriegsbriefe gefallener Studenten [War Letters from Fallen Students]*. Tübingen and Stuttgart: Rainer Wunderlich Verlag, 1952.

Bailey, Beth and David Farber. *The First Strange Place: Race and Sex in World War II Hawaii*. Baltimore, MD: The Johns Hopkins University Press, 1992.

Barr, Ruth. *Ruth's Record: The Diary of an American in Japanese-occupied Shanghai 1941–45*. Hong Kong: Earnshaw, 2017.

Beebe, Lewis and John M. Beebe. *Prisoner of the Rising Sun: The Lost Diary of Brig. Gen. Lewis Beebe*. College Station, TX: Texas A&M University Press, 2006.

Bem, Marek. *Sobibor Extermination Camp 1942–1943*. Amsterdam: Stichting Sobibor, 2015.

Benz, Wolfgang. *Theresienstadt: Eine Geschichte von Täuschung und Vernichtung [Theresienstadt: A History of Deception and Annihilation]*. Munich: C. H. Beck, 2013.

Bhattacharjee, Anuradha. *The Second Homeland: Polish refugees in India*. Los Angeles, CA: Sage, 2012.

Bioletti, Harry. *The Yanks are Coming: The American Invasion of New Zealand, 1942–1944*. Auckland: Century Hutchinson, 1989.

Blair, Clay Jr. *Silent Victory: The US Submarine War against Japan*. Philadelphia, PA and New York, NY: J. P. Lippincott, 1975.

Boberach, Heinz, ed. *Meldungen aus dem Reich: Die geheimen Lageberichte des Sicherheitsdienstes der SS 1938–1945 [Intelligence from the Reich: The Secret Situation Reports of the SS Security Service 1938–1945]*, vol. 12. Herrsching: Pawlak Verlag, 1984.

Boelcke, Willi A., ed. *Kriegspropaganda 1939–1941. Geheime Ministerkonferenzen im Propagandaministerium [War Propaganda 1939–1941. Secret Ministerial Conferences in the Propaganda Ministry]*. Stuttgart: Deutsche Verlags, 1966.

Bogdanov, V. M. "A Daring Raid." *Soviet Military Review*, no. 11 (November 1982): 38–9.

Bohnhoeffer, Dietrich. *Widerstand und Ergebung: Briefe und Aufzeichnungen aus der Haft [Resistance and Devotion: Letters and Notes from Jail]*. Gütersloh: Gütersloher Verlagshaus, 1998.

Bose, Sugata. *His Majesty's Opponent: Subhas Chandra Bose and India's Struggle against Empire.* Cambridge, MA and London: The Belknap Press of Harvard University Press, 2011.

Bratteli, Trygve. *Fange i natt og tåke [Prisoner in Night and Fog].* Oslo: Tiden Norsk Forlag, 1980.

Braubach, Max. *Der Weg zum 20. Juli 1944: Ein Forschungsbericht [The Road to July 20: State of the Research].* Cologne and Opladen: Westdeutscher Verlag, 1953.

Breslin, Ed. *Patton: The Pursuit of Destiny.* Nashville, TN: Thomas Nelson, 2010.

Brodhurst, Robin. *Churchill's Anchor: The Biography of Admiral Sir Dudley Pound.* Barnsley: Pen and Sword, 2000.

Brostoff, Anita and Sheila Chamovitz, *Flares of Memory: Stories of Childhood during the Holocaust.* New York, NY: Oxford University Press, 2001.

Carafano, James Jay. *Brutal War: Jungle Fighting in Papua New Guinea 1942.* Boulder, CO: Lynne Rienner Publishers, 2021.

Century, Douglas. *Barney Ross: The Life of a Jewish Fighter.* New York, NY: Shocken Books, 2006.

Chadwick, Owen. *Britain and the Vatican during the Second World War.* Cambridge: Cambridge University Press, 1986.

Chaudhuri, Nirad C. *Thy Hand, Great Anarch! India 1921–1952.* London: Chatto & Windus, 1987.

Chiang Kai-Shek, Albert French Lutley, Frank Wilson Price and Pin-ho Ma. *Resistance and Reconstruction: Messages during China's Six Years of War, 1937–1943.* New York, NY: Harper and Brothers, 1943.

Christensen, Claus Bundgård, Niels Bo Poulsen and Peter Scharff Smith. *Under hagekors og Dannebrog: Danskere i Waffen SS 1940–45 [Under Swastika and Dannebrog: Danes in the Waffen-SS 1940–45].* Copenhagen: Aschehoug, 1998.

Chunn, Calvin Ellsworth. *Of Rice and Men: The Story of Americans under the Rising Sun.* Los Angeles, CA: Veterans' Publishing Company, 1947.

Churchill, Winston S. *The Second World War, vol. 4: The Hinge of Fate.* London: Cassell, 1951.

Ciano, Galeazzo. *The Ciano Diaries,* edited by Hugh Gibson. Garden City, NY: Doubleday & Co., 1946.

Clark, Mark W. *Calculated Risk: His Personal Story of the War in North Africa and Italy.* London: George G. Harrap, 1951.

Cohen, Elie A. *The Abyss.* New York, NY: W. W. Norton, 1973.

Cohen, Laurie R. *Smolensk under the Nazis: Everyday Life in Occupied Russia.* Woodbridge: Boydell & Brewer, 2013.

Collie, Craig and Hajime Marutan. *The Path of Infinite Sorrow: The Japanese on the Kokoda Track.* Crows Nest: Allen & Unwin, 2012.

Collier, Basil. *The Defence of the United Kingdom [History of the Second World War: United Kingdom Military Series].* London: Her Majesty's Stationery Office, 1957.

Collingham, Lizzie. "The human fuel: Food as global commodity and local scarcity." In *The Cambridge History of the Second World War. Volume 3: Total War: Economy, Society and Culture,* edited by Michael Geyer and Adam Tooze, 149–73. Cambridge: Cambridge University Press, 2015.

Conger, Sarah Pike. *Letters from China.* Chicago, IL: A. C. McClurg & Co., 1909.

Cordingly, Eric. *Down to Bedrock: The Diary and Secret Notes of a Far East Prisoner of War Chaplain 1942–45,* edited by Louise Cordingly. Norwich: Art Angels, 2013.

Czech, Danuta. *Kalendarium der Ereignisse im Konzentrationslager Auschwitz-Birkenau 1939–1945 [Chronology of Events in the Concentration Camp Auschwitz-Birkenau 1939–1945].* Hamburg: Rowohlt, 1989.

Darian-Smith, Kate. *On the Home Front: Melbourne in Wartime, 1939–1945.* Melbourne: Oxford University Press, 1990.

——"The Home Front and the American Presence in 1942." In *Australia 1942: In the Shadow of War,* edited by Peter Dean, 70–88. Port Melbourne: Cambridge University Press, 2013.

——"Remembrance, Romance, and Nation: Memories of Wartime Australia." In *Gender & Memory*, edited by Selma Leydesdorff, Luisa Passerini, and Paul Thompson, 151–64. New York, NY: Routledge, 2017.

Das Deutsche Reich und der Zweite Weltkrieg, vol. 9/1: Die deutsche Kriegsgesellschaft 1939 bis 1945. Politisierung, Vernichtung, Überleben [The German Reich and the Second World War, vol. 9/1: German War Society from 1939 to 1945. Politicization, Annihilation, Survival], edited by Jörg Echternkamp. Munich: Deutsche Verlags-Anstalt, 2004.

Davies, Hannah. *Among Hills and Valleys in Western China.* London: S. W. Partridge & Co., 1901.

Desroches, Samantha. "Tanks and Tinsel: The American Celebration of Christmas during World War II." PhD diss., University of Western Ontario, 2018.

Dieckhoff, Martin. *Die Stimmen meines Onkels: Ein Lesetagebuch gegen das Schweigen [The Voices of My Uncle: A Diary against Silence].* n.p., 2015.

Diedrich, Torsten. *Paulus: Das Trauma von Stalingrad [Paulus: The Trauma of Stalingrad].* Paderborn: Ferdinand Schöningh, 2009.

Dönitz, Karl. *Zehn Jahre und zwanzig Tage [Ten Years and Twenty Days].* Munich: Bernard & Graefe Verlag für Wehrwesen, 1977.

——*40 Fragen an Karl Dönitz [Forty Questions for Karl Dönitz].* Munich: Bernard & Graefe Verlag für Wehrwesen, 1980.

Dooley, Thomas, Jerry C. Cooper, John A. Adams Jr. and Henry C. Dethloff. *To Bataan and Back: The World War II Diary of Major Thomas Dooley.* College Station, TX: Texas A&M University Press, 2006.

Draenger, Gusta Davidson. *Justyna's Narrative*, edited by Eli Pfefferkorn and David H. Hirsch. Amherst, MA: University of Massachusetts Press, 1996.

Duffy, Michael and Nick Hordern. *World War Noir: Sydney's unpatriotic war.* Sydney: University of New South Wales Press, 2019.

Durlacher, G. L. *Quarantaine [Quarantine].* Amsterdam: Meulenhoff, 1993.

Dyreborg, Erik. *The Lucky Ones: Airmen of the Mighty Eighth.* San Jose, CA: Writers Cub Press, 2002.

Eden, Anthony. *The Memoirs of Anthony Eden, Earl of Avon: The Reckoning.* Boston, MA: Houghton Mifflin Co., 1965.

Edmundson, James. *Letters to Lee: From Pearl Harbor to the War's Final Mission.* New York, NY: Fordham University Press, 2009.

Eichelberger, Robert L. *Our Jungle Road to Tokyo.* New York, NY: The Viking Press, 1950.

——*Dear Miss Em: General Eichelberger's War in the Pacific 1942–1945.* Westport, CT: Greenwood Press, 1972.

Eisenhower, Dwight D. *Crusade in Europe.* Baltimore, MD and London: The Johns Hopkins University Press, 1997.

Elrod, Roy H. *We Were Going to Win, or Die There: With the Marines at Guadalcanal, Tarawa, and Saipan.* Denton, TX: University of North Texas Press, 2017.

Emerson, Geoffrey Charles. *Hong Kong Internment, 1942–1945: Life in the Japanese Civilian Camp at Stanley.* Hong Kong: Hong Kong University Press, 2008.

Epstein, Karl Iosifowitsch. *Weihnachten 1942: Ein jüdischer Junge überlebt deutsche Massaker in der Ukraine und erlebt als ukrainischer "Ostarbeiter" eine deutsche Weihnacht in Berlin [Christmas 1942: A Jewish Boy Survives German Massacres in the Ukraine and Experiences a German Christmas in Berlin as a Ukrainian 'East Worker'].* Konstanz: Hartung-Gorre Verlag, 2017.

d'Este, Carlo. *Patton: A Genius for War.* New York, NY: Harper Perennial, 1995.

Fiset, Louis. *Imprisoned Apart: The World War II Correspondence of an Issei Couple.* Seattle, WA: University of Washington Press, 1997.

Forbes, Bruce David. *Christmas: A Candid History*. Berkeley, CA: University of California Press, 2007.

Foreign Relations of the United States. Diplomatic Paper 1943, vol. 2: Europe. Washington, D.C.: US Government Printing Office, 1964.

Friedländer, Saul. *Pius XII and the Third Reich*. New York, NY: Knopf, 1966.

Fussell, Paul. *Wartime: Understanding and Behavior in the Second World War*. Oxford: Oxford University Press, 1989.

Galen, Dick van Last and Rolf Wolfswinkel. *Anne Frank and After: Dutch Holocaust Literature in a Historical Perspective*. Amsterdam: Amsterdam University Press, 1996.

Gilbert, Martin. *Winston S. Churchill, Vol. VII: Road to Victory 1941–1945*. London: Heinemann, 1986.

——*The Holocaust: The Human Tragedy*. New York, NY: Rosetta Books, 2014.

Goebbels, Joseph. *Die Tagebücher von Joseph Goebbels [Joseph Goebbels' Diaries]*, Part 2, vol. 6 (October–December 1942), ed. Hartmut Mehringer. Munich: K. G. Sauer, 1996.

Goebeler, Hans with John Vanzo. *Steel Boats, Iron Hearts: A U-Boat Crewman's Life Aboard U-505*. El Dorado Hills, CA: Savas Beattie, 2005.

Goldstein, Donald M. and Katherine V. Dillon, eds. *Fading Victory: The Diary of Admiral Matome Ugaki 1941–1945*. Annapolis, MD: Naval Institute Press, 1991.

Gollancz, Victor. *Let My People Go*. London: Victor Gollancz Ltd., 1943.

Golovchansky, Anatoly, Valentin Osipov, Anatoly Prokopenko, Ute Daniel and Jürgen Reulecke (eds.) *"Ich will raus aus diesem Wahnsinn." Deutsche Briefe von der Ostfront 1941–1945 aus sowjetischen Archiven ["I Want to Escape from this Madness." German Letters from the Eastern Front 1941–1945 in Soviet Archives]*. Wuppertal: Peter Hammer Verlag, 1991.

Goñi, Uki. *The Real Odessa: How Perón Brought the Nazi War Criminals to Argentina*. London: Granta Books, 2003.

Gorbachevsky, Boris. *Through the Maelstrom: A Red Army Soldier's War on the Eastern Front, 1942–1945*. Lawrence, KS: University Press of Kansas, 2008.

Granatstein J. L. and Norman Hillmer. *Battle Lines: Eyewitness Accounts from Canada's Military History*. Toronto: Thomas Allen Publishers, 2004.

Grupe, Friedrich. *Jahrgang 1916: Die Fahne war mehr als der Tod [Born in 1916: The Flag Meant More than Death]*. Munich: Universitas, 1989.

Guardia, Mike. *American Guerrilla: The Forgotten Heroics of Russell W. Volckmann*. Philadelphia, PA: Casemate Publishers, 2010.

Gumpert David E. and Inge Joseph Bleier. *Inge: A Girl's Journey through Nazi Europe*. Grand Rapids, MI: William B. Eerdmans, 2004.

Haaest, Erik. *Frostknuder [Frostbites]*. Copenhagen: Bogan, 2005.

Halsey, William F. and J. Bryan III. *Admiral Halsey's Story*. New York, NY and London: McGraw-Hill Publishing Co., 1947.

Hamer, Heyo. "Die letzten Japan-Missionare der Ostasien-Mission (OAM). Ein Beitrag zur Geschichte der Auflösung der OAM 1947" ["The Last Japan Missionaries of the East Asia Mission (OAM): A Contribution to the History of the Dissolution of the OAM in 1947"]. In *Wege und Welte der Religionen [Roads and Worlds of the Religions]*, edited by Jürgen Court and Michael Klöcker, 177–92. Frankfurt am Main: Verlag Otto Lembeck, 2009.

Hamilton, Hope. *Sacrifice on the Steppe: The Italian Alpine Corps in the Stalingrad Campaign, 1942–1943*. Havertown, PA and Oxford: Casemate Publishers, 2011.

Handel, Paul. *The Vital Factor*. Sydney: Australian Military History Publications, 2004.

Hartley, F. J. *A Christmas in New Guinea*. Melbourne: The Book Depot, 1944.

——*Sanananda Interlude*. Melbourne: The Book Depot, 1949.

Hassett, William D. *Off the Record with F. D. R., 1942–1945*. New Brunswick, NJ: Rutgers University Press, 1958.

Hayward, Joel S. A. *Stopped at Stalingrad: The Luftwaffe and Hitler's Defeat in the East, 1942–1943*. Lawrence, KS: University Press of Kansas, 1998.

Hegi, Benjamin Paul. *From Wright Field, Ohio, to Hokkaido, Japan: General Curtis E. LeMay's Letters to His Wife Helen, 1941–1945*. Denton, TX: University of North Texas Libraries, 2015.

Hegland, Jon Rustung. *Nortraships flåte [Nortraship's Fleet]*. Oslo: Dreyers Forlag, 1976.

Heintel, Hans. "Weihnachten bei Matka" ["Christmas with Matka"]. In *Unter den Sternen: Weihnachtsgeschichten aus schwerer Zeit erzählt von Freunden und Förderern des Volksbundes Deutsche Kriegsgräberfürsorge [Under the Stars: Christmas Stories from Difficult Times Told by Friends and Supporters of the German People's League for the Care of War Cemeteries]*, edited by Martin Dodenhoeft and Henning Unverhau, 17–21. Kassel: Volksbund Deutsche Kriegsgräberfürsorge, 2007.

Hibbs, Ralph Emerson. *Tell MacArthur to Wait*. New York, NY: Carlton Press, 1988.

Hillen, Ernest. *The Way of a Boy: A Memoir of Java*. London: Penguin, 1993.

Hillesum, Etty. *Etty: The Letters and Diary of Etty Hillesum 1941–1943*. Grand Rapids, MI: William B. Eerdmans Publishing Company, 2001.

Hodgson, Vere. *Few Eggs and No Oranges*. London: Dennis Dobson, 1976.

Hoffman, Hilmar. *The Triumph of Propaganda: Film and National Socialism, 1933–1945*, translated by John A. Broadwin and Volker Rolf Berghahn. Providence, RI: Berghahn Books, 1997.

Holloway, Eric. *The Stars Are My Friends*. Darlington: Serendipity, 2005.

Holmes, W. J. *Double Edged Secrets: U.S. Naval Intelligence Operations in the Pacific*. Annapolis, MD: Naval Institute Press, 1979.

Howe, George F. *Northwest Africa: Seizing the Initiative in the West [United States Army in World War II: The Mediterranean Theater of Operations]*. Washington, D.C.: Center of Military History, 1957.

Jacobs, Eugene C. *Blood Brothers: A Medic's Sketch Book*. New York, NY: Carlton Press, 1985.

James, D. Clayton. *The Years of MacArthur*, vol. 2. Boston, MA: Houghton Mifflin, 1975.

Jersey, Stanley Coleman. *Hell's Islands: The Untold Story of Guadalcanal*. College Station, TX: Texas A&M University Press, 2008.

Jung, Richard. "90 Minuten Aufenthalt (Begegnung mit einem Engel)." ["90 Minute Stop (Meeting an Angel"]. In *Weihnachtsgeschichten aus schwerer Zeit erzählt von Freunden und Förderern des Volksbundes Deutsche Kriegsgräberfürsorge [Christmas Stories from Difficult Times Told by Friends and Supporters of the German People's League for the Care of War Cemeteries]*, edited by Martin Dodenhoeft, 44–8. Kassel: Volksbund Deutsche Kriegsgräberfürsorge, 2017.

Kaplan, James. *Irving Berlin: New York Genius*. New Haven, CT and London: Yale University Press, 2019.

Keegan, John. *Six Armies in Normandy: From D-Day to the Liberation of Paris, June 6th – August 25th, 1944*. New York, NY: Viking Press, 1982.

Keller, Sven, ed. *Kriegstagebuch einer jungen Nationalsozialistin: Die Aufzeichnungen Wolfhilde von Königs 1939–1946 [War Diary of a Young National Socialist: The Notes of Wolfhilde von Koenig 1939–1946]*. Berlin: Walter de Gruyter, 2015.

Kenney, George C. *General Kenney Reports: A Personal History of the Pacific War*. New York, NY: Duell, Sloan and Pearce, 1949.

Klemperer, Viktor. *Ich will Zeugnis ablegen bis zum letzten [I Will Bear Witness to the Last]*, vol. 2. Berlin: Aufbau-Verlag, 1996.

Knappe, Siegfried with Ted Brusaw. *Soldat: Reflections of a German Soldier, 1936–1949*. New York, NY: Dell Book, 1992.

Koehne, Samuel. "Were the National Socialists a Völkisch Party? Paganism, Christianity, and the Nazi Christmas," *Central European History*, vol. 47 (2014): 760–90.

Krakowski, Shmuel and Orah Blaustein. *The War of the Doomed: Jewish Armed Resistance in Poland, 1942–1944*. New York, NY: Holmes and Meier, 1984.

Kriegstagebuch der Seekriegsleitung 1939–1945 Teil A, Band 40: Dezember 1942 [War Diary of the Naval Command 1939–1945 Part A, vol. 40: December 1942. Herford and Bonn: Verlag E. S. Mittler & Sohn, 1993.

Kriegsweihnachten 1942: Eine Scheswig-Holsteinische Infanteriedivision im Osten [War Christmas 1942: A Schleswig-Holstein Infantry Division in the East]. Riga: Deutsche Verlags- und Druckerei-Gesellschaft im Ostland, 1942.

Kuklick, Bruce. *The Fighting Sullivans: How Hollywood and the Military Make Heroes*. Lawrence, KS: University Press of Kansas, 2016.

Kulka, Otto Dov and Eberhard Jäckel, eds. *Die Juden in den geheimen NS-Stimmungsberichten 1933–1945 [The Jews in the Secret National Socialist Public Opinion Reports 1933–1945]*. Düsseldorf: Droste Verlag, 2004.

Kuon, Peter. "Weihnachten im Konzentrationslager" ["Christmas in the Concentration Camp"]. In *Poetik des Überlebens: Kulturproduktion im Konzentrationslager [The Poetics of Survival: Cultural Production in the Concentration Camp]*, edited by Anne-Berenike Rothstein, 33–48. Berlin De Gruyter Oldenbourg, 2015.

Langbein, Hermann. *Against All Hope: Resistance in the Nazi Concentration Camps, 1938–1945*. New York, NY: Paragon House, 1994.

——*People in Auschwitz*. Chapel Hill, NC: University of North Carolina Press, 2004.

Leckie, Robert. *Helmet for My Pillow: From Parris Island to the Pacific*. London: Ebury Press, 2010.

Lévy, Jean-Pierre. *Mémoires d'un franc-tireur: Itinéraire d'un resistant (1940–1944) [Memoirs of an Irregular: A Resistance Fighter's Journey (1940–1944)]*. Brussels: Éditions Complexe, 2000.

Lindgren, Astrid. *Krigsdagböcker [War Diaries]*. Lidingö: Salikon förlag, 2005.

Logue, Mark and Peter Conradi. *The King's War*. London: Quercus, 2018.

Longerich, Peter. *Politik der Vernichtung: Eine Gesamtdarstellung der nationalsozialistischen Judenverfolgung [Politics of Annihilation: A Comprehensive Account of the National Socialist Persecution of the Jews]*. Munich: Piper, 1998.

——*Der ungeschriebene Befehl: Hitler und der Weg zur 'Endlösung' [The Unwritten Command: Hitler and the Road to the 'Final Solution']*. Munich: Piper Verlag, 2001.

——*Goebbels*. Berlin: Pantheon, 2012.

Lucas, Celia. *Prisoners of Santo Tomas*. London: Leo Cooper, 1975.

MacLaren, Roy. *Canadians Behind Enemy Lines, 1939–1945*. Vancouver: UBC Press, 2004.

Manchester, William. *American Caesar*. New York, NY: Little, Brown and Company, 1978.

Maronari, Antonio. *Un sommergibile non è rientrato alla base [A submarine has not returned to base]*. Milan: Libreria Rizzoli, 1957.

Marshall, George C. *The Papers of George Catlett Marshall, vol. 3, "The Right Man for the Job," December 7, 1941 – May 31, 1943*. Baltimore, MA and London: The Johns Hopkins University Press, 1991.

Mazower, Mark. *Inside Hitler's Greece*. New Haven, CT and London: Yale University Press, 1993.

McCarthy, Dudley. *South-West Pacific Area – First Year: Kokoda to Wau [Australia in the War of 1939–1945. Series 1 (Army), vol. 5]*. Canberra: Australian War Memorial, 1959.

Merridale, Catherine. *Ivan's War: The Red Army at War 1939–45*. London: Faber & Faber, 2005.

Mickle, Isaac. *A Gentleman of Much Promise: The Diary of Isaac Mickle, 1837–1845*. Philadelphia, PA: University of Pennsylvania Press, 1977.

Mielert, Harry. *Russische Erde: Kriegsbriefe aus Russland [Russian Soil: War Letters from Russia]*. Stuttgart: Reclam-Verlag, 1950.

Mikosz-Hintzke, Teresa. *Six Years 'til Spring: A Polish Family's Odyssey*. San Jose, CA: Authors Choice Press, 2001.

Miles, Milton E. *A Different Kind of War*. Garden City, NY: Doubleday & Company, 1967.

Milner, Samuel. *Victory in Papua [United States Army in World War II]*. Washington, D.C.: US Government Printing Office, 1957.

Molesworth, G. N. *Curfew on Olympus*. Bombay: Asia Publishing House, 1965.

Monahan, Evelyn M. and Rosemary Neidel-Greenlee. *All This Hell: U.S. Nurses Imprisoned by the Japanese*. Lexington, KY: University Press of Kentucky, 2003.

Monro, Mary. *Stranger in my Heart*. London: Unbound, 2018.

Montgomery, Bernard Law. *The Memoirs of Field-Marshal the Viscount Montgomery of Alamein*. London: Collins, 1958.

Morriss, Mack. *South Pacific Diary, 1942—1943*, edited by Ronnie Day. Lexington, KY: University Press of Kentucky, 1996.

Mukherjee, Ishan. "The Elusive Chase: 'War Rumour' in Calcutta During the Second World War." In *Calcutta: The Stormy Decades*, edited by Tanika Sarkar and Sekhar Bandyopadhyay, 65–92. London: Routledge, 2017.

Mukherjee, Janam. *Hungry Bengal: War, Famine and the End of Empire*. Oxford: Oxford University Press, 2015.

Nansen, Odd. *Fra dag til dag [From Day to Day]*. Oslo: Dreyers Forlag, 1946.

Nutter, Ralph H. *With the Possum and the Eagle: The Memoir of a Navigator's War over Germany and Japan*. Denton, TX: University of North Texas Press, 2005.

O'Connell, Gene and Tony Bilek. *No Uncle Sam: The Forgotten of Bataan*. Kent, OH: Kent State University Press, 2003.

Olson, James C. "The Gilberts and Marshalls." In *The Pacific: Guadalcanal to Saipan, August 1942 to July 1944 [The Army Air Forces in World War II]*, edited by Wesley Frank Craven and James Lea Cate, 281–310. Chicago, IL: University of Chicago Press, 1951.

Ortiz, Ezequiel L. and James A. McClure. *Don Jose: An American Soldier's Courage and Faith in Japanese Captivity*. Santa Fe, NM: Sunstone Press, 2012.

Ossemann, Nico. "Chor der Chöre" ["Choir of Choirs"]. In *Stille Nacht, Heilige Nacht. Weihnachtsgeschichten aus schwerer Zeit erzählt von Freunden und Förderern des Volksbundes Deutsche Kriegsgräberfürsorge [Silent Night, Holy Night: Christmas Stories from Difficult Times Told by Friends and Supporters of the German People's League for the Care of War Cemeteries]*, edited by Maurice Bonkat, 51–4. Kassel: Volksbund Deutsche Kriegsgräberfürsorge, 2008.

Papuan Campaign: The Buna-Sanananda Operation 16 November 1942–23 January 1943. Washington, D.C.: Center of Military History, 1990.

Perry, Joseph B. *Christmas in Germany: A Cultural History*. Chapel Hill, NC: University of North Carolina Press, 2010.

Pimlott, Ben. *The Queen: Elizabeth II and the Monarchy*. London: HarperCollins Publishers, 2001.

Plating, John D. *The Hump: America's Strategy for Keeping China in World War II*. College Station, TX: Texas A&M University Press, 2011.

Plaut, Joshua Eli. *A Kosher Christmas: 'Tis the Season to Be Jewish*. New Brunswick, NJ: Rutgers University Press, 2012.

Pogue, Forrest C. *George C. Marshall, vol. 3 Organizer of victory, 1943–1945*. New York, NY: Viking Press, 1973.

Potter, E. B. *Nimitz*. Annapolis, MD: Naval Institute Press, 1976.

Potts, Eli Daniel and Annette Potts. *Yanks Down Under, 1941–45: The American Impact on Australia.* Melbourne: Oxford University Press, 1985.

Presser, J. *Ashes in the Wind: The Destruction of Dutch Jewry.* London: Souvenir Press, 1968.

Raeder, Erich. *My Life.* Annapolis, MD: United States Naval Institute, 1960.

Random House Book of Poetry for Children. New York, NY: Random House, 1983.

Rashke, Richard. *Escape from Sobibor.* Urbana and Chicago, IL: University of Illinois Press, 1995.

Redlich, Gonda. *The Terezin Diary of Gonda Redlich.* Lexington, KY: University Press of Kentucky, 1992.

Restad, Penne Lee. *Christmas in America: A History.* Oxford: Oxford University Press, 1997.

Rill, James. *A Narrative History of the 1st Battalion, 11th Marines.* Bennington, VT: Merriam Press, 2003.

Ritter, J. R. *From Texas to Tinian and Tokyo Bay: The Memoirs of Captain J. R. Ritter, Seabee Commander during the Pacific War, 1942–1945.* Denton, TX: University of North Texas Press, 2019.

Robbins, Jane M. J. "Tokyo Calling: Japanese Overseas Radio Broadcasting, 1937–1945." PhD diss., University of Sheffield, 1997.

Roberts, Walter R. *Tito, Michailovic and the Allies, 1941–1945.* New Brunswick, NJ: Rutgers University Press, 1973.

Robinett, Paul McDonald. *Armor Command.* Washington, D.C.: McGregor & Werner, 1958.

Rolf, David. *The Bloody Road to Tunis: Destruction of the Axis Forces in North Africa, November 1942 – May 1943.* Redbridge: Greenhill Books, 2001.

Romanus, Charles E. and Riley Sunderland. *Stilwell's Mission to China [United States Army in World War II: China-Burma-India Theater].* Washington, D.C.: United States Army Center of Military History, 1953.

Romeiser, John B. *Combat Reporter: Don Whitehead's World War II Diary and Memoirs.* New York, NY: Fordham University Press, 2006.

Romulo, Carlos P. *I Saw the Fall of the Philippines.* Garden City, NY: Doubleday, Doran & Co., 1942.

Roosevelt, Eleanor. *This I Remember.* New York, NY: Harper & Brothers, 1949.

Roskill, S. W. *War at Sea 1939–1945, vol. 2: The Period of Balance [History of the Second World War: United Kingdom Military Series].* London: Her Majesty's Stationery Office, 1956.

Sajer, Guy. *The Forgotten Soldier.* Washington, D.C.: Potomac Books, 1990.

Savary, Gladys. *Outside the Walls.* New York, NY: Vantage Press, 1954.

Sereny, Gitta. *Into That Darkness.* London: Andre Deutsch, 1974.

Sheridan, Lisa. *From Cabbages to Kings: The Autobiography of Lisa Sheridan.* London: Odhams Press, 1955.

Sierakowiak, Dawid, Alan Adelson, and Kamil Turowski. *The Diary of Dawid Sierakowiak: Five Notebooks from the Lodz Ghetto.* New York, NY: Oxford University Press, 1996.

Simmet, Helmut. "Bethlehem kann überall sein" ["Bethlehem can be everywhere"]. In *Weihnachtsgeschichten aus schwerer Zeit erzählt von Freunden und Förderern des Volksbundes Deutsche Kriegsgräberfürsorge [Christmas Stories from Difficult Times Told by Friends and Supporters of the German People's League for the Care of War Cemeteries],* edited by Martin Dodenhoeft, 187–90. Kassel: Volksbund Deutsche Kriegsgräberfürsorge, 2017.

Skrjabina, Elena with Norman Luxenburg. *After Leningrad: From the Caucasus to the Rhine, August 9, 1942 – March 25, 1945: a Diary of Survival during World War II.* Carbondale, IL: Southern Illinois University Press, 1978.

Smith, Kathleen E. R. *God Bless America: Tin Pan Alley Goes to War.* Lexington, KY: University Press of Kentucky, 2003.

Stabler, Hollis D. and Victoria Smith. *No One Ever Asked Me: The World War II Memoirs of an Omaha Indian Soldier.* Lincoln, NE: University of Nebraska Press, 2005.

Stephens, Ian. *Monsoon Morning*. London: Ernest Benn, 1966.

Stevens, Frederic H. *Santo Tomas Internment Camp*. New York, NY: Stratford House, 1946.

Stresau, Hermann. *Als lebe man nur unter Vorbehalt: Tagebücher aus den Kriegsjahren 1939–1945 [As If You Lived Only Conditionally: Diaries from the War Years 1939–1945]*, edited by Peter Graf and Ulrich Faure. Stuttgart: Klett-Cotta, 2021.

Taggart, Caroline. *Christmas at War: True Stories of How Britain Came Together on the Home Front*. London: John Blake Publishing, 2019.

Tapert, Annette. *Lines of Battle: Letters from American Servicemen, 1941–1945*. New York, NY: Pocket Books, 1989.

Taylor, Nancy M. *The Home Front Volume I [The Official History of New Zealand in the Second World War 1939–1945]*. Wellington: Historical Publications Branch, 1986.

Tenold, Stig. *Norwegian Shipping in the 20th Century: Norway's Successful Navigation of the World's Most Global Industry*. London: Palgrave MacMillan, 2019.

Thompson, Julian. *Forgotten Voices of Burma: The Second World War's Forgotten Conflict*. London: Ebury Press, 2009.

Tittmann Jr., Harold H. *Inside the Vatican of Pius XII*. New York, NY: Image Books, 2004.

Towne, Allen N. *Doctor Danger Forward: A World War II Memoir of a Combat Medical Aidman, First Infantry Division*. Jefferson, NC and London: McFarland & Co., 2000.

Treadwell, Mattie E. *The Women's Army Corps United States Army in World War II [United States Army in World War II: Special Studies]*. Washington, D.C.: Center of Military History, 1954.

Trials of the Major War Criminals before the International Military Tribunal, vol. XXXIX and XL Documents and Other Material in Evidence Bormann-11 to Raeder-7. Nuremberg: International Military Tribunal, 1949.

Trials of War Criminals before the Nuremberg Military Tribunals under Control Council Law No. 10, vol. 4, 5, 11 and 13. Washington, D.C.: United States Government Printing Office, 1950.

Twiss, Frank. *Social Change in the Royal Navy, 1924–1970: The Life and Times of Admiral Sir Frank Twiss, KCB, KCVO, DSC*, compiled and edited by Chris Howard Bailey. Stroud: Sutton Publishing, 1996.

Vause, Jordan. *U-boat Ace: The Story of Wolfgang Lüth*. Annapolis, MD: Naval Institute Press, 1990.

Vetlesen, Leif and Ingvald Wahl. *Syv fortellinger fra Norges krig på havet [Seven Tales from Norway's War at Sea]*. Oslo: Gyldendal Norsk Forlag, 1993.

Vinson, J. Chal. *Thomas Nast: Political Cartoonist*. Athens, GA: University of Georgia Press, 2014.

Voglis, Polymeris. "Surviving Hunger: Life in the Cities and the Countryside during the Occupation." In *Surviving Hitler and Mussolini: Daily Life in Occupied Europe*, edited by Robert Gildea, Olivier Wieviorka, and Anette Warring, 16–41. Oxford and New York, NY: Berg, 2006.

Vrba, Rudolf. *I Escaped from Auschwitz*. Fort Lee, NJ: Barricade Books, 2002.

Wagner, Bernd G. *IG Auschwitz* [vol. 3 in *Darstellungen und Quellen zur Geschichte von Auschwitz [Accounts and Sources of the History of Auschwitz]*]. Munich: K. G. Sauer 2000.

Wainwright Jonathan M. and Robert Considine. *General Wainwright's Story: The Account of Four Years of Humiliating Defeat, Surrender, and Captivity*. Garden City, NY: Doubleday, 1946.

Walling, Michael G. *Forgotten Sacrifice: The Arctic Convoys of World War II*. Oxford: Osprey 2016.

Wassner, Fernando. "Feldpostbrief" ["Letter from the Front"]. In *Unter den Sternen: Weihnachtsgeschichten aus schwerer Zeit erzählt von Freunden und Förderern des Volksbundes Deutsche Kriegsgräberfürsorge [Under the Stars: Christmas Stories from Difficult Times Told by Friends and Supporters of the German People's League for the Care of War Cemeteries]*, edited by Martin Dodenhoeft and Henning Unverhau, 28–30. Kassel: Volksbund Deutsche Kriegsgräberfürsorge, 2007.

Waterford, Van. *Prisoners of the Japanese in World War II*. Jefferson, VA: McFarland and Company, 1994.

Watson, Bruce Allen. *Exit Rommel: The Tunisian Campaign, 1942–43*. Mechanicsburg, PA: Stackpole Books, 1999.

Weatherford, Doris. *American Women during World War II: An Encyclopedia*. New York, NY: Routledge, 2010.

Weber-Kellermann, Ingeborg. *Das Weihnachtsfest: Eine Kultur- und Sozialgeschichte der Weihnachtszeit [The Christmas Celebration: A Cultural and Social History of Christmas]*. Luzern and Frankfurt am Main: Verlag C. J. Bucher, 1978.

Weichherz, Béla and Daniel H. Magilow. *In Her Father's Eyes: A Childhood Extinguished by the Holocaust*. New Brunswick, NJ: Rutgers University Press, 2008.

Wheeler-Bennett, John W. *King George VI: His Life and Reign*. London: Macmillan, 1958.

White, Joseph R. *The United States Holocaust Memorial Museum Encyclopedia of Camps and Ghettos, 1933–1945, vol. 2*. Bloomington, IN: Indiana University Press, 2009.

——*The United States Holocaust Memorial Museum Encyclopedia of Camps and Ghettos, 1933–1945, vol. 3*. Bloomington, IN: Indiana University Press, 2012.

Wittmann, Rebecca. *Beyond Justice: The Auschwitz Trial*. Cambridge, MA: Harvard University Press, 2012.

Wituska, Krystyna and Irene Tomaszewski. *Letters of Krystyna Wituska, 1942–1944*. Detroit, MI: Wayne State University Press, 2006.

Yamato Ichihashi and Gordon H. Chang. *Morning Glory, Evening Shadow: Yamato Ichihashi and His Internment Writings, 1942–1945*. Stanford, CA: Stanford University Press, 1997.

Yellin, Emily. *Our Mothers' War: American Women at Home and at the Front During World War II*. New York, NY: Free Press, 2004.

Zapruder, Alexandra. *Salvaged Pages: Young Writers' Diaries of the Holocaust*. New Haven, CT: Yale University Press, 2014.

Zuckerman, Yitzhak. *A Surplus of Memory: Chronicle of the Warsaw Ghetto Uprising*, translated and edited by Barbara Harshav. Berkeley, CA: University of California Press, 1993.

Magazines

Atlas Obscura
Australian Women's Weekly
Billboard
CBI Roundup
Spiegel
Women's Home Companion

Newspapers

Amrita Bazar Patrika
Baltimore Sun
Bee
Birmingham Post
Boston Globe
Charleston Daily Mail

Chicago Daily Tribune
Chicago Tribune
Cincinnati Enquirer
Corpus Christi Caller-Times
Council Grove Republican
Courier-Journal
Courier-Mail
Culver Citizen
Cushing Daily Citizen
Daily Oklahoman
Daily Telegraph
Desert Sun
Evening Herald
Evening Post
Fitchburg Sentinel
Fort Lauderdale News
Fort Worth Star-Telegram
Gisborne Herald
Guardian
Honolulu Advertiser
Honolulu Star-Bulletin
Imperial Beach Star-News
Japan Times Advertiser
Kansas City Times
Knoxville Journal
Leader-Post
Leader-Telegram
Life, The
Lincoln Journal Star
Liverpool Daily
Los Angeles Times
Mainichi Daily News
Manawatu Standard
Marshall News Messenger
Marylebone Mercury, Middlesex Independent and West London Star
Minidoka Irrigator
Missoulian
Nelson Evening Mail
New York Times
New Zealand Herald
Newcastle Morning Herald and Miners' Advocate
News Journal
Oakland Tribune
People, The
Pomona Progress Bulletin
Portage Daily Register
Province

San Francisco Examiner
South Bend Tribune
South Wales Gazette and Newport News
Spokesman Review
Standard-Speaker
Sun
Sunday Sun
Surrey Leader
Sydney Morning Herald
Tampa Daily Times
Times of India
Town Talk
Tribune
Völkischer Beobachter
Vancouver Sun
Washington Post
Welt am Sonntag
Western Morning News
Western Times

Websites

Burma Star Memorial Fund: https://burmastarmemorial.org
Chronicles of Terror, Pilecki Institute: https://www.zapisyterroru.pl
Eleanor Roosevelt Papers Project, Columbian College of Arts & Sciences, The George Washington
    University: https://erpapers.columbian.gwu.edu/my-day
Faculty of Medicine, University of Queensland: https://medicine.uq.edu.au
Far Eastern Heroes: https://www.far-eastern-heroes.org.uk
Forces.net
Memorial and Museum Auschwitz-Birkenau: http://auschwitz.org
National Museum of the Pacific War: https://www.pacificwarmuseum.org/
Naval History and Heritage Command https://www.history.navy.mil
Philippine Diary Project: https://philippinediaryproject.com/
Smithsonian National Air and Space Museum: https://airandspace.si.edu/
Tennessee State Museum: https://tnmuseum.org/

Index